ECONOMIC POLICY:
PRINCIPLES AND DESIGN

ECONOMIC POLICY: PRINCIPLES AND DESIGN

BY

J. TINBERGEN

Professor of Development Planning
at the Netherlands School of Economics

4th revised printing

1967

NORTH-HOLLAND PUBLISHING COMPANY
AMSTERDAM

RAND McNALLY & COMPANY
CHICAGO

4th revised printing 1967

This book is Volume 10 of the North-Holland Series "Contributions to Economic Analysis" under the Editorship of J. SANDEE, R. STROTZ, J. TINBERGEN and P. J. VERDOORN

Publishers: NORTH-HOLLAND PUBLISHING COMPANY – AMSTERDAM
Sole distributors for U.S.A. and Canada: RAND MCNALLY and COMPANY – CHICAGO

PRINTED IN THE NETHERLANDS

INTRODUCTION TO THE SERIES

This series consists of a number of hitherto unpublished studies which are introduced by the editors in the belief that they represent fresh contributions to economic science.

The term *economic analysis* as used in the title of the series has been adopted because it covers both the activities of the theoretical economist and of the research worker.

Although the analytical methods used by the various contributors are not the same, they are nevertheless conditioned by the common origin of their studies, namely theoretical problems encountered in practical research. Since for this reason, business cycle research and national accounting, research work on behalf of economic policy, and problems of planning are the main sources of the subjects dealt with, they necessarily determine the manner of approach adopted by the authors. Their methods tend to be "practical" in the sense of not being too far remote from application to actual economic conditions. In addition they are quantitative rather than qualitative.

It is the hope of the editors that the publication of these studies will help to stimulate the exchange of scientific information and to reinforce international co-operation in the field of economics.

THE EDITORS

FOREWORD

This book originates from two main sources: from my experience in the Netherlands Central Planning Bureau and from my participation in discussions about the wider aspects of economic policy; discussions often centred in or around the Netherlands Labour Party. It is an attempt at a systematic treatment of the main lines, rather than of details. As such it is an amplification of the two small volumes, published earlier, on quantitative policy. It also deals with qualitative policy but, as a necessary consequence of the state of research in this field, in a much more primitive way than in the case of quantitative policy.

I hope it may be of some use for universities as well as for some of the planning experts in governments. The whole approach has been kept very simple; even the simple algebra used in the examples need not be read by those who do not like it, although they will then, of course, miss some of the points.

The book does try to bring within the sphere of scientific discussion some of the controversies which are, nowadays, often dealt with by slogans; it is the firm belief of the author that contributions can be made and must be made by objective analysis, even in the world's most important contemporary controversy. He certainly does not claim to have contributed much already; still he hopes to have stimulated the application of the idea. Two points seem to be outstanding here: first, that there are not only two alternative systems for the economic organization of society, but many shades; and secondly, that our choice between them is, in essence, a choice on the grounds of efficiency: only a few really fundamental human values have to count, but many traditional prejudices must be eliminated. The choice depends, too, on the country and circumstances considered.

In view of the overproduction of scientific literature it seems desirable to the author that each writer should himself indicate, in a foreword or a summary of any kind of publication, what he considers new in his own work. This may facilitate reading to a large extent. In this book the arrangement, rather than the subject matter, seems to have some novelty. Most of the models presented here have already been presented elsewhere; but not models 08 and 20, and some of the problems illustrated with the aid of models 14–16. In addition, some of the suggestions regarding aims, as given in section 1.6, would appear to be new.

The author wants to express his thanks to his collaborators in the Central Planning Bureau, who have contributed much to his education by their stimulating criticism; more particularly, he wants to thank Professors Bent Hansen of Stockholm and H. J. Witteveen of Rotterdam for having read the manuscript; Mr. Kelvin Lancaster of The London School of Economics, for having improved the idiom, Mr. Maarten Eisma for having made a large number of calculations and Mrs. H. C. H. Voskuil-de Vries for her incessant care in typing the manuscript. The remaining errors are mine.

J. TINBERGEN

CONTENTS

SUMMARY

CHAPTER 1

THE CONTRIBUTION OF ECONOMIC ANALYSIS TO THE DESIGN OF ECONOMIC POLICY

1.1. Objective of this Study; (1) to describe the process of economic policy; (2) to judge the consistency of its aims and means; (3) to indicate the optimum policy for attaining given aims; (4) to make suggestions as to aims. Explanation of structure of book.

1.2. Summary Description of the Economic Process and Its Determinants

Data and economic phenomena; policy-makers; available means, and other data; foundations and structure of an economy; instruments of economic policy. Foundations referring to spiritual aspects and to qualitative relations between human beings. Examples of foundations: existence or absence of certain freedoms and rights, of certain opportunities for education, the degree of specialization and division of labour. Structure referring to the details of the organization and the quantitative aspects of an economy. Examples of elements of structure: number of social groups and institutions and their behaviour, number of goods, system of exchange (free or rationed), degree of monopolization, numbers of policy-makers. Foundations and structure, as a rule, change gradually; certain other data subject to frequent changes: crops, technical factors, "world market data". Definition and examples of instruments of economic policy: tax rates, items of public expenditure, rate of discount, reserve ratios, wage rates, rates of exchange. Variables and constants; various degrees of constancy; economic relations or equations, and models.

1.3. The Logic of Economic Policy; the Contribution of Economic Analysis to the Design of Economic Policy

Economic policy consists in the deliberate variation in means in order to attain certain aims. Such changes in means may be used to offset the effect of changes in other data. In particular, changes in instrument variables are meant to offset rapid changes in other data, which continuously tend to disturb short-term equilibrium. If these changes in other data have undesired effects on the economy it may be desired to "cure" the "evil", and the "causes" of it may be seen in these changes in other data. The cure cannot consist, however, in reversing the change in the other data, since these latter cannot deliberately be changed. There need not therefore be any correspondence between causes and "cures", and the causes may even be irrelevant to the indication of "cures".

The economic policy of a certain area may be in the hands of one, or of several, policy-makers; to begin with the case of one policy-maker will be considered. According to the nature of means involved, policy may be "reform" (change in foundations), "qualitative policy" (change in structure) or "quantitative policy" (change only in values of instrument variables). Qualitative policy may consist of a change in the number of policy-makers themselves. Also, according to the nature of the aims, a distinction may be drawn between qualitative and quantitative policy; quantitative policy being mainly directed towards a change in the numerical values of some of the economic variables, to be called targets. Distinction between policy of fixed targets and one of flexible targets.

Necessity of considering economic policy at any moment as a coherent whole; possibility of "partition" only exceptional. "Range" of economic policy: number and nature of aims and means involved. Logic of economic policy an inversion of the logic of economic analysis. Logic simplest with quantitative policy and fixed targets: target values are given, instrument values are "unknowns". Problem with flexible targets a maximum problem: to find values of instrument variables rendering some welfare function a maximum. Qualitative policy problems usually of the "trial and error" type, i.e. optimum has to be found by trying alternative solutions. Contribution of economic analysis may be (a) to judge consistency of aims, and of aims and means as a combination; and (b) to find optimum policies where aims and means are given and consistent.

Procedure of policy-making: planning, i.e. making a forecast and considering consequences of conceivable changes in means; appraisal of possible consequences and making a choice; all this to be called "design". The final stage is that of the execution of the policy chosen. Planning of a policy has nothing to do with the particular policy sometimes called "planning", i.e. one of centralized production decisions.

1.4. Aims of Economic Policy

Policy-makers base their acts, consciously or unconsciously, on preferences, which, when consistent, may be represented by some welfare or utility concept. This welfare concept will coincide largely, but not necessarily completely, with a representative individual welfare concept; it will depend on quantitative and qualitative elements that also enter into these individual utility functions; in addition, collective preferences will come in. The elements entering into the policy-maker's welfare function refer to (*a*) elements determining individual material and spiritual well-being, such as the quantity of food and shelter available, the efforts needed, the opportunities for education, the right to take part in decisions; (*b*) elements determining relations between individuals, such as (i) the degree of freedom, (ii) the frequency of conflicts (or the degree of social and international peace) and (iii) the positive elements in social relations (e.g. justice). Some of these elements will be specified later on; sometimes they assume special legal forms, at least in the short run, as e.g. the maintenance or introduction of a number of constitutional rights. For each quantitative element not only the average value, but also various "distributions", are important, as e.g. the distribution over groups of the population or the distribution over time.

Policy-makers' "social welfare functions" are often streamlined by political parties emphasizing certain "principles" of economic (and general) policy; liberals stressing freedom since they rely on the self-adjusting forces in economy, communists stressing certain aspects of equality, nationalists stressing national interest etc.

"Similarity" between various social welfare functions defined for certain variables. Similarity between individual and social welfare functions; in the latter, collective needs and adjustments for inconsistencies in individual preferences may come in (among other things, corrections against human "vices"). Should social welfare functions be derived from individual ones and can they?

Historically the aims of economic policy have been influenced by some development in general individual aims, but much more by fluctuations in what was believed to be the possibility of self-adjustment of the economy. Liberal policy believed in it to the greatest extent and this consequently reduced the range of aims of policy-makers. In recent decades this belief has fluctuated and, on the whole, diminished. According to circumstances (normal or extreme scarcity, wealthy or poor regions) a narrower or a wider range of aims is now accepted.

Aims of modern economic policy may be summarized as (*a*) maintenance of international peace; (*b*) maximum real expenditure per capita with "full" employment and monetary equilibrium; (*c*) improvement of distribution of real expenditure over social groups and countries; (*d*) emancipation of certain underprivileged groups; and (*e*) as much personal freedom as is compatible with the other aims. Qualifications as to the meaning of "maximum" real expenditure if development in time is considered; limits to human needs.

1.5. Inconsistencies in Individual and Collective Aims

Inconsistencies in the aims of economic policy will to some extent derive from inconsistencies in the aims of individuals. Aims are called inconsistent if their ultimate consequences are incompatible. They may be regarded as due to imperfections in the human mind and are most likely to occur when great distances between cause and effect are involved. Inconsistencies in individual behaviour are often to be found in decisions as to education and the creation of a family. Lack of concern for other people's well-being is another example and this is connected with the belief in the unlimited needs of man. In the collective sphere this lack of concern is reflected in the doctrine that every country should use its own resources for its own well-being only.

The most appalling inconsistencies in collective aims are those responsible for the outbreak of war. Further inconsistencies are to be found in aims relating to the size of population, to the facilities for education and to social and geographic inequality. In certain countries inconsistencies in aims with regard to development exist, leading to inflation. Foreign assistance may reduce these inconsistencies.

1.6. Some Suggestions as to Aims

Suggestions as to aims may be meant to take account of new facts or new insights, as e.g. the situation created by atomic weapons, or the insight that human needs have a ceiling.

Further suggestions concerning aims may be made in order to remove inconsistencies. On this basis more family planning and more education may be suggested as aims. In some countries more orthodox financial aims need to be suggested. Finally, suggestions may be made in order to give shape to aims so far only vaguely felt. A sharper definition of social justice would be one of the most important contributions that could be made. Such a definition depends, essentially, on the comparison of the satisfaction of different individuals. Such comparisons are declared impossible by many economists. Nevertheless they seem to be the basis for many decisions taken by family heads as well as organizers, judges, etc. Furthermore, individuals who have undergone a "transformation" such as training or a medical treatment seem to be able to make comparisons. Finally it would sometimes seem possible to determine, with the help of medical and similar standards, the compensations needed to neutralize certain "handicaps" and by so doing to find a method of making different individuals "equally happy".

1.7. Means of Economic Policy

The means of economic policy used also affect welfare, by material and immaterial costs (sacrifices in resources or in friction and conflicts). The range of socially and politically acceptable means may be wider and narrower, and during the liberal era was narrowed down. During the great depression and in war time the range widened quickly, and narrowed down afterwards. Various political parties have pre-conceived ideas about the desirable range. Such ideas may represent side conditions to the problems of economic policy as e.g. a restriction on the type of instruments to be used (no nationalization; no price control; no increase in working hours). Choice of means should be based on their probable effects, i.e. their efficiency. It follows that a wider range of means will be needed, the more difficult is the situation. The disadvantages connected with an intensive use of certain means may impose limitations (i.e. boundary conditions) on their use (limit set to tax increases, or wage reductions). Certain sets of aims and means may appear inconsistent, i.e. that the aims cannot be attained by the means proposed or admitted. Or it may be that long-term effects are unfavourable to the aims.

CHAPTER 2

ECONOMIC MODELS

2.1. Scope of Models

To specify assumptions as to foundations and structure of economy, i.e. natural, technical and legal data and behaviour of subjects. Such specification—usually meaning strong simplification—enables the economist to give precise answers to precise questions and clarifies discussion. Applications to real situations are bound to introduce divergencies. "Micro" and "macro" models, for closed and open economies, static or dynamic. Complete description of model requires a large number of details; systematic survey of all conceivable models difficult. Important features: as to "actors" considered: (a) number, (b) nature and behaviour of their income, (c) spending habits, (d) nature and origin of wealth, (e) investment habits; as to "markets" considered: (a) number, (b) stock or flow character of commodity; as to technical relations (in the widest sense, including legal): (a) number, (b) nature of phenomena involved, (c) mathematical shape.

Logical structure of model may show a certain "ordering", different for analytical and political problems.

2.2. Some Conclusions from Models

Danger of aprioristic propositions in economics. Under specified conditions total value of production at free-market prices will be a maximum if free pricing and production is applied. This presupposes, however, the full use of all factors of production, and the non-interruption of exchange possibilities. Free pricing impossible, too, with decreasing marginal costs. It has further to be assumed that productivity does not depend on the time the technique of production has already been in use, and maximum production may be at variance with maximum real expenditure or with optimum distribution. "Dynamic" features such as lags, speculative attitudes and the role of stocks may make the adjustment to a changed situation an unstable process. Changes in the annual flow of production of a commodity of very long lifetime cannot be important for the market of such a commodity. Therefore short-term changes in the rate of savings are not important for the rate of interest. Changes in the price of a commodity or service which is only a minor factor in the production of a certain product will not influence the supply of that product very much; hence the restricted importance of the short-term interest rate for general activity.

Statistical inference is bound to yield only conditional results. If profits and equipment prices are the most important variables affecting investment fluctuations, the influence of the rate of interest on investment activity has been only weak. If income is the most important factor influencing demand, price elasticity for most goods has been only low. If product prices are primarily dependent on costs, their flexibility has been rather high. If incomes and prices are the most important factors in demand, short-run elasticities of substitution in international trade have been moderate.

2.3. Survey of Models Used as Examples in this Book, indicating variables occurring in them (cf. Appendix 3). Notations used.

2.4. Closed Static Models

Macro-models: (01) money-flow model: simplest Keynesian model; (02) money and product flow; specifies quantity and price components; (03) money, product and factor flow: distinguishes between product and factor market (labour); (04) money flow and public finance: introduces government decisions; (05) money flow, public finance and assets: introduces complications caused by liquidation and formation of assets.

Micro-models: (06) horizontal money and product flow: introduces multiplicity of final products; (07) horizontal money and product flow with monopolies: introduces monopolistic price formation; (08) income distribution: a model introducing personal abilities and other attributes making for income inequality.

2.5. Closed Dynamic Models

(09) development: specifies interaction between income, savings and capital in the process of long-term development; (10) cycle (money flow, paper profits): one of the simpler models of the busines cycle, with the emphasis on lags in income spending and the role played by paper profits in overspending and underspending.

2.6. Open, Static Macro-models

Models (11)–(15) correspond to models (01)–(05) with the only difference that they all refer to open economies; meaning that imports and exports are among the variables. Public finance has not, however, been introduced explicitly in these models, as was the case in (04) and (05); instead the rate of exchange is introduced as a separate variable in model (14).

2.7. Open, Static Micro-models

(16) money, product and factor flow and public finance: here public finance is introduced again; (17) money-flow and banking: introduces a more complete description of monetary aspects; (18) horizontal money, product and factor flow: a model illustrating complications of fostering isolated increases in productivity in open economies: (19) horizontal money and product flow: being a combination of (03) and (06) for an open economy.

2.8. Open Dynamic Micro-models

(20) investment project appraisal: a model to be used for the explanation of certain methods of "project appraisal" (priority calculations).

2.9. Group of Economies Model

(21) money and product flow: a model thought appropriate for dealing with short-term adaptations in employment and balance of payments between several countries.

CHAPTER 3

QUANTITATIVE POLICY: REGULATING THE POSITION WITHIN A GIVEN STRUCTURE; (I) CLOSED ECONOMY

3.1. Nature of Problem; Practical Approach so far Mostly Used

Quantitative policy, leaving structure unchanged, mainly short-term policy, but not always. Often takes form of trial and error. Tendency to incoherent treatment based on supposed one-by-one correspondence between targets and instruments. Choice often made on qualitative arguments. Interrelation should not be neglected; requires simultaneous consideration of all targets and instruments. Formal versus material aspects.

3.2. The Logic of Quantitative Economic Policy

Distinction should be made between problems with fixed or flexible targets, those with many or only few instruments and according to the possibility of boundary conditions intervening. Basis for design to be initial situation, or forecast, and effects of changes in "other" data to be expected. Criteria for policy to be found in divergency between "actual" and most desirable situation (targets). Choice of instruments should be a question of efficiency. Model should be realistic and "manageable". Stochastic nature of problem.

3.3 Provisional Solution; Efficiency of Instruments

Optimum values of instrument variables to be estimated with help of model. In case of fixed targets and an equal number of instrument variables, without boundary conditions, the solution will as a rule be unique. If the number of instruments is larger, some degrees of freedom will remain; if it is smaller, there will, as a rule, be no solution (inconsistency of given combination of aims and means). In the case of flexible targets, there will be a solution irrespective of the number of instrument variables; but it may depend on boundary conditions. The efficiency coefficient of a certain instrument, with respect to a certain target variable, may be defined as the ratio between the change obtained in the target variable and the change needed in the instrument variable; it depends on side conditions as to the other variables. For a comparison between various instruments and targets, their changes have to be valued. The final measures of efficiency then boils down to the net increase in social welfare obtainable.

3.4. Appraisal and Amendment of the Solution

The provisional solution found in 3.3 may be inacceptable because of too large changes in certain instrument variables, deemed to be impossible physically (e.g. capacity limit to production), or for psychological or political reasons (wage reduction or tax increase). "Conditional" targets may have to be dropped or additional instruments have to be introduced. Where degrees of freedom were left, a closer study of alternative instruments and their influence on social welfare are in place.

3.5. Methods to regulate employment and monetary equilibrium

Discussion of meaning to be attached to expressions "full employment" and "monetary equilibrium". Problems 011–061 (cf. Appendix 2). Money flows (government expenditure or taxes) more reliable instruments for regulating employment than factor prices (wage rates or interest rates). Choice between tax reduction and increase in government expenditure should depend on marginal utility of private and public expenditure and on delays involved. Multiplier for taxes lower than that for expenditures. Possibility of increasing total demand by expanding balanced budget. In depression, indirect taxes more efficient than direct taxes. Banking system may influence money flows mainly by restriction of credits. Financing of government deficit by loans to be preferred to credit creation with a view to avoiding future inflation; but credit creation not to be excluded for that reason, since loans may be impossible.

Monetary equilibrium may be maintained by the regulation of money flows, or of wage rates; but two simultaneous targets can be attained only if two instruments are applied. Apart from indirect taxes, wage rates seem to be the most appropriate instrument to be applied in addition to public finance.

Long-term targets may be added to the short-term ones; in particular the avoidance of future inflation. And the number of short-term targets may be increased by requiring "full" employment in a number of industries.

Indirect taxes or subsidies most efficient instrument for short-run regulation of employment in separate industries.

3.6. Main Problems of Development Policies

Investment the key to increased production. Problem 091. Fundamental choice of rate of development. Desirability and possibility of foreign aid, in order to reduce divergence in standards of life.

3.7. Example of Sector Policy in a Closed Economy: Transportation

Sector policy requires, among other things, decisions as to position with regard to other sectors. Characteristics of transportation: (*a*) low elasticity of demand; (*b*) bulky investment in some and (*c*) small units in other sub-sectors, implying high fixed cost leading to unstable prices in the former and a tendency towards over-investment in the latter: (*d*) a large number of partly noncompeting market compartments. Aims of policy: maximum contribution to national income, continuity and stability of facilities, income reasonable in comparison to other sectors. Instruments: price regulation, restrictions on entry to market, formation or control of monopolies. Price regulation may be needed to avoid both too low and too high prices; restrictions to entry of market in order to avoid over-investment in small units; formation of monopolies in order to prevent cut-throat competition; control of monopolies to avoid too high prices.

CHAPTER 4

QUANTITATIVE POLICY (II) IN AN OPEN ECONOMY; AND IN SETS OF ECONOMIES

4.1. Methods of Regulating Employment, Monetary Equilibrium and Balance-of-payments Equilibrium in an Open Economy

Open countries are dependent, for the volume of demand as well as for their price level, on the world market. They may be forced to "import" inflation from abroad but are sometimes able to "export" their own inflationary tendencies. Importance of ample reserves. Definition of monetary equilibrium "as the realization of the most desirable price level", to be distinguished from balance of payments equilibrium. Dependence on policies followed in other countries. Problems 111–152 (cf. Appendix 2). Policy requirements depend on the degree of similarity between the targets set abroad and at home. Necessity, in the long run, to maintain balance of payments equilibrium. In addition, nowadays, the further goals of "full" employment and monetary equilibrium will be maintained. Most efficient single instrument again public expenditure, although its multiplier is lower in an open country than in a closed one and varies according to the cyclical position. Together with money flows, price levels will now also have to be used as instruments; either exchange rates or the internal price structure, i.e. wage rates and commodity prices; perhaps both exchange rates and the internal price structure. Both will be needed if it is desired to maintain stable internal prices as well as balance of payments equilibrium. Efficiency of devaluation very different in different phases of cycle, and according to structure of country; the "critical elasticity" issue. Short-term and long-term effects; differences between wage policy and exchange-rate policy. Exchange-rate policy usually will not leave wages unchanged. Isolated wage policy tends to place the full burden of a difficult position on the workers, and a wage-adjusted devaluation tends to place the full burden on the other groups; sharing the burden is preferable. The interest rate only represents a weak instrument of regulating activity.

4.2. Multiple-target Policies for Open Economies

This represents the general type of quantitative policy for most countries. International ties in some respects reduce, but in others increase, freedom. "Imported inflation" as an example of reduced, and the possibility to "export inflation" as an example of amplified, freedom. Advantages of increases in productivity may have to be handed over to the other economies. Problems 161–191 (cf. Appendix 2).

Formal and material aspects (cf. 3.1.). Numerical combination of targets relevant. As long as each instrument acts on the various target variables in different ratios, any combination of targets may be obtained. Usually a problem of simultaneous algebraic equations. Sometimes the set of instrument values may be obtained by consecutive arithmetical operations. The target of full employment determines level of production, and hence imports; the target of balance of payments equilibrium then determines exports and these again determine the country's price level in international currency. With given exchange rate the wage level can be determined. With the internal price level as a further target, the exchange rate or the wage level will follow.

There may be inconsistencies in targets in that they are contradictory irrespective of the instruments used (i.e. since they do not obey a structural equation); or in that they are not attainable with the instruments admitted. This may be due to the fact that, even if the number of instruments is equal to the number of targets, some instruments are relevant to some targets, in a fixed combination only, so that other instruments will have to "do two jobs at the same time".

Also, boundary conditions on some of the instruments may reduce the possibility of solving a problem in economic policy. Importance of using a larger number of instruments than is strictly necessary in order to distribute pressure. Conflicts between short-term and long-term aims may be solved by the use of more instruments. For reasons of short-term employment it may be desirable to increase taxes, whereas for reasons of long-term development their reduction would be needed. If no other instrument is used, a compromise has to be made; but both targets may be served at the same time if two instruments are used, e.g. taxes and investment subsidies. "Trial-and error" policy usually requires a succession of steps whereas systematic policy tries to attain the target in one step; trial-and-error policy will not always be successful, but systematic policy will not always be possible.

Materially, this section confirms some of the conclusions as to the relative efficiency of wage rates, indirect taxes and credit policy. It is difficult to present general statements; one specific conclusion refers to the feasibility of "directed productivity increases".

4.3. Example of Sector Policy in an Open Economy: Agriculture

Most agricultural products have international markets. Foreign policies therefore influence national agriculture; home price policy only possible if trade impediments are accepted. Foreign policy may or may not be in accordance with home policy. Characteristics of agriculture: (a) random fluctuations in production; (b) low elasticity of supply; (c) low elasticity of demand; (d) a time-consuming production process; (e) seasonal fluctuations; (f) agriculture well organized in a number of countries; (g) land in short supply; (h) for Holland: land very fertile. Aims of Dutch policy: maximum contribution to national income; stable income, reasonable in comparison with other industries, regionally well distributed; seasonal pattern in labour demand with not too wide fluctuations. Instruments: import duties or subsidies, export duties or subsidies, price subsidies to consumer, quantitative restrictions, regulation of production, periodic stock accumulation and liquidation, and rent and wage control. Policy has to be flexible, adapted to changing circumstances; complicated. Only a few examples can be given; maximum contribution to national income fundamentally requires free trade pattern. Modifications: rather less production of commodities whose labour requirements are subject to overlarge seasonal fluctuations. If because of exceptional world crops prices are temporarily abnormal, normal prices may be maintained at home by duties or subsidies— on the import side for deficit products, on the export side for surplus products. A regulation of production will be usefull for products with a long period of production (pork); seasonal levelling out of prices by stock manipulations is another contribution to stability. To the extent that incomes of farmers are high in comparison to other industries (because of fertility of soil) reduced prices to consumers and rent control may be appropriate. If a certain region, largely dependent on one product, suffers from incomes which are too low, special regulations for that product may be appropriate.

4.4. Quantitative Economic Policy where Policy-makers are Many: (1) International Quantitative Economic Policy

Represents a case of decentralized policy. Introduces complications since policy also influences others' welfare and policy of other policy-makers influences welfare at home. Assumptions will have to be made about other countries' policy. Similarity with the problems of polipoly. Problem 211. Better results will be obtained if it can be assumed that other countries will follow a similar policy than if this is not the case.

4.5. Quantitative Policy where Policy-makers are Many: (2) Pressure Groups

Pressure groups are "states within the state" and their behaviour may be contrary to the general interest. Example of employers and workers.

CHAPTER 5

QUALITATIVE POLICY: CHANGING THE STRUCTUR WITHIN GIVEN FOUNDATIONS

5.1. Qualitative Policy consists of changing the less fundamental elements of social organization, those not affecting spiritual aspects or essential relations between individuals. Sometimes changes in quantitative data may bring about circumstances that require another type of organization (extreme scarcity, changing cost structure, better administrative techniques, etc.), but new ideas about organization may also come up spontaneously. No systematic way of summing up conceivable alternatives. Less knowledge available to make precise statements. Discussion of means one by one and an attempt at a synthesis at the end of Chapter 6.

5.2. Quantitative Restrictions (Q. R.) are an efficient means in the short run to attain the aims of equilibrium and equitable distribution under circumstances of extreme scarcity in markets showing a low elasticity of demand. Examples are food rationing and quantitative restrictions on imports if elasticities of demand for imports and exports are low. In the longer run the necessity to make the systems increasingly complicated makes them less attractive and freedom, partial at least, is preferable.

5.3. Built-in Stabilizers represent a structure of public expenditure that automatically counteracts cycles and hence to some extent replace *ad hoc* adjustments as discussed before (3.5 and 4.1). Problem 101.

5.4. Changes in Pricing and Taxation Schemes

Non-flat-rate charging an example of an efficient change in pricing techniques; it should, however, be based on correct cost calculations. With full use of capacity, marginal costs become high. Sliding scales for wages and other incomes lessen flexibility of economy; dangerous unless they would make financial authorities and organized income recipients more conscious of necessity to avoid inflation. In a well-administered state *direct taxes* are an indispensable instrument for influencing the rate of investment and for redistributing income. *Import duties* may increase a country's welfare (a) if they reduce unemployment; (b) because of the "infant-industry" argument and (c) because of the "optimum-tariff" doctrine. The same results for the country concerned may be obtained with less sacrifices from others by the use of subsidies in the case (a) and (b) and international redistribution of income instead of optimum tariffs.

5.5 Monopolies

Monopolies are an instrument to compensate for cut-throat competition in cases of over-capacity and high fixed costs. Their prices should not exceed long-term competitive prices; if they do, welfare is below optimum. Problems 071–074. Cumulative monopolies appear to be much more restrictive than vertically integrated monopolies.

5.6. Decentralization or Centralization in Administration may refer

to geographical as well as to institutional decentralization or centralization; there are stronger and weaker forms of centralization. Supporting, conflicting, neutral and mixed means of economic policy. Decentralization likely to lessen the use made of supporting and increase the use made of conflicting means. Decentralization to be recommended for means whose handling does not show economies of scale and whose affects are nearly neutral. *Centralization* to be advocated for clearly supporting or conflicting means. Trade impedimets, rates of exchange or wage rates and public finance surplus or deficit important examples of instruments to be centralized. Negative and positive integration.

5.7. Appraisal of Investment Projects to be based on net increase in real national product or expenditure they create (with possible modification for effects on income distribution), taking account of indirect and secondary effects and using equilibrium prices for products and factors. Problem 201. Priority figures cannot, strictly speaking, be calculated for separate projects, with a view to select some and rejecting others; among alternative sets of projects, requiring the same sacrifices of factors, the set has to be chosen which yields the maximum net increase in real income. Possible simplifications of procedure. Estimation of accounting prices. Labour-intensive industries as a rule more attractive to countries with little capital and much labour. "Industries" to be considered as technically inseparable combinations of complementary industries; "labour" to be understood as unskilled labour.

CHAPTER 6

REFORMS: CHANGES IN FOUNDATIONS

6.1. Reforms

Reforms are changes in the more fundamental features of social organization, affecting spiritual aspects and essential relations between individuals. Still less known about effects of these changes.

6.2. Social Security Schemes are important instruments of social justice, especially for the handicapped. Distinction to be made between formal and factual contributors to a scheme. Except when financed out of profit or income taxes most of the benefits are in the long run paid out of wages, since market forces determine the total of wages and benefits. Beyond a certain limit social security may lessen incentives to produce.

6.3. Minimum Incomes and Guarantees for Minimum Employment work the same way; minimum incomes cannot be an important portion of wages without endangering incentives to produce.

6.4. Equalization of Opportunities by cheap education, apart from being very important from a spiritual and social viewpoint, will raise the supply of qualified workers (in all ranges) in relation to non-qualified. Problem 081. Education will raise production and lessen inequality. Little is known about the distribution of desired and factual abilities, and about the possibilities of raising the quality of abilities.

6.5. Monetary Reforms may eliminate some of the instabilities, or un-necessary complications, of the present monetary system. Aim of "100 % money", meant to reduce violent expansion of circulation, may be attained by a wise monetary policy under present regulations as well. Problem 102. The "raw material standard" will reduce fluctuations in raw material prices in a much simpler way than would a set of commodity agreements.

6.6. Centralization of Production Decisions may avoid certain incon-sistencies (over-production), but would require a very complicated technique and would lead to power concentration, with dangers for individual freedom. Such centralization may recommended for industries with a long period of production and in a situation of extreme scarcity.

6.7. Industrial Democracy may be the best means to satisfy the need for self-respect and dignity with those occupying modest jobs. Important possibilities explored in European countries; need for further experimenting.

6.8. Nationalization

Nationalization is one of the most controversial subjects in economic policy, partly because of the vested interests involved. Nationalization may avoid over-production and eliminate unearned income, but it may en-danger efficiency and lead to a dangerous concentration of power. Scientific comparisons between nationalized and private industries are difficult be-cause of non-comparable situations. Such restricted evidence as is available suggests that the differences in efficiency are not large. Since there are other means to obtain the advantages claimed for nationalization, its importance seems to have been over-estimated. There are some secondary advantages to be found, however, in the control of certain vital national interests and the possibility to carry out an anti-cyclical policy in the field of investment.

6.9. Summary and Conclusion

A coherent treatment as recommended for quantitative policy is hardly possible yet for qualitative policy and reforms. The author tries to summarize his views on the probable effects, in an "average" country, of the policies discussed, in Table 6.9. Recommendations: to devote more effort to inter-national integration, including income transfers, stabilizing devices (including the raw-material standard), family planning, industrial democracy and the equalization of opportunities.

CHAPTER 7

UTOPIAS: MISCONCEPTION OF HUMAN NATURE?

7.1. Certain reforms have proved to be inefficient, mostly because a misconception of human nature was involved. They indicate certain limits set to reforms. These limits need not be lasting.

7.2. Complete Freedom means the jungle: the rule of the strong and brutal. Regulation of freedom by law recognized by all to be necessary. Even the regulated freedom of the 19th century led to unacceptable exploitation and inequality.

7.3. Complete State Regulation is inefficient and hence only acceptable in extraordinary circumstances. War economies have to some extent been abolished everywhere.

7.4. Productive Co-operatives (Associations) are attempts to replace hierarchy in productive organization by cooperation on an equal footing. The attempts have failed almost completely.

7.5. Abolition of Money as a means of saving, a proposal repeatedly made, is closest approximated by war-time rationing and inflation, when money loses its meaning. The attempts to "monetize" rationing coupons as well as the success of monetary purges illustrate the usefulness of money for accumulating reserves.

7.6. Complete Equalization of Incomes was attempted in Russia and Israel and appeared not, or not yet, to be possible. It disturbs the equilibrium between demand and supply of different types of labour, since it reduces the willingness to perform hard jobs.

7.7. Completely Free Services seem to be insufficiently appreciated by most people and are wasted therefore. Moderate charges even for vital services would seem to be a better device.

CHAPTER 8

SOME REMARKS ON THE ORGANIZATION OF ECONOMIC POLICY

8.1. Number and Nature of Agencies and Their Tasks

Economic policy, being a complicated activity, is divided over a large number of agencies, and requires deliberate organization. Organization dependent on type of policy and quality of officials. Since the handling of instruments is the task to be performed, executive agencies should be organized according to means. Coordinating and supervising agencies have to consider all the means and all the aims together. Means should be clearly allocated to the various agencies. The phases of planning, co-ordination and decision, execution and supervision. Time lags involved.

8.2. Planning of Economic Policy

The underlying principles are formulated by political parties; actual policy is planned by government agencies; such planning should already be based on provisional directives. Role of "declarations of intent"; desirability of contacts with private sector already in planning phase.

8.3. Co–ordination and Decision

Co-ordination commences with the issue of directives and ends with decision as to aims and means to be used and to what extent. Co-ordination requires the existence of inter-departmental bodies and staff organs and its general design should be a well-defined task of a well-defined unit. There will have to be clarity about the division of tasks between Parliament and Government. There should be a simultaneous proposal, at regular intervals, about important changes in policy, preferably on Budget Day.

8.4. Execution

The execution of economic policy is distributed over a large number of agencies, which partly have a certain autonomy and then have to be guided in an indirect way, e.g. by grants in aid. Numerous smaller decisions have to be taken in accordance with the general policy. Large numbers of non-economic factors, rightly or wrongly, influence the execution.

8.5. Supervision

Supervision of economic policy not only a means of control for Government, Parliament and citizens, but essential also to future planning and decisions. Largely a question of good statistics and analytical studies.

8.6. International Economic Policy

In the international field economic policy is scarcely organized at all. Responsibilities are often ill-defined. A large role is played by negotiations between autonomous governments. There is scope for more co-ordination and integration.

CHAPTER 1

THE CONTRIBUTION OF
ECONOMIC ANALYSIS TO THE DESIGN
OF ECONOMIC POLICY

1.1. Objective of this Study

1.11　This study is primarily an attempt to deal with problems of economic policy in a somewhat more systematic fashion than seems usual today. It tries to approach the subject from a scientific angle and has, therefore, to be careful in distinguishing between what contributions can be made by economic analysis and what contributions are, by their nature, not of a scientific character. The contributions this book tries to make may be presented under four headings, three of which are scientific while the fourth is based on intuition. They may be briefly formulated as:

(1) a description of the process of economic policy;
(2) methods for judging the consistency of the aims and means used in a number of types of economic policy;
(3) methods for indicating the optimum policy to attain given aims, and
(4) suggestions as to some of the aims.

1.12　The terminology used will first be explained at some length. Basic for all discussions—and discussions on economic policy are no exception to this rule—is a clear and precise *setting out of the problems* to be discussed. It avoids misunderstandings—which are very frequent in matters like this—and prevents those taking part in discussions from posing irrelevant questions. In the terminology to be developed in this book the setting out of the problem implies, among other things, that the aims and means of a policy should be explicitly stated before any discussion on it is started. Thus it will be found e.g. that in several cases lengthy discussions about the "causes" of certain economic difficulties are irrelevant because of the lack of correspondence between "causes" and "cures".[1] In other cases, apparent controversies appear to be due to differences in setting out of the problem discussed. [2]

1.13   It should also be made clear from the outset what this book does not cover. Practical details of a legal, administrative or technical nature will not be discussed; problems of general policy will only be taken up where they are vital to economic policy.

1.14   Since this study is primarily devoted to the logical structure of the problems of economic policy, its broad subdivision is derived from the fundamentally different *types of means* applied, to be called quantitative policy, qualitative policy and reforms; terms explained also in the headings of the chapters. Only the secondary subdivisions refer to the "outer form" or the particular type of means used. This does not imply, however, that no importance is attributed to the applications to practical cases. An attempt is made to clarify the main text by a large number of applications, using simplified models of some twenty types. A survey of the models used will be found in appendix I; and one of the problems dealt with in detail in appendix II. The models have been simplified for heuristic reasons. References will be made, for the specialists, to more complicated models, as needed in most practical situations. It is believed to be an advantage that most of the models are based on statistically tested relations.

1.15   The type of analysis offered will be found to vary greatly between the various chapters. Whereas it is hoped that chapters 3 and 4, dealing with quantitative policy, satisfy reasonable standards

---

[1] In a situation without international co-ordination, where each country acts autonomously, it is irrelevant, to quote an example, whether a decline in exports of country A is due to a decline in income of country B or to a decline in income of country C; no influence can be exerted by country A on these incomes and the decline in exports has to be met by other measures anyhow.

[2] A well-known example is the difference between depression and prosperity; a policy that is correct in a period of depression may be wrong during prosp' and if the phase of the cycle is not mentioned in a discussion, there may be considerable confusion.

of rigour, chapters 5 to 7, dealing with qualitative policy and reforms, are of a more sketchy nature. The author believes this to be a necessary consequence of the state of our knowledge and hopes it to be a challenge to further research. Notwithstanding this unsatisfactory state of affairs the author does believe that a summary of the kind he offers can be useful to many young economists working in the field of economic policy and planning.

1.2. Summary Description of the Economic Process and Its Determinants

1.21   The description to be given here is the economist's description; and even the theoretical economist's. The scene described is that of an *economy*, i.e. a group of human beings acting so as to satisfy their wants, with the emphasis on the material side, but without neglecting spiritual elements. The organization and operation of an economy is described by a number of elements, some of which are considered to be given and to come from outside the economist's realm, whereas others have to be explained by economic science and are considered to be a consequence of those in the first category. The given elements are called "data"; they refer to the natural, technical, psychological, institutional, and international elements which the economic action of man has to take for granted. Examples are climate, the crops, technical processes, human preferences, habits, laws, political agreements, world market prices and world market demand. As details which are, however, important in some questions of economic policy, one might add, among the psychological elements, the limited capacities of man, his hobbies, aversions, animosities and inertia. The elements of economic action itself will be indicated as "economic phenomena"; their quantitative aspects also as "economic variables"; examples are volume of production, prices, incomes, expenditure, capital etc. They are supposed to be logically explicable in terms of the data.

1.22   In an economy there are one or more institutions that will be called "*policy-makers*". They are, first of all, certain public authorities and may, in addition, be private bodies like trade unions, farmers' unions, big private corporations. As a first approximation we shall often consider the central government as the only policy-maker[1].

1.23   Among the data there are some that can be changed—to a greater or lesser degree—by policy-makers. They will be called *"means"* of economic policy; those that cannot be changed by policy-makers are called the *"other data"*. Not all means will be at any time actually controlled by the policy-makers; they may abstain from doing so. There are means of different types: they range from a change in the import duty on fish below 2 inches of length to the nationalization of the steel industry. We will distinguish qualitative from quantitative means; the former will again be subdivided into changes in "foundations" and changes in "structure". As every subdivision it is only a help to approximate the real character of things and its border-lines are to some extent arbitrary. Some means might be classified either as changes in foundations or as structural changes.

1.24   *Foundations* are, of course, the more fundamental elements in the organization of human society; those connected with spiritual values and those defining the essential relations between human beings. Examples of the former type of foundations are the freedom of confession or belief, voting rights, property rights, the opportunities for education; examples of the latter type of foundations are privileges of certain groups, the degree of division of labour and specialization, the degree of decentralization in production and in policy, the existence of certain forms of social security, and industrial democracy.

1.25   The group of elements in the organization of human society which we call *structure* are less fundamental; and there are qualitative as well as quantitative elements. The qualitative elements may be described as the details of economic and social organization, e.g. the number of policy-makers, the types of taxes in existence, or the system of distribution of consumer goods (rationing or free distribution)[2], or the degree of monopolization various industries show. The quantitative elements may be exemplified by: the number of social groups and institutions, their behaviour (e.g. their demand elasticities or their

---

[1] For a fuller description cf. chapter 8.
[2] One might prefer to consider this one of the foundations.

propensities to consume), the number of goods handled or the quantitative composition of an economy's real wealth. The futility of too precise a scheme of subdivision is illustrated by the border-line cases between qualitative changes and quantitative changes in structure. The abolition of an existing tax may be called a qualitative change as well as a quantitative one: a reduction to zero of the tax rate concerned. The transformation of a duopoly into a monopoly is another example.

The distinction between foundations and structure has not been made by most of the econometric authors writing on economic policy, but it is very common in literary economics and, in the present author's opinion, is of considerable importance. The common characteristic of foundations and structure is that they only, as a rule, change gradually or infrequently. There are many good, and some less good, reasons for this slow change, reasons which we are going to discuss later on (cf. ch. 5 and 6).

1.26   There remains the class of means which, as a rule, are of a quantitative character and are used for frequent changes, in fact for the adaptation of the economy to small and frequent changes in some of the other data. This class will be called *"instruments"* or "instrument variables" and may be exemplified by tax rates, items of public expenditure, the rates of discount, reserve ratios, and foreign exchange rates; in the Netherlands also the wage rate might be called an instrument of economic policy.

1.27   For all data, i.e. potential means and other data, a distinction can be made between those which, in certain problems, are considered constant and those which are assumed to vary; a datum need not be a constant. Usually the data that vary only gradually will be considered constant, but sometimes, for long-run problems, data showing rapid fluctuations, like seasonal data or crops, may be considered constant or stochastic over somewhat larger time units and then the "development data", like population and technology, will be considered to vary. As a rule, various meanings of constancy will have to be distinguished. For example, in the problem of short-term adaptation of an economy to the world market, the world market data may be considered as given and constant; constant, that is, relative to the alternative methods of adaptation studied. Once the most appropriate method has been found, however, it will be the changes in world market data that interest the policy-maker and at the second level of investigation they are therefore considered variable. Careful distinction between such levels of analysis will eliminate misunderstandings.

1.28   The process of adaptation of an economy to changing data, being the essential problem of "economic man" in practice, and of the economist in theory, emerges as a consequence of certain behaviour of economic subjects (citizens, firms), within the framework of the "laws" of nature, technology, and the juridical laws of the area concerned as well as other rules of the game. This behaviour and these laws and rules are formulated as *economic relations* or *equations*. Examples are the "demand relation", telling us how much of a certain good will be demanded under specified circumstances; or the "balance equation for a good", saying that production plus imports equals consumption plus exports plus stock accumulation; or the "production equation", expressing that one pound of yarn can be obtained from 1.07 lb of raw cotton; or finally, the "institutional relation" saying that income tax is a certain percentage of income above the exemption limit. These relations are, mostly, approximations: demand is subject to personal whims, qualities of cotton vary and taxes are evaded.

1.29   A system of relations, describing, in an approximate way, the adaptation process of an economy is called an *economic model*. It describes the behaviour of the mechanism which the policy-makers have to handle, or borrowing a musical metaphor, have to "play". Models will be discussed at length in chapter 2.

1.3. The Logic of Economic Policy; the Contribution of Economic Analysis to the Design of Economic Policy

1.31   As was already stated, economic policy consists of the deliberate manipulation of a number of means in order to attain certain aims. Taxes may be lowered to stimulate employment; social security may be introduced to further an equitable distribution of the national product. Such changes in means may be used to offset the effect of changes in other data: to offset, for example, a decline in employment caused by a change in taste or by an increased propensity to hoard. If such changes in other data have undesired effects on the economy, it may be desired to "cure" this "evil", and the "causes" of it may be seen in these changes in other data—in our example the change in taste or in hoarding habits. The cure cannot consist in reversing the initial change in the other data, however, since these latter cannot be changed deliberately. There need not, therefore, be any *correspondence between causes and cures*: a change in taste may be offset by a change in taxes. The causes may even be irrelevant to the indication of the "cures". The decline in employment may have been due to a change in commercial policy in some foreign country and yet the same measure will have to be taken as if the deline had been due to an internal change in taste. The causes do not always matter; what does matter, however, is how the means used will affect other phenomena in the economy.

1.32   The economic policy of a certain area may be in the hands of one or several policy-makers: to begin with, the case of *one policy-maker* will be considered. The problems created by the existence of several policy-makers at the same time will be studied later (cf. §§ 4.4, 4.5 and 5.6). According to the nature of the means used, we will make a distinction between *reforms, qualitative policy* and *quantitative policy*. Combinations between these types will, of cource, occur. Reforms, being equivalent to changes in foundations, are the most far-reaching types of policy. An example of a reform is the introduction of a social security scheme. By qualitative policy we mean changes in structure, that is, in the less essential aspects of social organization, such as a change in the number of taxes. Finally, by quantitative policy, we mean the changes that can be brought about in the values of the instruments of economic policy. This is the least ambitious type of policy, most frequently applied, and is particularly used to quickly adapt the position of the economy to variations in those data of the frequently changing type. Examples are adaptations in government expenditure, taxes, discount rates or reserve ratios.

1.33   While qualitative changes will, in most cases, also affect the quantitative aspects of the economy, quantitative means do not, as such, change the qualitative situation, although they may lead to

qualitative changes (cf. chapter 5). Quantitative policy in our sense
(i.e. the handling of quantitative means, or instruments), will be
directed towards the attainment of changes in quantitative aims, that
is changes in certain of the economic variables to be called target
variables or just *targets*. It may take one of two different forms: either
the targets may be *fixed*, or they may be *flexible*. With fixed targets
we mean targets of which the value has been fixed numerically, as,
for example, in the case where the government would aim at a level
of "full" employment (say 97% employment), and balance of payments
equilibrium (the deficit in the balance of payments then being equal
to zero), or at a numerically specified investment programme. We shall
speak of a flexible target, if the aim of policy is formulated as, for
example, maximum real income per head, leaving it to circumstances
what that maximum would mean numerically. This is clearly the more
general type, since there is always, in some sense, the intention to
attain maximum welfare, whatever its interpretation. It also represents
the analogue of the action of individuals, the difference being, among
other things, that the side conditions imposed on the action of the
individual are more stringent than those which the policy-maker has
to obey.

1.34   It is necessary to consider the economic policy at a certain time
as a *coherent whole*, because of the interdependence between most
economic phenomena. A change in one instrument will as a rule
influence all target variables; the cases where a certain group of
instruments acts only on a certain group of target variables and
another group of instruments on another group of target variables,
to be called cases of "partition", are only exceptional. It follows that
the fixation of any one of the instrument variables at a certain level
should be based on the complete set of targets. A practical example is
that credit policy should not, for example, be based on the requirements
of the balance of payments only, but also on those of employment.

1.35   Economic policy may show a wider or a narrower *"range"*, this
being the number of aims and means involved. Policies with a wide
range, therefore, are the more ambitious types, those with a narrow
range the more cautious.

1.36   The logic of finding the best economic policy, that is, of finding the extent to which certain means should be used in order to achieve certain aims, is, in a sense, an inversion of the logic to which the economist is accustomed. The task of economic analysis is to consider the data (including the means of economic policy) as given or known, and the economic phenomena and variables (including the aims of economic policy) as unknown. The problem of economic policy considers the aims as given and the means as unknown, or at least partly unknown. Its logic is simplest in the case of a problem of fixed targets in quantitative economic policy. Here the unknowns are simply the numerical values of the instrument variables (supposed to be indicated qualitatively by the setting of the problem) whereas the numerical values of the target variables are given.

The logic of problems of quantitative economic policy with flexible targets is different: it is a maximum problem, namely to find the values of instrument variables that render a certain welfare function a maximum. Its mathematical nature is more complicated. In certain cases it can be handled systematically, in others it cannot, particularly if the instrument variables are subject to certain boundary conditions. The problem then becomes one of trial and error. For problems of qualitative economic policy trial and error is the rule: here the various alternative possibilities have to be studied separately before an optimum can be found. This is the main reason why we have chosen to treat these types of problems one after the other.

1.37   As has already been observed, economic analysis cannot provide a complete treatment of problems of economic policy. "Extra-economic" elements are involved: especially the choice of aims, and, to some extent, the choice of means. But, nevertheless, analysis can make some important contributions. It can (a) help to judge the consistency of the aims assumed, and of the aims and means as a combination; subjects to be discussed further in sections 1.4 and 3.3. By detecting inconsistencies it may (b) narrow down the possibilities and so contribute to the solution. Finally it can also, as has already been shown, and will be shown in much more detail in chapters 3 and 4, (c) determine the values of instrument variables in problems where targets or more general aims have been sufficiently specified and cannot be shown to be inconsistent.

1.38 The *procedure of policy-making* can be subdivided in certain phases, between which it is useful to distinguish. Since policy usually emerges as a consequence of tensions between the actual state of the economy and some desired state (the aims), the first stage consists in *ascertaining the actual state of affairs*. Being given that both this stage and the following stages require time, it will often be wise to try to make a *forecast* under the assumption of no change in policy. This means that the probable changes in "other" data have to be determined as well as their effect on the economic situation. It may, for example, be expected that population will go on rising as well as productivity, that the world market price level will fall by a certain percentage, and so on. In order to estimate the consequences of these changes for national income, employment, prices in the country concerned and other variables use will have to be made of a particular economic model, explicitly or implicitly.[1] Once an estimate has been made of the prospective state of affairs, the second stage of the procedure consists of finding out *whether this state diverges from what is considered the most desirable situation*. If this is found to be the case, the third stage commences: the effects of possible alternative economic policies have to be estimated. To a certain extent this will also be possible on the basis of economic analysis; the more so, the simpler the policy changes are. If a fairly reliable model of the economy exists and if quantitative policies are considered, more can be said than if little only is known about the functioning of the economy or if more fundamental changes are envisaged. The first three stages may be said to represent the *"planning stage"*. This use of the word planning has nothing to do with the type of policy involved. Planning in our sense can be applied to any type of policy, including, of course, that type of policy sometimes called "planning". This latter type of policy will be briefly discussed as a policy of "centralized production decisions" (cf. § 6.6). The fourth stage of policy-making is that of making a choice, i.e. *taking a decision*. The fifth stage is that of the *execution*. The first four stages may be indicated as the *"design"* of policy and are more particularly the subject of this book.

[1] For examples of the operations just indicated the reader may be referred to the "Central Economic Plans" for the Netherlands, published by the Central Planning Bureau of that country.

1.4. Aims of Economic Policy

1.41　Policy-makers base their acts, consciously or unconsciously, on *preferences*. They choose certain aims because they think them worthwhile; they sometimes choose between alternative aims or they give reduced weight to one aim in favour of another, all of which presupposes certain preferences. They are not prepared to apply certain means if they consider the cost or trouble involved is not compensated by the aims reached. It is not certain beforehand that the preferences used in different decisions are always consistent. There will, however, be a tendency towards consistency, since inconsistency is only a lack of understanding or of foresight. If the preferences are consistent, they may be represented by some central, all-embracing, concept in the minds of the policy-makers, which we usually call *welfare* or utility of the economy to which the decisions refer. This welfare concept will largely, but not always completely, coincide with a certain representative individual welfare concept. In other words, the welfare function according to which the policy-maker acts will depend, among other things, on the quantitative and qualitative elements that also enter into these *individual* utility functions. In addition, *"collective preferences"* will come in, that is, preferences taken into account by the policy-maker because of feeling himself responsible for the economy in a collective sense. The elements of importance to the community as a whole will, at least, count strongly to him.

1.42　The elements entering into the policy-maker's welfare function thus refer to:

(*a*) elements determining individual material and spiritual well-being, such as the quantity of goods available (food, shelter, etc.), the efforts to be made, the opportunities for education, the right to take part in decisions;

(*b*) elements determining relations between individuals such as:

(i) the degree of freedom left to individuals,

(ii) the frequency of conflicts, or the degree of social and international peace, and

(iii) the positive elements in social relations, e.g. the degree of justice or the "social climate".

Some of these elements will be specified later on; sometimes they take special forms, at least in the short run, e.g. the form of the maintenance of a number of constitutional rights. [1] Many difficult problems in even the definition of these "elements" have to be solved before they can be used in a more rigorous analysis, one interesting question being how many independent elements are needed. For each element not only the "average" value or quality, but also various "distributions" are important. Not only the average quantity of food and shelter available, but its distribution over various groups of population—social, industrial, regional—are important. Not only the quantity available today, but also that for future periods, and hence, indirectly, the equipment to produce it, is relevant. Policy-makers will be interested, too, in the question as to whether future development will be regular or not. Very often they will group and summarize the interests of the population with the help of concepts which do not play a direct role in the minds of the majority, such as real national income or expenditure, national wealth, the balance of payments surplus, etc.

1.43   Policy-makers' social welfare functions are often influenced also by some *general theories* or *"principles"* concerning economic policy, these tending to summarize experience with, or scientific insight into, this complicated matter, and more or less streamlining it. Liberal politicians, for example, tend to emphasize the importance of economic freedom of the individual, since they think they can rely on a number of self-adjusting forces in the economy for letting it adapt itself to changes and blindly find its optimum state. Communists tend to doubt the usefulness of these forces and are much more impressed by deliberate organization, directed towards more equality. They stress the immorality of private property of capital, but do not consider forced labour immoral, just to quote a few examples. Nationalists are especially impressed, in most cases, by "national interests", about which they have numerous mythical concepts, not primarily economic in character. Socialists, while also sensitive to more equality between individuals, and not dogmatically in favour of free enterprise, have

---

[1] An important attempt at formulating the fundamental human rights was made by the General Assembly of the United Nations (cf., "Universal Declaration of Human Rights," U.N. Publ. 1949 1.3).

drawn conclusions from their experiences with dictators and have a higher valuation for freedom than communists.

1.44   In order to make comparisons between welfare functions the concept of *"similarity"* will be used. Two welfare functions will be called completely similar, if the same variables enter into them in the same mathematical form, but the variables in the one function refer to one individual or group and those in the other to another individual or group. Complete similarity is equivalent to equal tastes or preferences of the individuals to which the welfare functions refer; these individuals may also be policy-makers. Some of the variables in a welfare function of a policy-maker will refer to the distribution of certain phenomena (say, real income) over the individuals of the economy. Since the distribution in a large group is a more complicated concept than in a small group these variables may not be the same in both cases; this would preclude the existence of complete similarity between policy-makers' welfare functions referring to economies of different size. As an extreme example it may be stated that in an individual welfare function the concept of distribution over the individuals in the group does not even apply. However, as soon as the distribution can be characterized, with sufficient exactitude, by some statistical measure independent of the size of the group, the possibility is reintroduced of similarity between welfare functions for economies of different size.

Similarity may also be incomplete, and we shall speak of this when the same variables occur in the welfare functions of two individuals or of two groups, but with co-efficients that are slightly different; or if variables occur in them which are not exactly the same, but comparable in type; or if both things occur.

A complication may arise if, among the variables in the welfare function, there are also instrument variables (or other "means"), representing the costs and frictions involved in the use of such means (cf. § 1.7). If we have to compare a large and a small community, the use of the same instrument to the same degree may have to be valued differently in the two cases, since, for a larger community, its costs and frictions may be different from what they would be in a smaller one. On the one hand there may be "economies of scale", making it cheaper to organize the same thing in a larger community than in a smaller one. On the other hand, and this will probably apply for such units as countries, it may become more expensive and troublesome to organize something over a very large area. Even with the same distribution of tastes among individuals there will no longer be similarity of policy-makers' welfare functions between the smaller and the larger community.

1.45   In this terminology there may be a certain degree of similarity between individual welfare functions and that of the policy-maker. The more democratic is the community, the more will the citizens be able to further this similarity, with the proviso that, for this comparison the representative individual defined in some reasonable way should be taken. It hardly pays, however, to make this definition more precise, since it is clear beforehand that the similarity cannot, and should not, be complete. As has already been observed, the policy-maker has to give a higher weight to some elements from among the community as a whole, which may be taken to mean that allowances to correct for certain inconsistencies within or between individual welfare functions have to be made. If people have a short-run preference for certain stimulants that in the long run are detrimental to their health, the policy-maker will sometimes correct for this (by imposing excises for example). If people individually tend to evade taxes, the policy-maker, nevertheless, will be in favour of measures against such evasion. If some groups of the population, because of shortsightedness, prefer not to be educated or trained, the policy-maker will perhaps force them to go to school, etc. Finally, the policy-maker may, and often will, have a more detailed knowledge about the variables that enter into the welfare function.

1.46   In the light of all this the author doubts the relevance of the question whether social welfare functions can or cannot be derived from individual ones; a question to which some high-quality analysis has been applied. [1] For the time being the margins of inaccuracy in the above allowances for inconsistencies would seem so large, and our exact knowledge of individual welfare functions so limited, that the

[1] Kenneth Arrow, Social Choice and Individual Values, New York 1951. Cf. also Leo A. Goodman and Harry Markowitz, "Social Welfare Functions Based on Individual Rankings", The Amer. Jl. of Sociol. LVIII (1952) p. 257.

theory of economic policy would be better to take the policy-maker's welfare function as its starting point. But, no doubt, this has to be a temporary attitude only.

1.47   The aims of economic policy have changed a good deal in the course of history. This has probably been partly due to changes in individual aims generally, but fluctuations in economic convictions have been more important. In particular, the belief that the economic mechanism might have sufficient inherent forces of self-regulation did, in the nineteenth century, exert considerable influence on public opinion. To the extent that this belief is still correct, economic policy may be one of abstention. Liberal politicians, on the basis of the liberal school of economic science, held this belief very strongly and consequently reduced the range of economic policy. They did believe it was necessary, nonetheless, to have a legal framework in order to prevent excessive exploitation of the weak by the strong.

In recent decades, the strength of this belief in the economy's power of self-adjustment has shown severe fluctuations. It shrank in the face of the great depression and nobody dared to rely on it during the two wars. Opposite beliefs came up, emphasizing the necessity for all sorts of regulations; and there were swings in public opinion corresponding to the heavy swings in economic conditions. On the whole, however, the opinion has gained support that the forces of self-adjustment are not universal but dependent on a number of circumstances that can be clearly specified. Under extreme scarcity, to quote the most important example, the self-adjusting forces can be shown to work with small effectiveness only (cf. §§ 5.2; 3.7; 4,3). This may be of importance to developed countries in times of extreme scarcity and to underdeveloped countries even in normal periods.

1.48   It may be useful to give a brief summary of what would seem to be the *aims of economic policy in modern times*. It will be clear, however, that there is quite some difference of opinion in this respect, and that our summary, therefore, can only be meant to be an "average" of existing preferences and may have been influenced by the author's own predilections. The following points, then, would seem essential:

(*a*) *Maintenance of international peace*. This point would not usually have been considered as an item on the agenda of economic policy, even up to a few decades ago. Today it has to be, since the very foundations of our existence are at stake. But it would have been wise if, by 1914, economists had already stressed peace as an element of human well-being and economic policy-makers had not considered it as an outside element.

(b) *Maximum real expenditure per capita with "full" employment and monetary equilibrium.* Whereas, in this phrase, real expenditure per capita stands for material welfare, full employment has been added in order to remind us of the importance of work as part of human life. A maximum material welfare at the cost of unemployment, other than temporary and restricted in size, would not be acceptable. The word "full" has been given in quotation marks, since it has to be accepted that a small percentage of unemployment will, for technical reasons, be unavoidable and need not be serious—if it does not always press too much on the same people. Monetary equilibrium, which will be defined more precisely later (cf. §§ 3.5 and 4.1), stands, roughly speaking, for the maintenance of the purchasing power of money, a point of interest to all those who have to live from savings and to the process of saving itself, and hence of development. It might rightly be doubted whether, in reality, the aim should be that of maximum material welfare; for some of the most wealthy communities it might be better that an optimum, instead of a maximum, be aimed at. Human needs are not infinite, as has been incorrectly maintained by some economists; but, in view of the utter poverty of the larger part of world population, the aim of maximum per capita real income is still a good approximation. Instead of real income, real expenditure has been chosen as the aim; the difference being only that the latter measures the quantity of goods made available after income has been spent; whereas the former measures the quantity of goods produced.

(c) *Improvement of distribution of real income or expenditure over social groups and countries.* The phrase is necessarily vague, since what means improvement to some will be what others would call a deterioration. The intention is to indicate that actual distribution is not optimal and should be a subject of study and change; the author's opinion being that both distributions are, in almost all respects, too unequal. More will be said on this subject in sections 3.6 and 6.4.

(d) *Emancipation of certain under-privileged groups.* This point, also,

will not be considered by some as a subject of economic policy. Since
economic and social life cannot, however, be separated and in view
of the overwhelming significance which the social problem has for a
large part of the world's population, this point does represent a major
item in world welfare. It refers, above all, to the workers and peasants
in the less prosperous countries, but also to some other groups, and
still applies to more prosperous countries as well.

(e) *As much personal freedom as compatible with the other aims.* The
significance of freedom to large groups, though more particularly to
the more independent groups in the population, has been increasingly
recognized since dictatorships have reappeared. The point is therefore
essential, and especially so if spiritual issues are involved. A certain
lack of freedom in economic matters is not too serious, if it is the
necessary counterpart of other economic or social advantages. The
formula given should perhaps have been that an optimum combination
between (a), (b), (c), (d) and freedom should be sought. Since our
knowledge, at present, about most of the qualitative elements in (c),
(d) and (e) is only vague the exact phrasing is irrelevant for the moment.

1.49   In order that practical decisions on matters of economic policy
can be taken it will often be necessary to know the relative importance
attached to the relevant aims. In most cases such knowledge has so
far not been collected explicitly, although it certainly would not be
difficult to do so, with, for example, the help of interviews. In technical
language, it would not be difficult to construct indifference curves of
policy-makers with regard to, say, employment, balance of payments
surplus, price rises and so on. The questions to be asked would be of
the type: how much price rise would you be prepared to accept if you
could attain a one per cent increase in employment? Such questions
should, of course, be put to various policy-makers and it should be
made clear that the answer will depend on the initial situation.

Apart from explicitly collecting such data one might try to discover
what implicit valuations have played a role in practical decisions. Such
implicit value judgments are of course made continuously; the choice
of a set of targets is one example. Upon closer investigation it might,
however, frequently appear that an explicit formulation would be
instructive to the policy-maker himself (cf. § 1.6).

One may, of course, also try to construct welfare functions on the
basis of some intuitive knowledge about policy-makers' preferences.
One simple statement to be made will be that there are two types of
target variables to be distinguished, namely those whose optimum
values are within the field of attainable values and those whose optimum values are outside that field. In many developed countries,
employment is an example of the former category; the optimum value
may be 97%, a value frequently surpassed. It is less desirable to have
100% than to have 99% employment. The relation between employment and welfare in such countries will be a curve with a maximum
and cannot be represented by a linear function. An example of the
latter category may be, even for many developed countries, real
expenditure per head. Within wide limits a rise in this target variable
will be considered an advantage. The relation between real expenditure
per head and welfare will have to be a rising curve and may be approximated by a linear function. [1]

1.5. Inconsistencies in Individual and Collective Aims

1.51   In the previous section we tried to describe the nature of the
aims of economic policy and the relations that may exist between the
individual preferences of the citizens and the preferences of a policy-
maker with regard to the collective unit for which he is responsible,
briefly called collective aims. As was set out in § 1.3, the contribution
that economic analysis may make to the design of economic a policy
consists, among other things, of judging the consistency of aims. In the
present section an attempt at such a judgment will be made.

Since the aims of economic policy are ultimately connected with the
aims of individual economic activity, inconsistencies in the former will
to some extent derive from inconsistencies in the latter. And because
of the intimate links between economic activity and general way of
life, the inconsistencies of human behaviour generally, including
cultural behaviour, cannot be disregarded; if we are on the search for
inconsistencies we shall meet sociologists in their search for explanations
of the cultural crisis of the present. Our remarks will only be brief

[1] For other examples and their application cf. J. Tinbergen, Centralization
and Decentralization in Economic Policy, Amsterdam 1954.

indications, however, and will probably be influenced by personal preferences of the author.

1.52   By an inconsistency in aims we mean a situation in which some things are aimed at which *are ultimately incompatible* with other aims held concurrently. A very simple example is the aim to eat a cake in conjunction with another aim to have it. The aim to have a good time and hence not to save may, later on, prevent the same man from having a good time. A government may keep wages very low in order to let the country develop itself rapidly; but if it went too far it might evoke a civil war which might destroy the advantages of development so far obtained.

Speaking of collective aims, we will not class as an inconsistency the divergency that may exist between individual aims of the citizens, or even those divergencies which may exist between the individual aims of all citizens, on the one hand, and those of the policy-maker, on the other hand. It is in the nature of things that different individuals have different aims; and if too big divergencies exist between the citizens' preferences and the policy-maker's, there is an imperfection in the system of representation. Interesting and difficult though this latter problem is we do not consider it a case of inconsistency. This we assume to exist only if the above definition applies, where the fulfilment of certain aims precludes that of other aims.

1.53   In a general way one may state that inconsistencies are a consequence of imperfections in the human mind or in the control of the mind over the desires. Its ability to penetrate into the interrelations of the world is limited; a state of affairs which is recognised in such expressions as "narrowmindedness", "shortsightedness" and "superficiality", applicable to most, if not all, human beings. The state of affairs is also illustrated by the underdevelopment of science. This is true of all science, but is relatively more so in the more difficult subjects than in the easier ones; it is more true, for example, of sociology than of economics. The result is a state of affairs which necessarily entails the substitution of dogma for real knowledge.

Inconsistencies, by their nature, are most likely to occur in those problems in which there exists a marked separation between cause and effect; separations in time as well as in terms of social or geographical distance. Where effects are far away, there is the greatest chance for decisions to be made, or desires to develop, that are later regretted.

1.54   Among the important and widespread inconsistencies in individual economic behaviour, and hence short-term aims, are those referring to the choice of education and to the creation of a family. Generally speaking, too many young people choose too little education and care too little about family planning; very evidently because of the shortsightedness of others as well as of themselves. The test of inconsistency is that, if they could have chosen again, they would have chosen differently, and that this continues to be true for successive generations.

Another important inconsistency in individual aims is the lack of concern for other people's well-being which is characteristic for present-day civilization and which may be partly due to the teaching of the Manchester school of liberalism that it is sufficient for the good of all if every one looks to only his own interests. It is associated with the belief, or doctrine, that there is no limit to man's wants, so that it continues to be worth while to go on accumulating personal wealth even if a fairly high level has already been reached. In fact the increase in satisfaction derived from additional quantities of goods, beyond a certain limit, rapidly declines. The well-known phenomenon of over-saturation observable among wealthy individuals, or even populations, and characterized by a tremendous waste of resources and the creation of invented wants, are among the consequences. The doctrine that every country should use its own resources for its own well-being only is another expression of this state of mind which bars the way to important possible methods of improving the world's social stability.

1.55   The inconsistencies in the aims of the citizens will, of course, be reflected, to some extent, in those of their policy-makers. This may not always be the case, for the policy-makers may successfully resolve the inconsistencies.

The most appalling inconsistencies in collective aims are those which are responsible for the outbreak of war, which, in modern times, may be said to be contrary to the aims of most governments, and of all populations. It is easy to say this, but less easy to say where the inconsistencies are to be discovered. The problems concerned are largely non-economic in character but their importance to economic policy is so overwhelming that they should at least be mentioned. Anything that can be done to prevent war ranks very high in the whole of economic aims.

Apart from this complex of aims, the author sees important inconsistencies in the aims fostered with regard to the size of population, to the facilities of education and to social and geographic inequality. Population aims underestimate the consequences of over-population; those with regard to education underestimate the consequences of lack of education, and the consequences of present-day inequalities are also underestimated. This latter applies to social inequalities inside each country as well as to inequalities between countries. It does not apply to an equal degree to all countries, and least to the Scandinavian and Anglo-Saxon countries, and a few others of a comparable kind.

Inconsistencies which are of local importance only, but which rank high in the countries in which they apply are to be found in the aims of development policy, wherever such policy leads to serious inflation. The existence of serious inflation proves that the sum total of aims attempted has been too ambitious. In most cases this is because it is desired to develop the country and at the same time maintain the existing level of consumption. Without foreign assistance this is an impossibility; insufficient foreign assistance may itself be the consequence of inconsistencies in international economic policy, however.

1.6. Some Suggestions as to Aims

1.61 Another contribution which economic analysis is able to make to the design of economic policy is to make suggestions as to aims. The suggestions may be meant:
 (i) to take account of new facts or new insight;
 (ii) to remove observed inconsistencies;
(iii) to give definite shape to aims only vaguely felt; to reformulate old, or create new, aims.

A few examples will be indicated without attempting to give a coherent treatment.

1.62 Perhaps the best example of new facts, of which account needs to be taken in the design of whatever policy, is the situation created by atomic weapons. It may be said that these weapons have introduced the probability that their use will obliterate a nation before obliterating its military power apparatus, whereas, up to date, it has been the other way round. This new situation requires a technique of international and military policy that may be quite different from what it has been so far. We will not go into important questions such as this, since they are not considered to be economic questions, but it is necessary to stress their vital importance for economic policy.

1.63   If our thesis is correct that human needs, instead of having no limit, have, in fact, a ceiling, then this thesis might constitute another example (this time of a purely economic character) of new insight whose consequences for the aims of economic policy need to be investigated. The general conclusion would seem to be that more emphasis needs to be placed on some degree of equality in distribution.

1.64   The removal of some of the other inconsistencies discussed in § 1.5 would lead to the suggestion that more family planning and more education should be included in present-day programs of economic policy. In addition, for a number of countries, more orthodox financial aims should be recommended.

1.65   The shaping or reformulation of aims which are only vaguely felt may be exemplified in the aim of *social justice*. Social justice, whatever its meaning, is an aim of economic and social policy which, in the minds of many citizens of many countries, ranks very high. An attempt at defining social justice, in such a way as to appeal to most people's feelings and to be amenable to scientific analysis, might be of great importance. Social justice has, essentially, to do with comparing the satisfaction of different individuals.

1.66   The contribution made to our problem by most of present-day economists has been to declare the comparison of different individuals' satisfaction an impossibility. This contribution is not very constructive, since it implies (i) that all feelings about social justice are meaningless, (ii) that the scientist cannot make any contribution, and consequently (iii) that it is left to others, who often lack scientific education, to make such contributions. The first implication is especially important since it implies that the numerous decisions actually made about questions of distribution could just as well have been made differently.

1.67   There is another attitude with a minority of to-day's economists. They do not preclude a priori that comparisons can be made; they only feel that, so far, no general method has been developed, even though there exist methods applicable to special hypotheses. That general methods may nevertheless be found is a possibility, for several reasons. First, decisions are continuously being taken which imply such comparisons; the simplest example being the decisions taken within the family. In the ideal case it may be said that the family head compares, in his own mind, the satisfactions of the members of the family; and if his "projection" of the welfare of the family members into his own mind is correct, the possibility of having made the comparison would have sprung from the fact that these projections are made by one individual, using one system of preferences to appraise them all. Decisons of this type are not restricted to the heads of families, but are taken by a large number of organizers, policy-makers, judges etc. The extent to which such decisions are consistent and systematic, at least, could be made the subject of serious study.

Secondly, comparisons about shifting situations are continuously being made by experienced people, when making their own decisions. The essence of this type of comparison is that those concerned have not only gone through different external situations, but may have undergone a change in internal conditions. An untrained man who undergoes a training course has been transformed from one type into another. A man who was healthy and becomes ill, a man who has lived well and then suffers a famine, both of these have undergone an internal transformation and may be able, in their minds, to make comparisons. Processes of transformation such as these are, perhaps, rare at present, but the development of medical and psychological sciences may well make it possible to expand their number and scope.

Thirdly, by the same development of medical and psychological sciences it may be possible to determine what compensations for a number of "handicaps" are sufficient to neutralize, in terms of satisfaction, these handicaps. This might be called the analytical, as distinguished from the two other synthetic, approaches. It might gradually become possible to "build up" type A man by superimposing on type B a number of "handicaps"; and type A man could then be given a number of compensations so as to make him "equally happy" as type B.

In ways like this it may be possible to make fruitful contributions to this problem, which is not the first in the history of sciences to have been regarded—by renowned scientists—to be insoluble in principle.

1.7. Means of Economic Policy

1.71   It is not a matter of indifference to welfare which means of economic policy are used: their application implies certain *costs*, both material and immaterial. Material costs are all sacrifices to be made in terms of resources, that is, the use, by the policy-maker, of manpower, capital (in the form of buildings and otherwise) and nature (e.g. areas for military exercises). Immaterial costs include the aversion of the citizens to certain restrictions on their freedom, or the frictions arising out of them: these may, indeed, also lead to material costs. Generally speaking, the costs will depend on the extent to which the means of policy are used, and they may be different for different types of means. In any case they enter into the welfare function of the policy-maker, or at least ought to. It follows that the unnecessary application of means will be avoided and so the range of means applied will be wider at one moment and narrower at the other. The range may also differ from one country to another. Variations also occur as a result of changes in prevalent ideas. During the liberal era there was a tendency for the range to narrow down, while during the great depression and during both world wars the range quickly widened: the nature of the emergencies to be met required the application of a greater range of means of economic policy. As we will show later, there are good reasons to advocate an increase in intervention both during periods of extreme scarcity, as in war time, and periods of extreme unemployment, since in those circumstances the automatic adaptation of the economy becomes less efficient.

1.72   Various political parties have *pre-conceived ideas* about the desirable range. Such ideas may represent certain side restraints in problems of economic policy, but most frequently they will mean a restriction on the type of instruments to be used. Various political groups in western countries e.g. would in principle exclude the means of nationalization; a certain number of them would also, in "normal" times, reject a priori the means of price control. Other groups are just as strongly opposed in principle to any lengthening of working hours, or to the reduction of certain social security benefits. Such dogmatic attitudes do not appeal to the scientist, of course, and they do not appeal, either, to those who try to find, with an open mind, the most efficient solution of a difficulty in each particular situation. A seemingly dogmatic attitude may have a partial justification if it is based on an attempt to take account of those ultimate consequences of a policy which do not bear directly on the situation in question. This element— real farsightedness—should not, of course, be rejected. It follows from the requirement that economic policy must always be considered as a coherent whole.

1.73   If the effects of a measure are taken account of, and its application is, as it should be, made dependent on its efficiency in dealing with the "evil" to be eliminated, it follows that more means will be needed the more difficult the situation is. In a difficult situation the advantages to be obtained by the application of certain means are larger and it follows that more "costs" can be borne before the optimum is reached.

1.74   The disadvantages connected with an intensive use of certain means may be relatively much higher than those connected with a moderate use only. This may impose limitations on their use, that is, it may lead to the practical rule that it hardly ever "pays" to apply them above a certain more or less well defined limit. Such a limit will be called a *"boundary condition"*, in accordance with existing mathematical terminology. It may be, for example that when income taxes are increased beyond a certain figure, evasion will assume large proportions, leading to much extra cost in the broadest sense. For that reason it may be wise not to raise these taxes beyond that limit—a limit which may be different for different countries and periods. [1]

---

[1] Colin Clark, Welfare and taxation, Oxford, 1954, considers 25% of national income to be a limit beyond which taxes cannot be raised without causing inflation. Cf. also "Public Finance and Changes in the Value of Money", The Econ. J. 55 (1945), p. 371.

Or it may be that a wage reduction of a certain extent may arouse such opposition among workers that a certain boundary condition should be recognised here. One may say that boundary conditions sometimes represent the defence lines of certain social groups, but they need not always be justified defence lines.

1.75   Certain means may be *inconsistent with regard to a given set of aims*. This term we will use for the situation in which the set of means considered cannot lead to the aims assumed. Or it may be that some, or all, of them are too restricted in their effects to attain the aims set. The tobacco excise alone, to whatever levels it be raised, cannot suffice to solve a problem of a serious balance of payments deficit. The discount rate, however vigorously handled, cannot draw a country out of a deep depression. Inconsistency of a set of means and aims need not be ascribed to insufficiency of the means considered, it may also be attributed to overambitiousness in the aims set. Examples will be given in chapter 3 and 4. Inconsistency may be imperceptible in the short run but only apparent if long-term consequences are brought into the discussion. A wage increase may be a way to improve the distribution of income but it may, if too strong, endanger future employment and by so doing, adversely affect the distribution of income in some later period.

CHAPTER 2

ECONOMIC MODELS

2.1. Scope of Models

2.11   As we already observed (§ 1.2), the way in which certain means of economic policy influence the economic situation depends on how citizens and institutions react (i.e. adapt themselves to the new data) and this behaviour is represented by the economic relations, or equations, which together form an economic model. The word "model" also indicates that the assumptions made about the nature of this behaviour are explicitly stated and that they are in many respects a simplified picture of reality. These assumptions are partly of a "natural" character, partly of a technical or legal, and partly of a psychological character, as has already been shown in brief. Together they specify the foundation and structure of the economy considered. Such specification has always to be a simplification because of the very complicated nature of economic life. As a rule, only a few of the most relevant characteristics of society are implied.

Exact specification is necessary to avoid confusion and misunderstanding, for, on the basis of such specification only can the economist put precise questions and try to give precise answers. Problems of practical policy have therefore to be interpreted in terms of such simplified models and, after the analysis has been made, an interpretation back (i.e. an application of the findings of the model back to the real situation) has to be attempted. Here, of course, divergencies of opinion may, and necessarily will, arise. It is an initial advantage for mutual understanding, however, if consensus of opinion can be obtained on the precise problems and answers constructed with the aid of the models; this helps to narrow down differences of opinion. And if somebody believes that model A does not fairly represent the actual situation to be discussed, he will be forced to indicate in what respect that model has to be changed. For the revised model, the problem can be considered anew.

2.12 Since a model has always to be a simplified picture of reality, and reality may widely differ from one situation to the other, it follows that there will have to be made many different models, each of them meant to focus on certain aspects of economic life. Accordingly, there is a great variety of models. Some categories may be mentioned. There are, on the one hand, *micro* models, in which a large number of "compartments" is assumed to exist (e.g. firms and households) and where, for example, a distinction is drawn between a large number of different goods. On the other hand there are *macro* models where such distinctions are not made, but certain features common to all compartments are considered, perhaps in more detail than would otherwise have been possible. There are models for *closed* economies (economies without international trade) and for *open* economies (with such trade). Still another distinction is that between *static* and *dynamic* models. Here the line of distinction is chosen differently by different authors. We will call a model dynamic only if, in one or more of its relations, economic variables occur which relate to different time periods. Most of our policy models will be static. This implies that for this year's situation this year's variables only are relevant, there being no variables referring to earlier dates or, if we use a quarter as a time unit, only this quarter's variables are relevant for this quarter's situation. This heavy simplification may be acceptable if the time units we are using are long ones, that is, if we are interested in long-term equilibrium. It is also acceptable in another situation, however: if we are only interested in what happens in the next time period, as is the case in short-term policies (including year-by-year policy decisions). In that case all economic variables referring to previous time periods are already known and may be considered as given. For this reason the model for the next time period, only, will be static in character, according to our definition, even if reactions are influenced by the previous values of economic variables.

2.13 A complete description of a model requires an enumeration of a large number of details; and hence a systematic survey of all conceivable models (indicating, for each detail. what other choices could have been made) is difficult. We will not therefore try to give a systematic survey, but we will mention some of the "details" or features in order that the reader may have some basis for judging models that will be presented to him.

2.14   Important features seem to be, first of all, a certain number of details about the *"actors"* (the acting firms, households or other entities) entering into the model:

(a) Their *number*, defining the degree to which the model is micro or macro in character. We will repeatedly work with only one or two actors, namely the combined private firms and households as one ("aggregated") actor and, perhaps, the state as the other.

(b) The *nature and behaviour of their income:* from what sources does it originate and how does it react to certain other phenomena? If one of the actors is "all wage earners", its income is payment for labour supplied: we need to know, how do wage earners react, as regards their supply of labour, to the wage rate? If an actor is a producer of goods, how does he react to changes in their price?

(c) *Spending habits:* what part of income of the actors is spent, what is left unspent (hoarded); what part of it is spent on investment, what on consumption; how is consumption expenditure distributed over various goods, if there are more than one?

(d) *Nature and origin of wealth:* Is it assumed that the actors are in the possession of wealth, or assets? Are they liquid or non-liquid assets? How does this wealth come into existence: by savings, or by value increments?

(e) *Investment habits:* how do the actors invest their savings, and how do they react to changes in prices and yield of assets?

2.15   Another set of details concerns the *markets* occurring in the model, and hence at the same time the goods handled at these markets.

(a) *Number.* It depends again on the degree of aggregation whether only a few, or many, markets are assumed; they may be markets for final commodities, for intermediate products and for factors of production (e.g. labour).

(b) *Stock or flow character* of commodity handled: is the market considered a market for the flow per time unit produced and exchanged, as it must be in the case of a non-durable commodity; or is it a market where the total stock of a commodity, whether produced recently or at some previous time, is handled? For durable commodities, including liquid assets, this is the more relevant market for somewhat longer time units: the price of new securities is not independent of the price of already existing ones.

The further details concerning markets, such as the elasticity of demand or supply are, in essence, already included in the details about the actors.

2.16   A third class of characteristics has to refer to the *technical relations* (including legal or institutional ones) involved:

(*a*) *Number* of each type: how many production relations, how many tax relations?

(*b*) *Nature of phenomena involved:* is one equation assumed to exist which tells us how much product will be obtained out of given quantities of factors of production (e.g. how much nitrogen monoxide is obtained from given quantities of nitrogen and oxygen); or is there one relation for each factor of production which tells us how much of that factor is needed to produce a given quantity of the product (e.g. one equation indicating how much sulphur is needed to produce a ton of sulphuric acid, one other telling us how much hydrogen is needed and a third one for the oxygen needed)? As is well-known, there are two alternative methods of describing the production process, corresponding fairly well to the situations prevailing in chemistry if the reaction is, respectively, an equilibrium reaction or a one-sided reaction.

(*c*) *Mathematical shape.* The relation between product and factor may be one of proportionality or one of decreasing returns, and so on. The relation between income and income tax may be less or more progressive, etc.

2.17   As has already been observed, the enumeration is not easily made a complete one. The list just given is by way of example only, but making it sufficiently clear, that there is a very large number of possible models.

A model will be represented most accurately by (i) a list of phenomena and variables distinguished, and (ii) a system of *mathematical equations*. Each of these equations contains a certain number of the unknowns and a certain number of the given variables and constants. Not all the unknowns need occur in every equation, but they may. If all of them occur in every equation, we may say there is complete interdependence. No single one can be determined independently of the others. But there may be other logical structures, such as that in which each equation contains only one unknown. Each unknown can then be determined independently of the others: this means that the constants that do not occur in the one equation containing a certain unknown do not influence that unknown. Suppose the unknowns are x_1 and x_2 and the given quantities are indicated by a's and b's, while the equations are:

$$a_{11} x_1 \qquad\qquad = b_1 \tag{1}$$

$$a_{22} x_2 = b_2 \tag{2}$$

then x_1 is not influenced by b_2 or a_{22}. If, however, as in the previous case, x_2 had also occurred in the equation (1), and x_1 in equation (2), e.g.

$$a_{11} x_1 + a_{12} x_2 = b_1 \tag{1'}$$

$$a_{21} x_1 + a_{22} x_2 = b_2 \tag{2'}$$

then x_1 is now also influenced by b_2 and a_{22}.

Still another, and interesting, logical situation is the one where x_1 occurs in the second equation, but x_2 does not occur in the first:

$$a_{11} x_1 \qquad\qquad = b_1 \tag{1''}$$

$$a_{21} x_1 + a_{22} x_2 = b_2 \tag{2''}$$

Now we say there is a certain "causal ordering" [1]; meaning that x_1 is independent of what occurs in equation (2''); but x_2 is not independent of what occurs in equation (1'') and may be said to depend on x_1. In a way, therefore, x_1 may be said to cause x_2, and not the other way round. The values of x_1 and x_2 may be found in succession and their determination can be easily explained in ordinary speech. This difference in logical structure has some practical consequences to be discussed later. It should now be clear that the type of logical ordering shown in a model may be different, for the problems of economic analysis, than it is for the problems of economic policy, since the unknowns are not the same set in both cases. (Cf. §§ 4.22 and 4.23).

[1] Cf. Herbert A. Simon, "Causal ordering and identifiability," in Studies in Econometric Method, ed. by W. C. Hood and T. C. Koopmans, Cowles Commission Monograph Nr. 14, New-York–London, 1953, p. 49.

2.18   The solution of a problem in economic analysis, as well as of a problem in economic policy, consists, in principle, of the solution of the unknowns of the whole system of equations which together form a model. The unknowns differ for different problems, a point which will be illustrated by many of our "problems" (cf. appendix 2). The advantage of working with models represented by sets of equations lies in the decomposition of the process of research into logically arranged elements, facilitating its being checked. The somewhat loose talk about direct and indirect "effects" of a certain measure of economic policy, usual in verbal analysis, may easily forget one or several of these effects. In the system of equations no such oversight is possible. In addition every "effect" of whatever order can be traced and localized, and its influence determined.

2.2 Some Conclusions from Models

2.21   In a sense it can be maintained that all economic reasoning has been based, and must be based, on models. All economic theory may therefore be classified as "conclusions from economic models". If we are here formulating some of them, in a very brief way, we are confining ourselves to those portions of economic analysis that seem to us to have a particular importance for economic policy. There are two types of conclusions from models; one refers to models that are completely aprioristic in nature and the other refers to models in which statistical material has been used, that is, to models that, on being tested statistically, have (in some way or another) proved successful.

2.22   Propositions derived from aprioristic models have been proved to be dangerous, primarily because so many aprioristic models are not realistic. The assumptions on which they rest must therefore always be borne in mind.

One of the very important conclusions drawn from economic models is what might be called the *optimum proposition of free exchange.*

Several attempts have been made to prove that some sort of optimum situation will be reached if the organization of production and distribution is based on perfect competition, or, in the practical terminologies often used, free enterprise and free pricing. It can indeed be shown [1] under certain conditions to be discussed later, that perfect competition leads to a so-called Pareto optimum. A Pareto optimum is a situation in which it is not possible to increase the utility of anybody without decreasing somebody else's utility. Inversely, any Pareto optimum can be obtained by a process of perfect competition.

The contents of these statements should not, however, be misunderstood, as they often are. The following points have to be kept in mind.

1. There is not just only one Pareto optimum, but there are a large number of them; and a choice between these is only possible if we have some social utility function, which, under certain further assumptions, may be equivalent to having a method of comparing utilities of different individuals. Each of the Pareto optima is characterized by certain income transfers, and the prices resulting for the different commodities will depend on these transfers.

2. It has not been proved that the one particular case where no income transfers take place at all is "better" than the other Pareto optima. On the contrary certain income transfers will even be necessary, if only because firms working under decreasing marginal costs may suffer permanent losses. There are strong further reasons for advocating income transfers.

3. Certain methods of transfer, as, for example, an income tax of the usual type, are, however, not compatible with a Pareto optimum if the only constraints accepted are those required by the necessities of production. [2]

4. Perfect competition without any further specification of economic organization—without a specification of either some income transfers, or other equivalent measures, for example—is not sufficient, therefore, to define the organization of society, and thus it cannot be said to lead to an optimum.

5. According to 1 and 4 some further specification of either the social utility function or income distribution has to be given before an

---

[1] I am indebted to professors Ragnar Frisch and Tj. C. Koopmans for their help in finding my way through the highly specialised literature in this field.

[2] It may, however, be that other methods of transferring income between the subjects of an economy are so difficult to organize that the method of income taxes of the usual type has to be chosen, nevertheless.

optimum situation can at all be deduced. A well-known choice is the existing income distribution (after allowance for income transfers as they exist already) and the resulting system of free-trade world-market prices that would result. For small countries existing world market prices are sometimes taken as given. Either price system can be used to define a "total value of production". This total value of production (either at free-trade world-market prices or at existing world-market prices) will then be made a maximum by perfect competition, provided the other conditions are fulfilled on which the optimum proposition is based.

6. The most important of the other conditions may be summarized as follows: (i) at least one factor of production is fully used; (ii) exchange possibilities will not be threatened with interruption; (iii) marginal costs of production should not ever be decreasing; (iv) production techniques should not depend on the length of time during which they have already been applied; (v) productivity does not depend on the way income is distributed.

2.23   This optimum proposition of free exchange has exerted an enormous influence on economic policy, as we already stated. It has led the liberals to advocate non-intervention in matters of economic policy. Indeed, without going as far as advocating complete non-intervention, almost any political party would use it as an argument for leaving certain sectors of economic life, at least, to themselves. It may be said to be the basis even of a good deal of socialist ideas, especially as far as the freedom of consumption, the freedom to choose one's job and a claim for freedom of minor management decisions of socialized enterprises is concerned. The main problems of economic policy may indeed be formulated as consisting of *finding out the limitations* to this general theorem and deriving the necessary modifications to a policy of fundamental freedom of action. These limitations will prove to be important enough; but still a good deal of modern economic policy, including socialist policy, may well be said to have the task of (i) providing a certain framework of institutions within which very much can be left to the free action of producers and consumers and of (ii) correcting certain less desirable consequences of the system of free exchange.

2.24   A discussion of some important factors that invalidate the central proposition is therefore needed.

(i) The *full use of at least one factor of production* is not at all times guaranteed. In periods of depression unemployment may develop, even if there is no lack of capital or land. If such unemployment develops, wages do not quickly react and even if they react, demand for labour does not increase quickly and sufficiently. For these reasons the full use of at least one factor of production has to be a subject of deliberate concern of the policymaker (cf. §§ 3.5 and 4.1).

(ii) If *interruption of the process of exchange* is a possibility, as in the case of war, it may be wiser to deviate from free pricing and production and, in particular, from relying on imports for essential goods.

(iii) Free pricing appears to be *impossible* for goods produced under *decreasing marginal costs* for the complete range of production. It would lead to prices equal to marginal costs and these would be below average costs and hence imply permanent losses to their producers. This has in practical life led to the creation of monopolistic organizations which then do seem to be justified.

(iv) If techniques *depend on the time during which they have been applied*, that is, if the element of experience plays an important role, there may also be good reasons to deviate, if only temporarily, from free pricing and production (the "infant industry argument").

(v) Finally, it may be that *maximum production* value or "efficient production" does not represent the aim of economic policy, or not the only one, and so deviations from free pricing seem justified. In particular, questions concerning the distribution of the product over the members of the community may have this effect.

2.25   One of the further limitations to the relevance of the central proposition of free-enterprise economics is caused by the *static* character of the assumptions from which it is derived. No account is taken of the difficulties that may arise from the process of adaptation, for this necessarily requires a dynamic analysis. Among the features of the processes of adaptation, to be called dynamic features, there are several which lead to unstable processes. An unstable process is one which, instead of moving from the old equilibrium directly to the new one, produces unnecessary swings or never even reaches the new equilibrium. This can be a consequence of the existence of "lags" in the reactions, or of the occurrence of speculative effects, or of the role played by stocks.[1] Sometimes, therefore, deviations from free pricing and trading will be justified and even necessary in order to avoid instabilities in the adaptation process.

2.26   Apart from the general theorem just discussed there are one or two minor conclusions of a theoretical nature, to be drawn from models, that deserve attention. The first refers to the implications of *durability*. For a durable good, especially if its life time is considerable, the annual flow of production is necessarily small in comparison with the total stock available. Changes in that annual flow, even if considerable as a percentage ot that flow, cannot, within a short time, influence the market position of that good to any appreciable extent. It is well known that rents, for example, cannot react appreciably on, say, an excess in building activity, except after some years. This is a reason for rents being a poor regulator of the housing market. For similar reasons the influence of the rate of savings in one individual year on the rate of interest is only a very remote one and so, therefore, is its influence on the inducement to investment.

A second statement that can be derived from a consideration of orders of magnitude is that changes in the price of a commodity or service which is only a minor factor in the production of a certain product will not influence the supply of that product very much: those changes have little affect on the cost and hence on the profit margin. Thus it is well-known that price changes in a minor raw material of any product do not influence the supply of that product. Similarly, the influence of the short-term rate of interest on general activity is very restricted: Short-term credits are only a minor component in the process of production as a whole.

2.27   Conclusions from *statistical testing* can only be conditional in nature. Statistical tests never can prove a certain causal relation to be "true". It can only be stated that if certain variables, x, y, z..., may be assumed to be the most important ones to cause fluctuations

---

[1] For a more detailed treatment of such processes see W. J. Baumol, Economic Dynamics, New York 1951.

in another variable u, and if the additional influences may be assumed to be stochastic, the most probable size of the influence of x, y or z on u is so and so much. So it has been proved that if profits and equipment prices are the most important variables affecting fluctuations in investment activity, the influence of the rate of interest on investment activity in the past has been relatively weak. Put in another way this means that if profits etc. are an important factor, the changes, in the past, in investment activity have been mainly due to changes in profits and to a much smaller degree to changes in interest rates. It does not follow that, should profits be much more stable in the future than they have been in the past, the influence of the interest rate would not then be relatively larger.

Similar statements can be made about the price elasticity of demand for a large number of goods. If it is true that fluctuations in income are the most important causes of changes in demand, then the price elasticity of the demand for many goods appears to be fairly low. Substitution, in other words, is of some importance only between goods as closely related as various types of meat, or as margarine and butter; not between the, say, twenty items into which the complete set of consumer goods will usually be subdivided.

Finally, if prices of manufactured products are primarily dependent on costs, their flexibility appears to be rather high, that is, these prices are only influenced to a small extent by the quantity demanded. Only if this quantity comes close to the capacity for producing these goods, will its influence on prices become important, that is, in the "bottleneck stage".

If incomes and prices are the most important factors making for demand in international trade, it appears that short-term elasticities of substitution are moderate. This comes to saying that a price decrease of country A's product, while country B's product does not change in price, will affect the demand for A's product in relation to B's only moderately. In many cases, a relative price reduction of 1% will only lead to a relative demand increase of some 2% and often no more than 0.5 or 1%. This is particularly true for nonstaples and for exports as a whole. For staples higher elasticities will be found. Long-term adaptations of total exports (i.e. after some 3 years or longer), will show elasticities up to about 4.

2.3 Survey of Models Used as Examples in this Book

2.31 In order to illustrate the use that may be made, in the design of economic policy, of economic models and in order to give a hard core to some of the propositions on economic policy that will be made in this book, some twenty models have been constructed or taken from literature and described in Appendix 3. These models are the basis of some thirty separate "problems" defined with some precision and spread through chapters 3 to 6 inclusive. Appendix 1 provides a survey of the models used and Appendix 2 a list of the "problems" treated with their aid. It has been thought useful to give a brief characteristic to each model—although for the reasons given previously such a characteristic cannot claim to be unambiguous. The choice of the models will be discussed in the remaining sections of this chapter. In the survey the number of variables involved, specified according to 35 categories, has also been indicated. The categories have been described in brief in the heading of the table of Appendix 1; certain further specifications can be found in Appendix 4, giving a list of variables used in the various models. Because of its completely different character, model 08 has not been summarized in Appendix 1 and the notation used has been explained separately. Some general remarks on the notation used for the other models will be given here.

2.32 *Latin* letters have been used to denote economic variables and some variables that are closely related to them but which sometimes play the role of instruments (wage rates, government expenditure). *Capital* letters indicate money sums (either flows or stocks); the other Latin characters therefore indicate either prices or quantities. *Greek* letters, which are not explained in Appendix 4, indicate data and more particularly coefficients in structural equations, that is multiplicative data usually representing elasticities, propensities, quotas and related concepts. These Greek letters usually are the same as the Latin letter representing the variable at the left-hand side of some structural equation. They are defined in the detailed description of models in Appendix 3. Greek symbols may be specified by lower indices if more of them occur in one equation. Lower indices with economic variables are used to indicate time periods and will therefore only be found in dynamic models. Top indices are used to indicate specifications of variables; if a larger number of "compartments" (either industries or countries) is distinguished, they are specified by a top index h, of which the highest value is H. In model 15, transactions between sectors are indicated by two top indices, characterizing the sector of origin and the sector of destination.

2.33　In some of the more complicated models it appears to be useful to introduce, apart from the *absolute* value of any variable, its *deviation* from a certain initial or equilibrium value. This deviation plays the major role in the computations and has then been denoted by the simplest symbol used, the symbol without any bar; if this is the case, it is mentioned explicitly. The initial value is then represented by a barred symbol and the absolute value by a doubly barred one. The same method has been followed in a single case where a Greek symbol represented a variable (namely, in model 18, symbols a_1 and a_2). In all other cases the unbarred symbol represents the absolute value of the variable or constant considered.

2.4 Closed Static Models

2.41　The models listed under this heading refer, as is clear, to closed economies and therefore disregard foreign relations. For the world at large this is evidently permitted, whereas for a country like the United States it is a possible first approximation. They may also be used for a group of countries of sufficient total "size", if "size" is used to refer to the degree of isolation. These models have the advantage of showing certain fundamental tendencies in the internal problems of the economies concerned, without confusing the student by the complications of foreign trade. They have been used by almost all economists.

A first group (01–05) is in addition of the *macro* type, which further simplifies them. Clearly, they are only useful so long as all sectors in the economy show almost parallel changes, but this is, as a rule, characteristic of both the general cycle and the process of general development. The models to be described here are very well known in literature and their advantage lies in their simplicity. They will all be indicated by short names summarizing their main characteristics. A full description is given in Appendix 3.

2.42 MODEL 01:   MONEY FLOW MODEL

The first to be discussed is the simplest Keynesian model, where only two variables are considered, national income and outlay. The model is essentially meant to represent the behaviour of the economy during short-term movements. The two relations represent, to put it briefly, the *income formation* and the *income spending equation*. The first says that, in a closed economy, income originates from total expenditure, from which no deductions have to be made, because no imports of raw materials take place. Expenditure as far as for investment goods should be taken net, however, i.e. gross investment expenditure minus depreciation allowances. To the extent that replacement exceeds depreciation it has to be included in gross investment. If replacement falls short of depreciation allowances, it contributes to gross investment by a negative amount.

The second equation, that of *spending* income, indicates the "laws" of spending, or the behaviour of income recipients with regard to spending. Keynes' simplest hypothesis is taken, in which it is assumed that expenditure depends only on income, i.e. consists of a constant "autonomous" portion X_0 and a portion varying with Y, but not necessarily proportionally.

2.43   MODEL 02: MONEY FLOW AND PRODUCT FLOW MODEL

The second model is derived from the simplest Keynesian model by the introduction of one further element. In the simplest model no distinction is made between the money flows of income and expenditure and their "real" counterpart, the quantities of goods they represent. It depends on the level of *prices*, whether the same flow of money commands a larger or a smaller quantity of goods. A third variable therefore intervenes, the price level. A third equation has now also to be added, expressing the action of those who fix prices. Usually the price level, in short-term cyclic movements especially, is itself dependent on the "economic position", i.e. on the level of demand, since, apart from autonomous elements such as cost changes, a higher price can be charged the stronger is the market position. Simultaneously, the higher the demand, the more need is there for the supply of marginal suppliers, which can only be attracted by a higher price. This is what equation (3) expresses. Equation (4) is a definition.

2.44   MODEL 03: MONEY, PRODUCT AND FACTOR FLOW MODEL

One further element is now being introduced, namely the most important factor of production (as far as short-term fluctuations in activity are concerned), *labour*. Not only will the money flow of demand and the price level (and therefore the product flow) vary in the course of short-term fluctuations, but also the flow of factor demand, in this case employment. This has various implications. It becomes possible for the composition of income to change with changes in its size. And, since expenditure may be dependent on income composition, it becomes necessary to specify income. Labour income will depend on employment, but also on the wage rate l, which therefore has to be added to the list of variables. Unless we consider it as an autonomous datum (which is justified in the case where the wage rate is considered to be an instrument of economic policy), we have to add an equation expressing the behaviour of wage-fixers. We will, however, consider l as an instrument of policy (except in § 6.4).

Finally employment a has also to be determined and will, as a first approximation, depend on the volume of production x. It need not be proportional to x and hence it has been assumed in equation (4) that the relation is again linear with an autonomous term.

2.45   MODEL 04: MONEY FLOW AND PUBLIC FINANCE MODEL

This is another generalization of model 01, where the role of government is somewhat more specified in that a distinction is made between *government expenditure* and other expenditure by the economy (private expenditure), while *taxes* are introduced at the same time. Government expenditure is considered to be an autonomous variable, namely an instrument of economic policy, whereas taxes are assumed to consist of both an autonomous part and a term depending on income.

2.46   MODEL 05: MONEY FLOW, PUBLIC FINANCE AND ASSETS
       MODEL

This again is a generalization of model 04, in that the "public" is now supposed to hold *assets*. Two types of assets are introduced, namely *money* and *bonds*, of which the quantities held are M and B, respectively. It is assumed that the issue of bonds is an instrument of economic policy and that therefore B represents a datum. The amount of money in the hands of the public at the end of each time period will then depend on their incomes, their expenditure and the value of the bonds $\varDelta B$ added to their assets; the nature of equation (3), expressing this, being that of a "balance equation" or a "finance equation".

2.47   The second group of "closed static models" will be a pair of *micro* models, though still of a very simple nature.

MODEL 06: HORIZONTAL MONEY AND PRODUCT FLOW MODEL

This is a generalization of model 02 in that it assumes the existence of a large number of different final goods that may be bought, the prices and quantities of which need not necessarily move in a parallel way.

2.48   MODEL 07: HORIZONTAL MONEY AND PRODUCT FLOW MODEL WITH MONOPOLIES

This model differs from the preceding only in that it is assumed that one or more of the products are monopolized and their prices accordingly fixed so as to maximize profits under certain conditions to be specified.

2.49   MODEL 08: MODEL FOR INCOME DISTRIBUTION

This model is of a completely different nature. Instead of making a distinction between different products it lumps them together as in the macro models, but here productive services are considered in detail. A large number (in fact an infinite number) of different jobs is introduced and the income formation process is presented as a price formation process with supply and demand as instruments of analysis. Each job is described by the intensities of the required abilities and each individual by the actual intensities of these abilities he shows. The choice made by each individual is assumed to be based on a utility function. It is further assumed that the income scale for the various jobs depends on the required intensities as well as on the quantity of product delivered and the scale is supposed to be fixed in such a way as to equate demand for and supply of jobs in each category.

2.5 Closed Dynamic Models

2.51   Dynamic models have an important part to play in the explanation of economic movements. They are less important, however, in policy designing. Decisions have, as a rule, to be taken with respect to relatively short intervals; and most of the problems will refer to what is to happen in the next short interval. The development up to the moment of decision can be considered as known and given. The unknowns (as a rule the values of the instruments) then refer to one, the next, time interval, and the nature of the problem is then a static one. This explains why dynamic models are often not needed even if problems of rapid change are being considered. Nevertheless there are problems of policy for which such models will be needed, namely problems in which a longer series of events has to be considered.

2.52 MODEL 09: DEVELOPMENT MODEL

A first example is supplied by the problems of development. Model 09 is a very simple model on the interdependency between *capital formation* and future production. It is a model in physical concepts only, considers a succession of time units, in which savings are accumulated and used to build up a growing stock of equipment, leading to a rise in production assumed, for simplicity's sake, to be proportional to the stock of equipment. A distinction is made between depreciation and replacement and between the stock of equipment (or capacity) and the stock of capital.

2.53 MODEL 10: BUSINESS CYCLE MODEL

The number of models of the business cycle that has so far been presented is embarrassingly large. Most of them contain a large number of variables, probably in agreement with reality. It would lead us much too far to try to introduce such complicated models here; our intention being to illustrate rather than to present complete schemes. This is why a very simple model bearing on certain features, only, of real cycles has been chosen in this series; features which appear to be interesting from the political point of view.[1] These features are, the cumulative process during upturn and downturn

---

[1] Readers interested in more realistic and refined models of the cycle may be referred to L. R. Klein and A. S. Goldberger, An Econometric Model of the United States, 1929–1952, Amsterdam, 1955 and J. Tinbergen, Business Cycles in the U.S., 1919–1932, Geneva, 1939.

(connected with lags between income and expenditure), the existence of an upper and a lower value of total expenditure and the influence of price movements (as distinct from price levels) on income calculations and hence expenditure. In the author's opinion, this latter feature, the phenomenon of *"paper profits"* has, wrongly, been somewhat neglected in many models of the cycle. It may be somewhat overemphasized in the present model.

2.6. Open, Static Macro-Models

2.61   After having dealt with a number of problems in countries (or combinations of countries) for which *foreign trade* can be neglected, we will also have to study policy problems in countries on which international trade has an important impact. In order to make comparisons easy, the models for this group of problems have been chosen in all other respects similar to models 01 to 05 inclusive and been numbered 11 to 15. There is one exception however: the separate variables of public finance, namely tax revenue and public expenditure, have not been introduced. Instead the rate of exchange has, in model 15, been introduced as a variable.

2.62   There is of course no clear-cut boundary line between macro and micro models. A micro model is one in which a number of different sectors of the economy are separately introduced: what number is a question of taste. We have chosen to call micro models some (to be treated in § 2.7) which others might have considered still as macro models. A model is included in which some details of public finance have been introduced.

2.63   In agreement with what has just been said, the characteristics of the models in the present section are the following:

MODEL 11: OPEN MONEY FLOW MODEL

This is the simplest Keynesian model which contains only money flows, but now including imports and exports. This is the model used for the *"foreign trade multiplier"* by Machlup and others. The money value of imports is assumed to depend in a very simple way on nominal national income, which evidently constitutes a heavy simplification.

2.64 MODEL 12: OPEN MONEY AND PRODUCT FLOW MODEL

Here again, a distinction between money flows and product flows is introduced, implying that prices also enter into the picture, prices being important in international competition and therefore even more essential in open than in closed economies. Here it is possible to make more precise assumptions as to the relation between imports and the internal economic situation. It has been assumed that the volume of imports is directly related to the volume of gross product.

2.65 MODEL 13: OPEN MONEY, PRODUCT AND FACTOR FLOW MODEL

In addition to the flow of products the flow of labour is now considered separately, and consequently its price, the wage rate, becomes an important potential instrument of economic policy. Because of the simplifying assumption that labour income is spent in the same way as non-labour income, and labour productivity is not supposed to change, it is not necessary, however, to introduce employment as a separate variable. This will be done in models 16, 18 and 19.

2.66 MODEL 14: OPEN MONEY, PRODUCT AND FACTOR FLOW AND
         EXCHANGE RATE MODEL

For open countries the target of balance of payments equilibrium may be added to the two discussed for closed economies, namely full employment and monetary equilibrium; and accordingly a third instrument of policy will also be needed (cf. § 4.1). This is why an open model with both wage rates and exchange rates is here presented.

2.67 MODEL 15: OPEN MONEY FLOW AND ASSET MODEL

The introduction of financial assets is also of particular importance to open economies since their exchange may influence the balance of payments. This has been done in model 15, where the principle of the monetary survey as conceived by Schouten has been introduced.[1]

2.7. Open, Static Micro Models

2.71   As already stated we have chosen the term micro to apply even

---

[1] J. Tinbergen und D. B. J. Schouten, "Die Anwendung des Nationalbudgets zur Beurteilung der Währungslage," Wirtschaftsdienst **34** (1954) p. 4.

to a model where, apart from a "macro" treatment of the business sector, public finance is described in some more detail, bringing the number of variables already to 13; we also apply it to models where some sector of the economy is treated in detail, a model which we may call a "focussing model". Like a looking glass it shows us part of the object in detail and sharply, whereas the rest is more vaguely described in outline. Accordingly the following models are being considered here.

2.72   MODEL 16: OPEN MONEY, PRODUCT AND FACTOR FLOW AND PUBLIC FINANCE MODEL

This model is a combination of more features than have so far been combined and will serve as a basis for a "multi-purpose policy" as it usually occurs in practice. It makes a distinction between consumption and investment, between factor-cost and the market-price value of consumption, introduces direct and indirect taxes, and a different spending pattern for workers and independents. It still does this in the very simplest way possible and might be made far more complicated if less simple assumptions concerning the same phenomena were made.

2.73   MODEL 17: OPEN MONEY FLOW, ASSETS AND BANKING MODEL

This is a focussing model for certain questions of banking policy. A complete, but still simplified, balance sheet for the banking system is introduced, in addition to what has to be the basis of every model, the main money flows of the economy.

2.74   MODEL 18: OPEN, TWO-INDUSTRIES PRODUCTIVITY MODEL

This model focusses on two industries, of different structure, and on the results that may be due to changes in productivity in an open country. In contrast to the previous models, it therefore varies the ratio between the volume of production and the volume of labour employed, and this independently in the two industries.

2.75   MODEL 19: OPEN HORIZONTAL MONEY, PRODUCT AND FACTOR FLOW MODEL

This model is comparable to model 06, but applies to an open economy. It has, in addition, been made somewhat more general in that now expenditure on each commodity is assumed to depend on all prices. This is a type of complication which brings this model very near to Leontief models in which inter-industry physical flows are considered.

2.8. Open Dynamic Micro Model

MODEL 20: PRIORITY CRITERIA MODEL

Only one example will be treated in this category, namely a model to be used for the discussion of *priorities* among a group of investment projects. In order to give a complete discussion it is necessary not only to distinguish between the projects, which makes the model clearly a micro model, but also between present and future time units, which makes it a dynamic one.

2.9. Groups of Economies Model

In many respects there is no difference between industries and countries as compartments of an economy. It is therefore for the economist rather than for the mathematician that a separate type of models is announced under his heading.

MODEL 21: GROUP-OF-ECONOMIES MONEY-FLOW, PRICE-LEVEL
        MODEL

In this model, with full employment and balance of payments equilibrium as targets and public expenditure and price levels as instruments, the most important short-run international policy, as dealt with by Meade in particular is discussed.

CHAPTER 3

QUANTITATIVE POLICY: REGULATING THE POSITION WITHIN A GIVEN STRUCTURE; I—CLOSED ECONOMY

3.1. Nature of Problem; Practical Approach so far Mostly Used

3.11   According to our terminology quantitative policy leaves the structure and the foundations (i.e. the organization of the economy) unchanged. It consists mainly in the current adaptation of the economy to the continuous changes in data that threaten to upset its equilibrium. Changes in the world market, caused by crop changes or changes in policies of other countries, changes in techniques applied or in the age structure of the stock of capital goods, and numerous incidental deviations in human decisions, are continuously interfering with the economy and make it dance up and down; sometimes, in the past, with long swings. Irrespective of whether the structure and the foundations are considered satisfactory or not, the economy has to be kept at a certain level of activity and certain other aspects have to be taken care of. Prices are to be kept from moving too violently, and perhaps certain internal ratios (say between farm income and total income) are to be kept from changing suddenly. All this requires adjustment: can it be carried out by adequate changes in some of the instruments of economic policy?

3.12   This type of policy therefore lays less emphasis on certain of the long-term aims which are taken care of by infrequent or slow changes in the more qualitative means of policy. The most important practical aspects of short-term quantitative policy will first be considered, each in isolation. The present chapter, for example, deals with problems of closed economies, whereas chapter 4 deals with the problems of open countries. To begin with, the adjustments in employment and monetary equilibrium will be considered. For open economies the adjustment of the balance of payments will then be added. There are also, however, elements in quantitative policy that are more of a long-term character; these will be dealt with in section 3.6. There are, in addition, problems of particular sectors of the economy that deserve separate attention and require separate instruments of a less general character. These will be exemplified in §§ 3.7 and 4.3. Real policy will have to be a synthesis and, finally, something about this synthesis will be said in chapter 4.

3.13 Quantitative economic policy, and short-term policy especially, often takes the form of a *trial and error* adjustment. If disturbances of equilibrium occur, more or less arbitrary changes in some of the instruments are made and, if after some time they appear to have been insufficient, something more is done. Or, if the first change overshoots the mark, a change is made back in the opposite direction. The justification for this method is generally considered to be our lack of knowledge about the reactions of the economy. Though our knowledge is certainly defective it has gradually improved and a more systematic policy is now possible.

There is, in addition, a tendency to an *incoherent* treatment. Measures regarding various instruments are taken separately, often at different moments and without much co-ordination. This tendency is to some extent based on the belief that there is a one-to-one correspondence between targets and instruments, that is, that each instrument has to serve one special target. Taxes and government expenditure are thought to be relevant to financial equilibrium, wage rates to employment, exchange rates to the balance of payments and so on. The interdependence is neglected or underestimated.

The choice between alternative instruments is also sometimes made on *qualitative* rather than quantitative arguments, which, again, was understandable at a time when little was known about the quantitative reactions of the economy.

3.14 It would seem that a better approach has now become possible. It is no longer necessary to neglect the interrelations, and a simultaneous consideration of all targets and instruments, as well as their quantitative relations, should be considered.

For heuristic reasons it is to be recommended, however, that a start be made with relatively simple situations and that complications be introduced gradually. For this reason we shall start our examples (§ 3.5 and following) with single-target problems and introduce more targets and instruments only gradually. The logic of the treatment will first be given, however, in its general form, in §§ 3.2 to 3.4 inclusive. This may be said to represent the formal aspect, the material aspect being discussed in the examples.

3.2. The Logic of Quantitative Economic Policy

3.21 The logical structure of problems of quantitative economic policy differs, first of all, as between problems with fixed targets and those with flexible targets. For problems with a given number of targets, the problem varies according to the number of instruments. Finally, the logical structure will be changed if boundary conditions are imposed (cf. § 1.5). Logically the simplest situation prevails if targets are fixed and instruments are available in a number equal to the number of targets, while no boundary conditions are interposed. The policy-maker cannot, however, choose all the aspects himself.

3.22 The basis for every design has to be the *initial situation* of the economy considered, either as it is known from the most recent statistics or, if that would mean too remote a picture, as taken from a forecast. Since the execution of measures of economic policy will itself also require some time, it is to be preferred to start with a forecast, i.e. an estimate of what the situation will be in, say, the following year, under the assumption of an unchanged economic policy. A forecast will itself have to be based on the most recent statistics and will then have to answer two questions:

(*a*) what changes will probably occur in the "other data", the data that are not instruments;

(*b*) what will the most probable influence of these changes in data on the economic variables be ? [1]

The answer to the first question will usually be based on expert estimates about these changes; examples of the type of data involved

[1] For a numerical treatment of these questions in a practical case (the economy of the Netherlands) cf. Central Economic Plan 1955, published by the Netherlands Central Planning Bureau, The Hague 1955.

are prices at the world market, changes in population, in productivity, in crops, etc. Some of these estimates might be, in principle, based on studies of foreign economies.

The answer to the second question has to be given by the substitution of the changes in data in the equations of the economic model for the economy concerned. In fact, these contain the data as given quantities and the economic variables as unknowns that can be solved. The solutions are of course only approximations [1]. Sometimes there may be a priori reasons to amend these solutions in the light of qualitative information.

3.23   The criteria for economic policy are now to be derived from a possible *divergency between the "actual" situation* as revealed by either the statistics or the prognosis *and* what is considered *the most desirable situation*. The deviations between these two—dependent on the nature and number of targets the policy-maker chooses to set himself—represent the given changes that have to be brought about in the target variables. The simplest situation is presented when the policy-maker has certain fixed targets in his mind. Let these be a degree of unemployment equal to 97% of the working force and balance of payments equilibrium, and let the forecast yield an employment of 95% and a balance of payments deficit of $0.5 milliards. Then the aim of the policy being sought is to increase employment by 2% and to reduce the balance of payments deficit by $0.5 milliards. The situation is less simple if the targets are, for example, balance of payments equilibrium and the highest possible volume of employment: here we have a flexible target. The situation is also more complicated if, apart from the targets set, certain boundary conditions are imposed on certain of the instruments to be used.

3.24   Setting the targets of the policy is only one side; in addition the *instruments* have to be indicated. As we discussed already (cf. § 1.5) there are a good deal of pre-conceived ideas about what instruments should be used; and in the short run the choice will often be determined by general political forces. If so, the problem is clearly defined. The

---

[1] For an appraisal of the forecasts made by the Netherlands Central Planning Bureau cf. Een vergelijking van de ramingen van het Centraal Planbureau met de feitelijke economische ontwikkeling 1949–1953, The Hague 1955.

more satisfactory attitude is, however, that the choice be itself also made part of the problem. And this choice should then be made on the basis of what was called the *efficiency* of the instruments (cf. also § 1.5). This requires a study of a number of alternative solutions to be discussed in § 3.3, and examples will be given in the § 3.5 and ff. The most complete investigation of efficiency should also reckon with the influence of the instruments on the social welfare function. In practice, however, it will often be on incomplete information, only, that decisions have to be taken. Examples of the type of considerations that may be decisive here will also be given in § 3.5.

3.25   The solution of the problems thus defined will depend on the model of the economy used in the analysis. It goes without saying that the more realistic the model is, the more accurate will be the results. The difficulty facing the adviser on economic policy is, however, that the model, apart from being realistic, should also be "manageable". First of all, it must be possible, with its aid, to make the calculations needed to find the values to be given to the instrument variables. Limitations here are rapidly diminishing with the development of calculation machines. There are, however, also other aspects of manageability. The data and variables appearing in the model should be available in quantitative form. This is not always the case if such concepts as "expectations" are coming in. Also here, to be sure, observation is rapidly increasing in volume and quality. Another important practical aspect of the manageability of models concerns their appeal to the policy-maker or -makers: they must be understandable. Here the most serious limitations are sometimes to be found. Again the situation is not fixed once and for all. The knowledge of policy-makers about economic matters is, on the whole, increasing. Furthermore, their confidence in economists may increase, permitting them to accept certain results of more refined technical analysis.

3.26   The problems described are of a stochastic nature, that is, the data, and hence the unknowns, of the problems are not exact figures, but figures subject to errors. As a consequence, a complete treatment requires the cooperation of mathematical statisticians. They can, in specified cases, indicate the probability distribution of the answers found or at least make certain statements about such distribution.

In particular they are able to find out, whether, in specific cases, the answers obtained by neglecting the stochastic element are or are not biased [1]. Since this book is meant to emphasize the economic aspect of the problems considered, the stochastic element has been left out. The reader should be warned, however, that this is not always admissable.

3.3. Provisional solution; efficiency of instruments

3.31 The optimum values of the instrument values, the unknowns in the problem of quantitative policy, have to be estimated with the help of the model used [2].

(a) *Fixed targets, number of instruments equal to number of targets; no boundary conditions violated.* The simplest case indicated in the previous section, one where targets are fixed and the number of instruments equals the number of targets, and where no boundary conditions are violated, presents a problem with as many unknowns as there are equations. The logical situation may be described more precisely with the aid of some symbols, indicating by:

x^i economic variables that are not targets (irrelevant variables);
y^j target variables;
z^k instrument variables, i.e. data controlled by the policy-maker; and
u^l data, not controlled by the policy-maker.

The number of each of these four categories, of which the first two represent the economic variables and the other two the data of economic analysis, will be indicated by the capital letter corresponding to the index used for each; so there are I irrelevant variables, J targets, K instruments and L data. In addition there will be a number of N equations describing the "structural relations" in the model:

[1] Professor H. Theil, "Econometric Models and Welfare Maximisation," Weltwirtschaftliches Archiv 72 (1954) p. 60 has proved that no bias occurs "if the covariance matrix of the deviations (of target variables) is independent of the instruments and if the welfare function of the policy-maker is quadratic in the indirect (target) variables, the coefficients of the quadratic terms being independent of the instruments".

[2] Instrument variables which are identical with target variables will not, of course, be unknowns.

$$\varphi_n \left(x^i, y^j, z^k, u^l \right) = 0 \quad n = 1,2 \ldots \ldots N$$

If the model is a consistent one, the number of equations will be equal to the number of economic variables, i.e. $I + J = N$; otherwise the model would not be able to "explain" the economic variables with the aid of the data. The problem of economic policy in this simplest case consists of finding the values of the instrument variables z^k; in addition the x^i are unknown, but the y^j are now given. The unknowns are now $I + K$ in number; since the number of instruments is assumed to be equal to the number of targets, $K = J$ and hence the number of unknowns equals that of the equations. The problem is soluble except in special cases. If the equations are linear, there will, as a rule, also be only one solution: it is unique. However, if by some coincidence the equations became dependent, the number of solutions would be infinite, or, if the equations became incompatible, the solution would be non-existent [1]. The interesting thing is that this may also occur if the original set of equations, with the economic variables as unknowns, is not dependent or incompatible in these variables; it only depends on the numerical values given to the targets and on the coefficients with which the new unknowns, i.e. the instruments, appear [2].

Linear equations are, of course, only an approximation to reality and do not represent the most general case. With non-linear equations a large number of different logical situations may present themselves. There may be more than one solution; there may be no solution. A general treatment is hardly possible.

With sufficiently complicated non-linear equations all phenomena of saturation, bottlenecks, etc., will be accounted for by the equations already and no boundary conditions will have to be added. Boundary conditions are needed only as corrections on too simple linear equations. The simplest well-known example is that of a supply curve of the shape indicated by fig. 3.31. This may be replaced by two straight lines

---

[1] An interesting case will be found in P. C. Mahalanobis: "Planning in India", Sankhya 1956, where four instruments $\lambda_1, \lambda_2, \lambda_3$ and λ_4 are considered, which have to satisfy the equation $\lambda_1 + \lambda_2 + \lambda_3 + \lambda_4 = 1$ in which no other variables occur. Evidently three only out of these four instruments can be chosen freely; three targets only can therefore be set.

[2] For an example the reader may be referred to J. Tinbergen, On the Theory of Economic Policy, Amsterdam 1952, p. 46.

(dotted) *a* and *b*. Using such linear function instead of the curve will simplify the mathematics of the solution of some economic problem in which the supply curve plays a role. If, however, a solution is found outside the range of *a* which coincides with part of the supply curve, this solution is of no value. A new attempt will then have to be made with *b* instead of *a*. Here then the boundary condition *b* comes in, as a consequence of the use of the linear approximation *a*. It will be clear that one might also have started with *b* as the approximation and then have added *a* as a boundary condition.

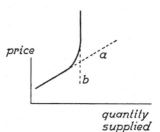

Graph 3.31. A curvilinear function (in this example a supply function) may be approximated by a linear function (a) and a boundary condition (b).

The use of linear equations, apart from being simple and being sometimes the only possible way of arriving at a solution, has an economic justification for most problems where small variations, only, are studied. For small variations, as is well known, curvilinear functions may often be replaced by their tangents. This makes linear equations suitable for cases in which only small variations are considered.

3.32   (*b*) *Fixed targets; number of instruments unequal to number of targets*. In these cases the necessary condition for a unique solution is not fulfilled. If the number of instruments is smaller than the number of targets, the number of unknowns in the political problem will be smaller than the number of equations they have to satisfy, and this will, as a rule, be impossible. A solution will only be possible by pure coincidence, i.e. for certain "happy" combinations of targets. In this case we will therefore say that the targets are *inconsistent* with the set of instruments chosen. Examples will be given in § 3.5.

If, on the other hand, the number of instruments surpasses the number of targets, there will be more unknowns than equations and, as a rule, an infinite number of solutions will be possible. This means that one or more of the instruments may be chosen arbitrarily, and the others will then follow. The number of instruments that can be chosen arbitrarily equals the difference between the number of instruments and that of targets: it will also be called the number of the degrees of freedom.

3.33 (c) *Flexible targets.* In this case the nature of the problem changes completely: it becomes a "maximum problem with side conditions", i.e. a certain function, the social welfare function, has to be made a maximum. This function depends on the variables y^j and possibly also on the instrument values z^k; thus: $\omega(y^j, z^k)$max.

Between the y^j and the z^k there are now a certain number of relations, namely, the relations that remain after the elimination of the irrelevant variables x^i from the structural equations. There will be $N - I$ such relations, which we will call the *"simplified relations"*; they may be symbolized by:

$$\varphi'_m (y^j, z^k, u^l) = 0 \quad \text{(side conditions)}$$

As a rule a maximum problem with side conditions will have a unique solution, irrespective of the number of side conditions.

Often the instrument variables cannot assume all values that are mathematically conceivable. Yet it may happen that the maximum value for welfare ω will correspond to such an impossible value of one of the instruments. We will then have to be satisfied with a lower value of ω, namely the highest within the possible region. This 'next best' will be determined by the boundary condition, or, if there are more than one, by one of these conditions. Often methods of trial and error will be the only ones available to find the solution. We will not here go into these complications and only quote a very simple example to illustrate the role of a boundary condition.

Suppose a wage level lower than the existing one can be shown to make welfare a maximum, but that trade unions do not accept any reduction in wages. This represents a boundary condition, putting a limit to the wage level. The maximum attainable under these conditions will evidently be reached at that limit.

In each of the cases dealt with, the solution, or solutions, if any, will also depend on the data. That is, the values the data u^l assume will also influence the optimum values of the instrument variables. If one is particularly interested in the influence exerted on these optimum values by a change in data, the solutions may be expressed "in terms of" these data, i.e. in the form of equations expressing the optimum values of the instrument values as functions of the data values. Such equations, since they contain directives as how the policy-maker should react on changes in data will be called *"directives"*. Examples will be found in §§ 4.151–4.156.

3.34   We will now discuss the concept of *efficiency* in economic policy. The approach will be made in two stages. We will call the efficiency coefficient of a certain instrument with respect to a certain target variable the ratio between the change obtained in the target variable and the change needed in the instrument variable. In a general way, the change in target variable may be indicated by Δy and that in instrument variable Δz; the efficiency coefficient will then be $\frac{\Delta y}{\Delta z}$. Its value evidently depends on the units in which the target and instrument variable are expressed. If an increase in employment is measured in million man-years and government expenditure in milliards of dollars and, if one million man-years can be obtained by an extra expenditure of 3 milliards of dollars, then the efficiency will be $\frac{1}{3}$.

The value of the coefficient also depends on the policy-problem considered, in particular on the hypotheses made as to the other target and instrument variables. It may be assumed, for example, that all other target variables are left unchanged, but it may also be supposed that all other instruments are unchanged. In the latter case the coefficient may be represented mathematically by $\frac{\partial y}{\partial z}$; for this symbol assumes (i) that the y's are functions of the z's (i.e. the "analytical problem" is set) and (ii) that all the other z's are kept constant. In the case where all other target variables are assumed constant, the simplest representation is $\frac{1}{\frac{\partial z}{\partial y}}$; this symbol assumes (i) that the z's are functions of the y's (the political problem) and (ii) that all the other y's are constant. In order, nevertheless, to obtain an expression with Δy in the numerator and Δz in the nominator, we have then to invert the partial differential coefficient $\frac{\partial z}{\partial y}$

The two measures for the efficiency coefficient thus obtained—and others would be possible, leaving some of the other instruments and some of the other target variables unchanged—need not be equal and usually will not be equal either. For example, it will take more dollars to increase employment by one million if the balance of payments is not kept in equilibrium and part of the expenditure therefore "leaks away" than if that balance is kept in equilibrium by simultaneous wage reduction.

Efficiency coefficients as defined are not comparable between different instrument variables. The knowledge, for example, that an increase of one million man-years can either be obtained by spending 3 milliard dollars or by devaluing the currency by 5% does not enable us to make a comparison. The two alternative changes in instrument variables have to be brought on the same denominator, i.e. they have to be valued. It goes without saying that the most natural valuation is the one to be taken from the policy-maker's welfare function. If 5% devaluation is believed to be twice as burdensome as the spending of $3 milliard, then evidently the efficiency of devaluation is half that of public spending.

The comparison between the efficiencies of two instruments therefore requires (i) the solution of two alternative problems of economic policy and (ii) the valuation of the changes in instrument variables needed.

3.35 The comparison may be brought still one stage further: results obtained for different target variables may also be compared. This is, again, only possible if the relative valuation of the changes obtained is made; as before, it can best be made on the basis of the welfare function. Suppose 1 million man-year employment is valued as high as 10 milliard additional national income; then, if with the same sacrifice in instrument variables either 1 million man-years employment or 2 milliard additional national income (with constant employment) can be obtained, the first policy is 5 times as efficient as the second. This latter comparison has no other significance than the measurement of the increase in "gross welfare" to be obtained with the same sacrifice in ,,cost", and the most appropriate definition might be derived from a comparison of the "net increases" in welfare obtained by two different policies.

3.4 Appraisal and Amendment of the Solution

3.41   The solution found as a result of the first stage described in the preceding section will not always turn out to be acceptable. The changes required in some or all of the instruments may appear to be too large, for some reason. There are in fact, as has already been observed, certain limits (or *boundary conditions*) to be set to some of the instruments. This may be so for physical reasons: if government building activity were an instrument, this activity cannot surpass the production capacity present in the relevant industries. It may also be so for psychological, and hence political, reasons: tax increases will be subject to certain maxima of this nature. These maxima are, to be sure, less clearly defined and one policy-maker or commentator may assume lower limits than the other. But there are limits, vague though they may be, of this kind. Wage decreases are another example. In this case it may even be maintained that the boundary is the figure zero, no wage decreases at all being, in present conditions, acceptable. This statement seems to be too general; it depends on the circumstances in which the economy finds itself, and on the changes in other instruments considered, whether the trade unions will be willing to accept reductions. It will depend, for example, on the composition of the government, on the influence given to unions in the general design of economic policy, and on the sacrifices required from other groups of the population, whether they are able to accept.

3.42   However this may be, the existence of boundary conditions makes it impossible to accept the solution sometimes found by the procedures described so far. In fact, this means that there is no solution to the political problem as set originally, including the boundary conditions. The same conclusion will have to be drawn if the value of the unknowns are found to be infinite or even, in certain cases, negative; in fact, these results are special cases of the same inacceptability.

If there is no solution, then evidently the problem itself will have to be changed. Some of the targets will have to be dropped, or changed numerically. These should be selected from the "less urgent" targets which we may bring together in a class to be called *conditional* targets, in contradistinction to the other *unconditional* targets to which we want to stick. This is evidently a question of practical judgment and only partly accessible to economic analysis. By dropping one or more conditional targets we obtain a new problem which we may then try to solve; it may again appear that some boundary conditions are violated. The search for another setting of the problem will then have to continue.

3.43 The procedure indicated may be illustrated by referring to an example treated elsewhere. [1] The example is a problem in which two unconditional, and two conditional, targets are set, the former being a certain requirement concerning the balance of payments and the volume of goods available for use in the country, the latter being full employment and a certain level of real wage rate. Since four targets are set, also four instruments have to be chosen; they are the nominal wage rate, labour productivity, the profit margin and the indirect tax rate. The choice of the targets as well as the instruments was based on the situation the Netherlands had to face in 1950 and the instruments then available: wages were, as well as a number of prices (and hence profit margins) under government control and there was a drive for the improvement of labour productivity, symbolized even by the presence in the Cabinet of a minister for productivity furtherance. In the situation of that year and as far as the model used was a true representation of the Dutch economy, the calculations showed that the targets set would require a wage decrease of 5%, a decrease in profit margins of some 13%, an increase in labour productivity of 4% and an increase in indirect taxes equal to 2% of prices. Both the wage decrease and the profit reduction seemed to be beyond the boundary conditions. A long list of alternative choices of targets was then studied. Accepting a boundary condition of no reduction in the nominal wage rate meant the necessity of still heavier reductions in profit margins and a heavier increase in indirect taxes; accepting a boundary condition of no profit margin reduction implied impossible requirements as to labour: either a reduction in real wages of 13% or a reduction of employment by the same percentage, both accompanied by increases in labour productivity. The only alternatives likely to be acceptable

[1] Cf. J. Tinbergen, On the Theory of Economic Policy, Amsterdam 1952, p. 45 ff.

were those in which no prior boundary conditions on either wage rates or profit margins were introduced, but a certain fixed relation was introduced between the sacrifices to be made by either group.

3.44 The situation will be simpler in all those cases where certain degrees of freedom are available; i.e. where the number of instruments surpasses that of the targets. To be sure, no number of instruments can ever help to violate fundamental conditions, such as the rule that a country cannot consume more than the total of its own production, its stocks and the foreign aid available. But with less ambitious programs there are sometimes degrees of freedom. An increase in indirect taxation necessary to reduce consumption to an accepted degree may still be obtained by increasing either one or another, or several other, individual tax rates. Here the choice may finally be made by a closer analysis of the influence of these alternative instruments on social welfare. The consequences for the volume of production of various separate industries may be taken into consideration; or the influence on public health, leading perhaps to increases in taxation on stimulants; or certain simplifications in the administration of taxes; or, finally, certain international agreements may be involved, as is the case of the Benelux countries, which have pledged the unification of indirect taxes.

3.5. Methods to Regulate Employment and Monetary Equilibrium

3.51 We are now going to apply the general methods set out in sections 3.1 to 3.4 to a number of practical situations and problems. As our first series of applications we choose the short-term adaptations needed to meet the continuous changes in the more variable of the data. These changes threaten to throw the economy out of equilibrium —either to create a certain amount of unemployment or to create inflationary situations—and it is the current task of any government so see to it that such deviations do not become too large. As we already stated (cf. § 2.2) the selfadjusting forces in this respect are none too reliable.

The two important targets of short-term quantitative policy involved will first have to be defined somewhat more precisely. The target of employment policy is often described as *full employment*, and also as *high and stable employment*. In the practice of economic policy the latter is often taken to be equivalent to an employment level that never falls below 97% of employable persons; but there are deviations to either side. Full employment is taken by some to be identical with high and stable employment; but others think of lower percentages of unemployment than 3. Among difficulties of unemployment rates below about 0.5% has been found to be [1] an increased turnover in the labour force, depressing efficiency. In countries, or regions, or occupations, with a high seasonal employment amplitude, an annual average of 3% will sometimes be more difficult to attain than in countries with less seasonal employment; in countries with a one-sided industrial structure it will be also more difficult to keep employment within small limits than in countries with a manysided structure. In this text we will consider the 3% level of unemployment as the "danger point", i.e. the point at which action will have to be taken if it tends to be exceeded. This is, admittedly, a rather arbitrary choice.

The concept of *monetary equilibrium* has also been defined in different ways. [2] The more sophisticated definitions are based on a comparison between an economy with and one without money; it is assumed that the latter will not show certain disturbances that are observed in the former; and monetary equilibrium is taken to mean that these disturbances are avoided. More specifically, it means that prices "only reflect changes on the commodity side of the market, and not changes in money supply", or, in other words, that the active circulation of money does not change. Our choice will be different. The thing to be avoided because it does harm to the economy is, we think, a violent movement in prices. Such violent movements lead to undesirable effects such as "unstable speculation" [3] and other disturbances. Slow movements in prices do not have these effects; from this point of view a slow upward as well as a slow downward movement are just

---

[1] Cf. B. Ohlin, The Problem of Employment Stabilization, New York 1949, p. 14.

[2] Professor F. de Roos, "Condities voor monetair evenwicht", De Economist, 102 (1954), p. 321 even advocates a definition consisting of two conditions.

[3] For a discussion of different types of speculation, cf. H. Rijken van Olst, Prijsstabiliteit en Speculatie, Rotterdam 1948.

as acceptable as no movement at all. On the other hand, abrupt movements, even if due to "the commodity side of the market" are undesirable. The dividing line therefore should not necessarily be between the "commodity side" and the "money side", but between what is, from the standpoint of general aims of economic policy undesirable and desirable. Among the general aims there should be, apart from the aspect, already mentioned, of avoiding certain disturbances, the protection of savings, which may require constant prices; and the technical verification of the aim should be simple. Finally, there should be similarity of definition for closed and open economies. [1] For all these reasons we define monetary equilibrium as the *realization of the most desirable price level* and for a closed economy we interpret this as a *constant price level*. Accordingly we shall speak of *"inflation"* if prices rise more than is considered desirable and of *"deflation"* if they fall more or rise less than is thought preferable.

As already announced, we will study the policy problems involved by considering a succession of well-defined, simplified problems which the reader will find listed again in Appendix 2. The models used will be indicated with their numbers and are to be found in Appendix 3.

A summary of our findings, also meant for those among the readers who do not like algebra, will be given at the and of this section.

3.521: PROBLEM 011. MODEL 01.

Target: high and stable ("full") employment
Instrument: public expenditure
Comment: it is assumed that there is a stable relation between national income Y and employment and that, therefore, the target can be expressed in terms of Y; i.e. that a certain value Y, namely Y^F, is the target. We have to do with a fixed-target quantitative-policy problem with one target and one instrument. In the equations (1) and (2) of the model we now substitute this desired value Y^F for Y; and we eliminate the variable X which, according to our terminology, since it is not a target, represents an irrelevant variable. We retain

$$Y^F = X_0 + \xi_1 Y^F \qquad (3501)$$

---

[1] This aspect was rightly emphasized by professor H. J. Witteveen. Cf. H. C. Bos, A Discussion on Methods of Monetary Analysis and Norms for Monetary Policy, Rotterdam 1956.

in which only the target variable and the instrument variable X_0 appear. Solving for the unknown value X_0 we find:

$$X_0 = (1 - \xi_1) \, Y^F \qquad (3502)$$

It follows that, in order *to attain a certain value Y^F a much smaller value of X_0 is sufficient:* as a rule, $1 - \xi_1$ is only a small fraction.

The formula obtained is of course the inverse of Keynes' well-known *"multiplier" formula:*

$$Y^F = \frac{1}{1 - \xi_1} \, X_0 \qquad (3503)$$

meant to be used for similar purposes.

A well-known difficulty arises with the interpretation of these formulae for the case where the marginal propensity to spend ξ_1 is equal to 1. The equations of model 01 then become either contradictory or dependent: they are contradictory if $X_0 \neq 0$, for then they run:

$$Y = X \text{ and } X = X_0 + Y$$

and they become dependent if $X_0 = 0$. When trying to interpret the equations one should, then, not forget that they are meant to determine the situation of lasting equilibrium; i.e. a situation of unchanged values of X and Y that can persist. The conclusion has to be reached that such an equilibrium does not, under these circumstances, exist. It should not be that the movements of the economy themselves are indeterminate. These movements have to be represented by a set of dynamic equations, dependent on the dynamic features of the economy. One very simple possibility is that expenditure depends on income one time unit before, or in symbols:

$$X_t = X_{0t} + \xi_1 \, Y_{t-1} \qquad (2')$$

and now it is easily found that, for $\xi_1 = 1$,

$$Y_t = X_t = X_{0t} + Y_{t-1}$$

that, therefore Y_t is rising every time unit by an amount equal to X_{0t} for that time unit. The movements of Y_t are thus perfectly determinate. They might have been different if another dynamic behaviour would have been assumed, however.

3.522 **PROBLEM 021. MODEL 02.**

Target: high and stable employment
Instrument: public expenditure
Comment: Since we are now making a distinction between money flows

and the product flow and since the latter is more relevant to employment, we will now express our target in terms of x and indicate it by x^F. Again we have a fixed-target quantitative-policy problem with one target and one instrument. We again eliminate all the irrelevant variables (now being, Y, X and p). From model equation (2) we get, with (4) and (1):

$$x^F p = x_0 p + \xi_1 x^F p \tag{3504}$$

We should now consider $x_0 p = X_0$ as the instrument; the other terms with p are expressed with model equation (3) in terms of x (and hence x^F):

$$x^F (1 - \xi_1) (p_0 + \pi x^F) = X_0 \tag{3505}$$

This formula at once expresses X_0, the value of the instrument, in terms of x^F, the target. It appears that no longer the simple relationship found in (3502) is valid, but that with increasing x^F it becomes more difficult to attain the target. One may also express the situation in this way: part of the X_0 is needed to pay for the higher price level that will occur as a necessary corollary of higher production. In Keynes' language: *the multiplier becomes less large* if prices are, as is usual in a closed economy, also dependent on the volume of production.[1]

3.523: PROBLEMS 031/2. MODEL 03.

Target: high and stable employment
Instrument: public expenditure (problem 031) or wage rate (problem 032)
Comment: As an alternative to the two previous problems—to be considered once more for this somewhat more complicated model in problem 031—we are now also considering the possibility of influencing employment with the help of wage rates. As is well known this was the usual pre-Keynesian method recommended for the cure of unemployment. Again we have fixed-target quantitative-policy problems with one target and one instrument.

Our target will now be a certain value of a, to be called a^F. The instrument is X_0 (problem 031) or l (problem 032). The other variables are irrelevant, i.e. Y, X, L, p and x. The first problem means that we are repeating the treatment of problems 011 and 021 with this, more complicated, model. Y and L are first eliminated:

$$X = \xi_1 X + \xi_2 l \, a^F + X_0 \tag{3506}$$

---

[1] Evidently the situation will be different when, in stead of money expenditure X_0, the corresponding volume x_0 of government spending is assumed to be the instrument. The reader may be invited to deal with this problem.

Elimination of X brings in x and p, which in turn can be eliminated with the help of model equations (4) and (5):

$$x = \frac{a^F - a_0}{a} \qquad p = p_0 + \pi_1 l + \pi_2 \frac{a^F - a_0}{a}$$

Hence:

$$(1 - \xi_1) \frac{a^F - a_0}{a} \left(p_0 + \pi_1{}^t + l \pi_2 \frac{a^F - a_0}{a} \right) = \xi_2 \, l \, a^F + X_0 \quad (3507)$$

Rearranged, this equation may express l or X_0 as a function of a^F:

$$- X_0 + l \left\{ \pi_1 (1 - \xi_1) \frac{a^F - a_0}{a} - \xi_2 \, a^F \right\} = - p_0 (1 - \xi_1) \frac{a^F - a_0}{a} -$$

$$- \pi_2 (1 - \xi_1) \left(\frac{a^F - a_0}{a} \right)^2 \qquad (3508)$$

PROBLEM 031.

For $l = 0$ we have the solution to this problem which appears to be similar to the solution of problem 021: in fact we easily transform formula (3505) into (3508) if instead of x^F we read $\dfrac{a^F - a_0}{a}$ and instead of π read π_2.

PROBLEM 032.

Formula (3508) also shows us, however, how a certain value of a^F may be obtained by a change in l, since for $X_0 = $ const., it connects l with a^F. In order to see how a change in l would affect a^F it is useful first to assume that $\xi_2 = 0$, i.e. that workers spend their income in the same way as non-workers. Formula (3508) without the ξ_2-term than reduces to:

$$\pi_1 l = - p_0 - \pi_2 \frac{a^F - a_0}{a} + \frac{a \, X_0}{(1 - \xi_1) \, (a^F - a_0)} \qquad (3509)$$

From this formula we deduce that a small change da^F requires a change in l:

$$dl = - da^F \left(\frac{\pi_2}{\pi_1 a} + \frac{a \, X_0}{\pi_1 (1 - \xi_1) \, (a^F - a_0)^2} \right) \qquad (3510)$$

i.e. a reduction of wages; in order to estimate the order of magnitude of the change needed, we take the realistic values of the coefficients as indicated in model 03: $\pi_{\mathcal{I}} = 0.1$ to 0.2; $\pi_1 = 0.4$ and $a = 0.4$; the resulting formula becomes

$$\frac{dl}{da^F} = \frac{-1.1}{0.16} \text{ to } \frac{-1.2}{0.16} \text{ or } -7 \text{ to } -8 \tag{3511}$$

Since the equilibrium value of l was taken equal to 1 and that of a^F equal to 0.5, this means that a change in employment of say 10 % would require a wage reduction of -0.35 to -0.4, or 35 to 40 % reduction. This already shows that the wage rate is not a very influential instrument.

If, however, the spending behaviour of workers should differ systematically from that of non-workers, the result would be very different. The formula would then read:

$$l = \frac{-p_0 - \pi_2 \dfrac{a^F - a_0}{a} + \dfrac{a\,X_0}{(1-\xi_1)\,(a^F - a_0)}}{\pi_1 - \dfrac{\xi_2}{1-\xi_1} \dfrac{a\,a^F}{a^F - a_0}} \tag{3512}$$

and it might happen that the denominator of this fraction would become near to zero; this may easily happen because both $1 - \xi_1$ and ξ_2 may be assuming small and rather uncertain values and these could be such as to make

$$\pi_1 = \frac{\xi_2}{1-\xi_1} \frac{a a^F}{a^F - a_0}$$

For certain combinations of values the sign of $\dfrac{dl}{da^F}$ may now even become positive. Choosing again the values of π_1, a, a_0 and a^F already quoted in model 03, and the value for p_0 as well as the initial value for X_0 which follow from this choice, we obtain:

$$\left(-0.4 + 0.5 \frac{\xi_2}{1-\xi_1}\right) d\,l = \left(\frac{-\xi_2}{1-\xi_1} + 2.5 + 2.5\,\pi_2\right) da^F \tag{3513}$$

It appears that for $\dfrac{\xi_2}{1-\xi_1} > 0.8$, $\dfrac{dt}{da^F} > 0$; such a situation could present itself when workers simply spend their income completely and non-workers do not; for then $\xi_2 + \xi_1 = 1$ or $\xi_2 = 1 - \xi_1$. The explanation is that in these circumstances a shift of income from non-workers to workers means an increase in demand; and this may overcompensate the negative effect of higher prices on demand.

The conclusion then must be that the *wage rate is an unreliable instrument to regulate employment* in a closed economy. Under certain circumstances it may work, under other circumstances it may not work.

3.524 PROBLEM 033. MODEL 03.

Targets: "Full" employment and monetary equilibrium
Instruments: Public expenditure and wage rate
Comment: Whereas "full" employment is now generally accepted as a desirable target, the danger of a continuous rise in prices which it might evoke is more and more being recognized and it may therefore be said that the targets set should be full employment and, at the same time, stable prices or, more generally, monetary equilibrium. For a two-target policy the use of two instruments will be necessary and for reasons set out at some more length in section 3.56, the wage rate has been chosen as the second one.

Solution: Evidently the values of a and p are now given; say

$$a = a^F \text{ and } p = p^D \text{ (desired price level)}$$

The unknowns are l and X_0. It is easily found, that, after substitution of equations (1), (2) and (6) of model 3 in the other equations, (5) will supply the value of x, which again may be substituted in (3) and (4). The solutions for l and X_0 will be found to be:

$$l = \frac{p^D - p_0 - \pi_2 \dfrac{a^F - a_0}{a}}{\pi_1}$$

$$X_0 = (1 - \xi_1) p^D \frac{a^F - a_0}{a} - \xi_2 a^F \frac{p^D - p_0 - \pi_2 \dfrac{a^F - a_0}{a}}{\pi_1}$$

The structure of these equations is much simpler than (3512) e.g., and accordingly there is much greater stability of the numerical values that will be found for varying values of the coefficients. Since π_2 is relatively small, it may be said, as an approximation, that the wage level is determined by the desired price level, whereas government expenditure primarily has the task to stabilize employment.

3.525 PROBLEMS 041/2. MODEL 04.

Target: high and stable employment
Instruments: public expenditure (problem 041) or taxes (problem 042)
Comment: Since there has, in principle, to be made a choice between in-

fluencing economic activity by an increase of government expenditure and a decrease in taxes, some closer investigation of the consequences in either case seems useful. The choice is, in principle, between an increase in government expenditure or an increase in private expenditure (or, as the case may be, a decrease in either of the types of expenditure). A first aspect to be considered is the utility, in any given situation, of each of these types. Since there are wide differences in incomes between various classes of the population, it is not possible to speak of "the" marginal utility of private expenditure. Still less is it possible, with our present knowledge, to indicate objective criteria of the relative usefulness of public expenditure on the one hand, and private expenditure, for any group of the population, on the other hand. Subjective judgment will have to play an important role anyhow, therefore, but it may be obtained in a more precise way than is usual, nowadays, by systematic study of (a) the type of expenditure involved on either side and (b) public opinion—both with policy-makers and with the general public—on their usefulness.

Apart from these considerations, there are, however, other aspects to the choice to be made. They are to be found in the *multiplier effects* of both instruments. It is the purpose of problems 041 and 042 to determine those effects.

The following cases will be considered separately:

(1) The marginal propensity to spend $\xi < 1$, autonomous changes in public expenditure and taxes;

(2) $\xi < 1$, and the changes in taxes are equal to those in expenditure ("balanced budget change");

(3) $\xi = 1$ and autonomous changes in expenditure and taxes;

(4) $\xi = 1$ with a balanced budget change.

In cases (2) and (4) it will first be assumed that the marginal rate τ of taxation is not changed and secondly that it is also permitted to change (cases 2A and 4A).

(1) Since in model 04 we again use the simplification of model 01 to disregard divergencies between money flows, product flows and factor flows, we consider as our target a value Y^F of the variable Y.

Again we have to eliminate the irrelevant variables, which are now X^P and T and we easily obtain:

$$Y^F = X_0{}^P + \xi (Y^F - \tau Y^F - T_0) + X^G \qquad (3514)$$

from which the analytical equation is deduced:

$$Y^F = \frac{-\xi T_0 + X^G + X_0{}^P}{1 - \xi + \xi \tau} \qquad (3515)$$

which shows the influence that can be exerted on Y^F by T_0 and X^G. Considering the marginal tax rate τ as given, it may be said that there is a multiplier $\dfrac{1}{1 - \xi + \xi\tau}$ to be applied to X^G if X^G is changed; and another multiplier $\dfrac{-\xi}{1 - \xi + \xi\tau}$ to be applied to T_0, i.e. to the autonomous component of tax revenue. The *multiplier for government expenditure is thus larger than that for taxation*, as long as $\xi < 1$. The reason for this difference is, as is easily understood, that a tax reduction is, according to our behaviour formula (2) of model 04, only spent to the proportion ξ; the rest, $1 - \xi$, being hoarded.

(2) Some special attention has, for this reason, been given [1] to increases in government expenditure and in taxes which are such as to maintain equilibrium in the government budget. It follows from the preceding paragraph that an equal increase in government expenditures X_0^G and autonomous taxes T_0 does not leave the national income unchanged, as long as $\xi \neq 1$; if we call this increase $\Delta'X^G$, where the ' indicates that there is the side condition of a balanced budget, we find from formula (3515) an increase ΔY in income

$$\Delta Y = \frac{1 - \xi}{1 - \xi + \xi\tau} \Delta'X^G \tag{3516}$$

i.e. an income effect with a multiplier $\dfrac{1 - \xi}{1 - \xi + \xi\tau}$; this multiplier is smaller than 1. If tax revenue is independent from income (no induced tax revenue changes) it becomes just 1, the case dealt with by Haavelmo. The way in which changes in the marginal rate τ of taxation would act on income is a little bit more complicated, since income Y is not linearly dependent on this parameter. It can be found from equation (3515) as well.

(2A) A combined change in T_0 and τ to the extent that the change in tax revenue equals the change X^G would require that $\Delta'X^G = \Delta T_0 + Y\Delta\tau + \tau\Delta Y + \Delta\tau\Delta Y$ and would lead to a much more complicated problem, which, however, is easily solved in principle by our formulae.

---

[1] Cf. Haavelmo, "Multiplier Effects of a Balanced Budget", Econometrica 13 (1945) and subsequent discussion with Haberler, Goodwin and Hagen in Econometrica 14 (1946). After this was written I came across Baumol and Peston's article, "More on the Multiplier Effects of a Balanced Budget," The American Economic Review 45 (1955), p. 140.

(3) The conclusions so far reached are valid for values of $\xi \neq 1$ and are meaningful for values of $\xi < 1$. It is worth its while to investigate what happens when $\xi = 1$, i.e. when private expenditure changes by the same amounts as private national income after tax. It follows from equations (3514) and (3515) that in that case

$$Y^F = \frac{-T_0 + X^G + X_0^P}{\tau} \tag{3517}$$

i.e. that now the multiplier equals $\dfrac{1}{\tau}$ for both an increase in government expenditure and a decrease in taxes.

(4) If also in this case the additional condition is set that the changes in X^G and T_0 should be equal—i.e. the hypothesis of a balanced budget is introduced and the marginal rate of taxation unchanged—the resulting income change appears to be zero. Here, for obvious reasons, the statement about a multiplier with a balanced budget does not therefore apply.

(4A) If, finally, the marginal rate of taxation τ is again also permitted to change, the analysis runs as follows. Both before and after the change in T_0, τ and X^G we have:

$$Y = Y - \tau Y - T_0 + X^G$$

and

$$X^G = T_0 + \tau Y$$

which, however, leads to a tautological equation for Y, namely:

$$Y = Y$$

Seemingly, then, Y would be indeterminate both before and after the change. Here we are again concerned with a situation similar to that dealt with at the end of problem 011. Again, therefore, we have to have recourse to a dynamic analysis. If we assume the same dynamic behaviour as in problem 011, we have:

$$Y_t = Y_{t-1} - \tau_{t-1} Y_{t-1} - T_{0,\, t-1} + X_t{}^G \tag{3518}$$

If, in addition:

$$X_t{}^G = T_{0t} + \tau_t Y_t \tag{3519}$$

we obtain:

$$(1 - \tau_t) Y_t = (1 - \tau_{t-1}) Y_{t-1} + \Delta T_0$$

which determines Y's movements. We could have assumed other dynamic features, however, in both (3518) and (3519) and might then have found different results.

Our findings may be summarized by saying that the multiplier for an increase in public expenditure is different from that for a decrease in autonomous tax revenue as soon as the marginal propensity to spend of the private economy is different from one; if public expenditure and autonomous tax revenue are varied by equal amounts, the multiplier for expenditure is smaller than one. If the marginal propensity to spend equals one, expenditure and autonomous taxes have numerically equal multipliers, equal to the inverse of the marginal tax rate. No change in income then results, therefore, for an increase in expenditure equal to that in autonomous taxes. The cases in which the marginal rate of taxation also changes are much more complicated.

So far, in problems 041/042, we have kept to the analytical method. The policy problems will have to be solved by the inversion of the equations after a choice of the instrument to be used has been made. Thus, equation (3515) would yield the value of T_0 if that instrument be chosen:

$$\Delta T_0 = -\frac{1 - \xi + \xi\tau}{\xi} \Delta Y^F = \left(1 - \tau - \frac{1}{\xi}\right) \Delta Y^F \qquad (3520)$$

Similar equations for other cases could be easily derived.

Here the procedure discussed in section 3.4 may be necessary. It may appear from (3520) that, for psychological reasons, the tax increase found is too high, as could be the case in a situation of threatening over-full employment. It may then be necessary to use not only the instrument of taxes but, in addition, that of expenditures; in the situation now referred to, this would mean that a decrease in expenditure would be necessary. Illustrations may be taken from the situation in both the United Kingdom and the Netherlands in 1955. The psychological situation was even such as to demand for a tax reduction after years of high post-war taxation. The instantaneous situation was one of over-employment. Reduction in public expenditure was the alternative to be considered. Another illustration may be taken from the situation prevailing in the Netherlands in 1951, again one of overemployment (and of balance of payments deficits). A combination of tax increase and decrease in expenditure was chosen; because of the balance of payments problem involved we will deal with this example in more detail in chapter 4.

A final example may be taken from the situation in the United States in 1954, one of recession. Tax reductions were applied that had been previously promised; and it was made clear by the government that, if these tax reductions should prove to be insufficient, an increase in expenditure would be considered.

3.531 PROBLEMS 051/053. MODEL 05.

Targets: high and stable employment; no potential inflation, that is, a fixed amount of money in circulation.

Instruments: public expenditure, debt policy

Comment: we are now going to consider the complication arising from possible future consequences of full-employment policies. To the extent that such a policy makes use of money creation, the danger of potential inflation may come up, i.e. the danger that money balances in the hands of the public will be spent at too high a rate during later time periods. One way to forego this danger is not to create money, but to finance deficit budgets with the aid of long-term or medium-term loans.

This feature in our problem provides an example of the complications that arise if not only short-term, but, at the same time, long-term targets have to be taken care of. As B. Hansen rightly observes [1] more instruments will then be needed.

It is useful to make a distinction between three situations regarding the provision of the economy with money. First, the "normal" situation may be considered where the circulation of money M is sufficient to finance desired transactions Y^F, or only slightly above it. In the second place, a situation may be considered where the supply of money is kept relatively low, to be called the situation of insufficient cash balances. This is the state of affairs if credit is made scarce or even rationed. In the third place, a situation of excess cash reserves will be given some attention, i.e. the situation prevailing after a period of sustained inflation, e.g. after a war.

It depends on the targets set with respect to M, whether we will be in a situation of sufficient, insufficient or excess cash balances.

We do not introduce the rate of interest as a separate variable. This more subtle instrument of regulating the provision of the economy with means of payments does not, it seems (cf. § 2.2) exert a very large influence [2]. Mostly it works to an appreciable extent only in co-operation with either psychological factors—if it is used as a warning signal, but then the inter-

---

[1] B. Hansen, Finanspolitikens ekonomiska teori, ch. XVI.

[2] J. Tinbergen, Business Cycles in the U.S., 1919–1932, League of Nations, Geneva 1939; Business Cycles in the U.K., 1870–1914, Amsterdam 1951.

pretation is what really matters—or with straightforward rationing. This is the second of our three cases to be considered. (For open countries, cf. § 4.1). Attempts to use interest rates in economic models were made by the present author in previous work.[1]

PROBLEM 051. SITUATION OF SUFFICIENT CASH BALANCES

We will for this problem specify the function $X_0{}^P (M, B)$ as a general linear one:

$$X_0{}^P (M, B) = X_{00}{}^P + \xi_2 M + \xi_3 B \tag{3521}$$

Since the increase in M and B rather than their absolute values are relevant to the problem, it is more appropriate to write this function as:

$$X_0{}^P (M, B) = X_{00}{}^{P'} + \xi_2 \Delta M + \xi_3 \Delta B, \tag{3522}$$

where

$$X_{00}{}^{P'} = X_{00}{}^P + \xi_2 M_{-1} + \xi_3 B_{-1};$$

M_{-1} and B_{-1} indicate the values of M and B, respectively, one time unit before, i.e. at the end of the previous time unit. (This can be applied only to somewhat long units, such as years.)

Our equations may now be written in the following form (cf. model 05):

$$Y^F - X^G = \xi_1 Y^F + X_{00}{}^{P'} + \xi_2 \Delta M + \xi_3 \Delta B \tag{3523}$$

$$\Delta M = X^G - T_0 - \tau Y^F - \Delta B \tag{3524}$$

In these equations $X_{00}{}^{P'}$ and T_0 are data; Y^F and ΔM are targets (where ΔM will depend on future values of Y^F) and hence also given; ΔB and X^G are unknown. If $\xi_3 = 0$, X^G may first be derived from (3523); and with X^G determined, and ΔM given, ΔB may then be found from (3524). The situation is so simple here, that algebra would seem superfluous: ΔB represents the deficit of the government which, if no financing through money creation is desired, has to be raised from the capital market, and which is determined by $X_{00}{}^{P'}$ (the autonomous private expenditures) and the standard Y^F set for full-employment income. In times of depression, there will have to be a government deficit; in times of boom, a surplus. Accordingly bonds will have to be issued or to be paid back.[2]

The problem becomes a bit more complicated and algebra then becomes

---

[1] This does not imply that the rate of interest does not vary. It varies, but it does not influence the other variables to any appreciable extent.

[2] These amortizations may, however, better be spread over time, and the surplus may partly be hoarded.

useful, if $\xi_3 \neq 0$, i.e. if the bond holdings of the public do also influence their spending. In this case there is interdependence and after solution of the equations we find:

$$\Delta B = \frac{(1 - \xi_1 - \tau) \, Y^F - X_{00}P' - T_0}{1 + \xi_3} \tag{3525}$$

The higher, with other data equal, the influence of bond holdings on spending, the lower the amount of loans to be floated now. On the other hand, however, a higher value of ξ_3 means an increase in the danger of potential inflation; for then the future propensity to spend will also be larger.

The question has to be raised whether not even the setting of the problem reflects too great a concern about the danger of potential inflation. At the moment that potential inflation would become actual inflation, i.e. when the excess of cash reserves would be spent, it is always possible to exert a counterforce by deflationary policies of the type discussed previously. This argument, taken together with the possibility that "consolidation" of cash reserves need not reduce the spending out of assets to zero, diminishes the importance of the problem now being considered. Nevertheless a better knowledge of the coefficients ξ_2 and ξ_3 seems desirable.

3.534 PROBLEM 052. SITUATION OF INSUFFICIENT CASH RESERVES.

The form so far given to the function $X_0{}^P$ can only be an approximation and in particular applies to the situation of sufficient cash reserves. This function assumes a different form if we reach the region where liquid assets are less than sufficient for a minimum transaction cash balance. Such a minimum balance depends on the organization of payments facilities and on habits. It is well-known that in developed countries cash-balances of between one quarter and one half of annual income are customary. If M falls below such a minimum, it will influence X^P to a much stronger degree, almost or exactly with a coefficient $\xi_2 = 1/\mu$, where μ is the ratio between minimum cash balances and annual income.

We have then to replace the spending equation by

$$X^P = \frac{1}{\mu} M \tag{3526}$$

i.e. $X^P{}_{00} = \xi_1 = \xi_3 = 0$. Ths relation may be said to represent a boundary condition to our variable X^P, transforming our equation (3523) and (3524) into:

$$Y^F - X^G = \frac{1}{\mu}(M_{-1} + \Delta M) \qquad (3527)$$

$$\Delta M = X^G - T_0 - \tau Y^F - \Delta B \qquad (3528)$$

and brings us back to the simpler logic where X^G can be derived from (3527) and consequently ΔB from (3528). The solution reads:

$$X^G = Y^F - \frac{M_{-1}}{\mu} \qquad (3529)$$

$$\Delta B = Y^F (1-\tau) - \frac{M_{-1}}{\mu} - T_0 \qquad (3530)$$

3.533 PROBLEM 053. SITUATION OF EXCESS CASH RESERVES.

In this situation we will again have to use formula (3521), but now the target to be set for M may be different. It may now be desirable to let M fall to a more normal level. Such a fall presupposes surplus spending during the period of the fall, however, the phenomenon well-known from the post-war period. That is to say, ΔM cannot fall by more than the public is willing to spend above its income, unless another type of measure should be introduced, such as a forced "monetary purge". The autonomous willingness to spend is expressed in our formulae by the level of X_{00}^P; it may be high in a post-war period, for reasons of back-log demand. If X_{00}^P happens to be high, ΔM may therefore be strongly diminished; otherwise it cannot. The limitation, or boundary condition, now involved, can be expressed in our formulae by an unwillingness, of the public, under such circumstances, to take bonds; i.e. by the boundary condition $\Delta B = 0$. Such a boundary condition changes the logical structure of our problem, in the way indicated in section 3.4. We cannot now impose a target with regard to ΔM unless we either give up our target with respect to Y and let Y go up into the inflationary region; or introduce further instruments, e.g. a forced purge. This latter solution comes down to imposing a certain value ΔB on the public, if a "blocked account", as it is usually created in the case of a monetary purge, is considered a type of bond.

3.534 PROBLEM 054.

Target: "full" employment
Instrument: money circulation
Comment: We may use formula (3523) or (3527) for other problems of economic policy also, namely problems where M is used as an instrument. In practical terms this represents credit policy, i.e. the regulation of the

quantity of means of payments in the hands of the public by regulating the extent of credits given to business. Here again the asymetric behaviour of the public with regard to cash balances comes into play. If the target of policy, is to reach a certain level of activity Y^F and for some reason X^G, cannot be changed sufficiently (there may be an upper as well as a lower boundary condition for X^G), it may be attempted to influence X^P (and so, according to equation (1) the level of Y) by the intermediary of M (according to equation (2) of model 05). The influence of M on X^P has been represented by the coefficient ξ_2 in equation (3521), and been specified to be $\dfrac{1}{\mu}$ under conditions of insufficient cash reserves (equation 3526)). As far as our knowledge goes, ξ_2 is only about 0.1 [1], whereas $\dfrac{1}{\mu}$ is 2 to 3. This "kinked curve" represents the well-known fact that the instrument of credit restriction by rationing (downward from the point of "sufficient cash balances") is very efficient, but that it is much less easy to increase expenditure by making ample credits available, if for other reasons there is no desire to spend. Credits can hardly be forced on people. One of the ways in which one could express this is that the stimulating effect of a (short-term) interest rate reduction is only limited. We believe it to be so limited that we think one might even disregard the short-term rate of interest as an instrument of economic policy. Its influence is no larger than the margin of error in most of our knowledge about the economic mechanism. This does not apply to all types of long-term interest rates, and still less to such types of "interest rates" as the yield on shares or the profit rate. They have a larger and fairly considerable influence.[2] (For an open country, cf. § 4.1.).

3.535 PROBLEM 061. MODEL 06.

Targets: high and stable employment in each industry.
Instruments: public expenditure, indirect tax rates for each industry.
Comment: This problem is given to illustrate certain short-term aspects of the problem of full employment: the inelasticity of labour supply in different industries. Even if it is admitted that in the longer run supply should be adapted to demand, it will be necessary to have available short-term instruments in order to regulate employment by industry. Here indirect taxes or

---

[1] Cf. L. R. Klein and A. S. Goldberger, An Econometric Model of the United States, 1929–1952, Amsterdam 1955, p. 05.

[2] Cf. references given in problem 051. The remark may be added that also, in the long run, a persistent change in short-term rates will influence long-term rates.

subsidies seem to be the most appropriate instruments. Since, in addition, we will maintain the instrument of public expenditure, the number of instruments surpasses that of targets by one, and there will be one degree of freedom. This may be used to satisfy some further condition, either a boundary condition or another target.

In accordance with this state of affairs we find, upon counting equations and variables, the following situation:

Number of equations: $3H + 3$

Number of economic variables: $3H + 3$, distributed over targets (number: H, namely the production volumes $x^h = x_0{}^h$) and irrelevant variables ($2H + 3$, namely X^h, p^h, X, X^P, Y).

Among the data there are the $H + 1$ instruments τ^h and X^G.

Elimination of the irrelevant variables may be undertaken as follows. From equations (5) of model 06 we deduce

$$x^h = \xi_1{}^h \frac{Y}{p^h} + \xi_2{}^h \tag{3531}$$

or

$$x^h - \xi_2{}^h = \xi_1{}^h \frac{Y}{p^h} \tag{3532}$$

Since $x^h = x_0{}^h$ is given (target), we may express p^h in terms of Y:

$$p^h = \pi^h Y \tag{3533}$$

where

$$\pi^h = \frac{\xi_1{}^h}{x_0{}^h - \xi_2{}^h} \tag{3534}$$

We may further express Y in terms of X^G, since:

$$Y = X = X^G + X^P = X^G + \Sigma X^h = X^G + Y\Sigma\xi_1{}^h + Y\Sigma\xi_2{}^h\pi^h$$

or:

$$Y(1 - \Sigma\xi_1{}^h - \Sigma\xi_2{}^h \pi^h) = X^G \tag{3535}$$

Putting

$$\frac{1}{1 - \Sigma\xi_1{}^h - \Sigma\xi_2{}^h \pi^h} = \eta \tag{3536}$$

we have

$$Y = \eta X^G$$

and can now write our H equations between the $H + 1$ unknown instrument variables in the form:

$$p_0{}^h + \tau^h = \pi^h\eta X^G \qquad h = 1 \dots H \tag{3537}$$

or, expressed in the original coefficients:

$$p_0{}^h + \tau^h = \frac{\xi_1{}^h}{x_0{}^h - \xi_2{}^h} \quad \frac{X^G}{1 - \Sigma \xi_1{}^h - \Sigma \xi_2{}^h \pi^h} \tag{3538}$$

It is now easily seen that we may freely choose e.g. X^G and having done so will then find τ^h. It appears that the higher X^G, the higher also all the τ^h have to be taken, for the obvious reason that if X^G already stimulates demand in a general way, the indirect taxes need not do so, and vice versa. On the other hand, the τ^h vary inversely with the targets $x_0{}^h$, also for obvious reasons. The only thing that could not have been found easily without our algebra is the exact form of the relationships (3538); as already observed, these are still simplified and would become more complicated as soon as the spending equations (5) would also depend on the prices of the other goods.

The degree of freedom present in (3538) may be used, as already observed, to fulfil certain boundary conditions. If X^G is subject to such a condition, this may be used to restrict the intervals to the admissable solutions. On the other hand, also the τ^h may be subject to certain boundary conditions. It may e.g. be thought that subsidies are not an appropriate instrument of economic policy. In such a case, each of the τ^h has to be > 0. The situations that can present themselves here are manyfold; as will be clear, it is easily conceivable that not all these conditions can be fulfilled at the same time; but just as well it may happen that all can be satisfied and that even a certain interval of freedom remains to some or all of the variables. The reader may be invited to construct numerical examples himself.

3.541   The isolated problems considered in §§ 3.521 to 3.535 inclusive may now serve as a few stepping stones to a reasoned discussion of the various alternative methods of regulating employment and monetary equilibrium. We start with policies where *only the employment target is set*. The alternative methods available may first be subdivided into money-flow methods and factor-price methods, indicating that the instruments are money flows in the former case and prices of productive factors in the latter, i.e. wage or interest rates.

The first point to be made is that in closed, or nearly closed, economies the *factor price instruments are unreliable* (cf. problem 032). Both wage rates and interest rates have only a restricted influence on the total activity of a closed economy. The influence of wage rates is uncertain even as to its direction: a fall in wage rates may lead, under conditions of depression, to a fall in total activity. The chief explanation is that its influence consists partly of positive and partly of negative elements, and that the size of these influences varies, but is about equal. The general reason why interest rates, at least short-term interest rates, are inactive has been discussed in § 2.2.

3.542 *Money-flow instruments* are mainly the money flows regulated by the government: *public expenditure and taxes*. Their influence on total activity is considerable, as has been characterized by Kahn's and Keynes' famous expression "multiplier" (problems 011, 021, 031). As far as a choice has to be made between both, the choice is between certain private expenditures, made possible by a tax reduction, or eliminated by a tax rise, and certain public expenditures made possible by their rise or eliminated by their reduction. A first criterion should be their utility, but this device has only a restricted value because of the fact that many very different individuals will mostly be involved, the marginal utility of money to whom differs widely. Not much more can be recommended than careful "public opinion polls", among the policy-makers and the citizens.

A clear-cut situation prevails, however, when huge expenditures simply have to be made, as in the case of war or other emergencies (floods, post-war reconstruction). There is no choice then and taxes have to be increased. They may even have to be increased to such an extent that the boundary condition for taxes is reached, meaning the limit where, because of evasion or lack of inducement to produce, a further increase in taxes has its own drawbacks. In this situation the extra expenditures, technically speaking, will have to be financed either out of loans or by credit creation. The choice here should be loans and not credit creation, since the latter would lead to over-employment.

In more normal circumstances the choice between increases in expenditure and decreases in taxation is, however, less unambiguous.

3.543 A second criterion for the choice between different money flows as instruments for regulating employment exists in the delay to be expected in their handling. This delay will be considerable if parliamentary approval is needed for the change to be brought about, as will be the case for changes in tax rates or increases in expenditure. The delay may also be considerable if complicated tax chemes that are usually applied to, say, annual assessments, should have to be changed. There are, however, numerous ways of avoiding delays. The government may, for example, accelerate or slow down the collection of taxes, or the execution of a certain spending program, without parliamentary consent, and, in urgent cases, it is certainly possible to obtain the quick co-operation of parliament.

A third factor that may then be of some importance is that the multiplier for an increase in expenditure may be somewhat larger than the one for a reduction in taxation (cf., problems 041 and 042). This is only true when the marginal propensity to spend is below one; and in those circumstances even an increase in public expenditure with an equal increase in taxes will increase total demand.

3.544   A further choice has to be made, or can be made, namely between *direct and indirect taxes*. The exact effects exerted by each of these instruments depend on many particular details: a reduction may be a general one, say proportional to the existing rates, or a specific one, say the reduction of rates on some specific income groups or goods. It will be clear that specific changes may have very different results according to their shape. Usually there are good reasons for maintaining a certain balance between the rates for different income groups or different goods (see, however, the end of this §). A proportional reduction of existing rates will mean, in the case of direct taxes, a reduction which primarily affects high incomes, whereas a proportional reduction in indirect taxes will affect lower incomes more. Accordingly, their influences on total demand will be different, and particularly so if they are applied during a depression. In such a period the marginal propensity to spend will be below one for the higher income brackets; and the probable effect on total outlay is less in the case of direct taxes than in the case of indirect ones. Under more normal conditions there need not be any differences in the total effect on outlay; but there will be a difference as to the composition of the increase in demand. The demand for investment goods as well as for luxury goods will be more affected by a change in direct taxes, whereas the demand for consumer goods generally will be more affected by a change in indirect taxes.

3.545   Money-flow instruments are mainly the government-controlled money flows; there is, however, the possibility of the banking system, and hence especially of the central bank, of influencing money flows spent by the private (and even the government) sector by credit policy. This policy is only efficient when it takes the form of credit restriction by rationing (cf. problem 052); it is to be compared with a cable, which can only be used to pull, but not to push. In an inflationary situation it may be very important. In a deflationary situation the initiative to spend is the decisive one and this cannot be imposed on the private sector; either the factors making for demand have to be changed (as e.g. taxes) or the spending has to be undertaken by the public sector.

3.546   A final remark to be made on the problem of regulating employment in the short run refers to the question, whether a government deficit should be financed by *credit creation* or by *loans*. For the instantaneous effect this is a matter of indifference, as long as total demand is unaffected. For this to be so the loans should attract only money flows that would not otherwise have been spent. If loans reduce the money flows for spending, financing by credit creation deserves preference. We are coming back to this subject after a while (§ 3.57).

3.55   We continue our discussion by asking what policy is required if *monetary equilibrium is the only target*, irrespective of the level of employment. From our problem 021 we deduce that as a rule the price level, also, is affected by changes in money flows; and that hence autonomous changes in price level, such as crop variations, technical changes or wage changes can be counteracted by changes in money flows. Such changes will, however, affect the employment situation at the same time, and it will, as a rule, not be possible to attain both monetary equilibrium and a certain employment target by the use of only one instrument. In the absence of any violent autonomous changes in prices, a well-known device will have to be employed, namely, to let total expenditure be just sufficient to buy the national product at the prices of the previous time unit.

Another instrument that may be used for the maintenance of monetary equilibrium is the *wage rate* (cf. model 03). If the only autonomous changes in price-determining factors are changes in productivity, the way to maintain a constant price level is to let wage rates rise in proportion to labour productivity, no less and no more. Wages may also be raised, of course, if the incomes of other than wage-earners are lowered, but this will affect employment at the same time.

3.56 Most modern policy-makers, however, prefer to pursue a *two-target policy* at least, i.e. to maintain both *high employment and monetary equilibrium*. Such a policy requires the use of at least also two intruments. One of them should be one of the government-controlled money flows, since the reliability of factor prices for the regulation of employment was found to be low. The most natural choice for the second instrument is the *wage rate:* as a regulator of the price level this is a quite efficient instrument. All the alternatives, with the possible exception of one, turn out to have serious drawbacks. The *interest rate* only exerts a very small influence on the price level. Direct regulation of prices themselves requires a complicated administration and considerable friction will be one of the accompanying phenomena. For certain bulk commodities, such as raw materials, it could be done, however (cf. § 6.5).

A third possibility might, in theory, be the use of two money flows (government expenditure and tax revenue) or two types of taxes. This would only work if the relative effects of each of these instruments on the two target variables were different. Suppose both instruments should affect employment and prices in the same proportion. Then any combination of these instruments would do the same, so that it would not be possible to affect employment and prices in any other proportion. It would also be, if not impossible, scarcely possible to affect the target variables, employment and price level, in a different proportion if the instruments should affect both in almost the same ratio. Suppose government expenditure would, if applied to a certain amount A, increase employment by 1% and prices by 0.9%, while taxes, when increased by A, would decrease employment by 1% and prices by 1.1%. Then it would theoretically be possible to attain any combination of changes in employment and price level. If an increase in employment of 2% and a decrease in price level of 2% were desired, a very large increase both in expenditure and in taxes should be applied, namely an increase of $21A$ in expenditure and an increase of $19A$ in taxes.

This would in all probability mean a bad policy since very debatable expenditures would have to be involved.

A less unfavourable alternative would seem to be the use of *indirect taxes* in order to influence prices. This would be possible as long as the indirect tax level were sufficient to allow a reduction of the size needed to counteract an excessive rise, say, in wage rates. Other purposes aimed at by the policy-makers in handling indirect taxes (cf. also end of this §) would then, however, have to be foregone. This alternative, therefore, also has some drawbacks, although to a smaller extent.

For these reasons, wage rates have to be a deliberate instrument of economic policy if employment targets and monetary equilibrium are to be pursued at the same time. There is an important and well-known argument against making wage rates an instrument of economic policy. It is felt by many that wages should be a subject for "free negotiation" between workers' and employers' organizations. Making wages subject to government approval or even decree would be, following this train of thought, a tendency towards totalitarianism. In the author's opinion the desire for "freedom" in wage negotiations is very close to an inconsistency. The real freedom of course is very small, since the choice of a wage rate deviating from the one required by "full" employment and monetary equilibrium will endanger one, or both, of these targets. And the assertion regarding totalitarianism seems to be exaggerated respecting countries in which trade unions have an important influence on the decisions taken by the government.

3.57 The problem again becomes a little bit more complicated if, not only short-term targets, but also some *longer-term targets* are aimed at. Monetary equilibrium, especially, should not only be maintained in the short run, but in the long run as well. Here the problem of choosing between credit creation and loan policy comes up again. If in a period of low private expenditure employment is to be maintained by increased government expenditure, and a resulting deficit is financed by credit creation, this may introduce the danger of potential inflation, i.e. the possibility of future inflation. The larger cash balances left in the hands of the public may later be spent by them in addition to their incomes. This makes it preferable to finance the budget deficit with the aid of loans (cf. problems 051–053). To the extent that the public is willing to take the bonds presented at not too high interest rates and without too great a reduction in their expenditures, this policy will work. The adaptation of the types of loans presented to the preferences of the public will be an important technical problem to be solved. The better the financial authorities succeed in attracting the exact unspent margin between income and private expenditure, the more successful this policy will be. As has been already observed, however, when discussing problem 051, there is no need to restrict extra government expenditure during a depression to the amounts that can be borrowed in the capital market. This safeguard against potential inflation is only a second line of defence; actual inflation at some later time can always be matched by appropriate measures at that time, namely reduction of government expenditure or an increase in taxes.

3.58   The last problem we will consider in this section is the problem of maintaining employment, not only as a whole, but in *a number of different industries*. It is necessary here to make a distinction between the long-run and the short-run problem. It would be erroneous to try to maintain employment in each separate industry over a long period since this would mean a lack of adaptation to changes in taste, or in techniques, with a consequent loss to national income. In the short run, however, the problem is different. Adaptations, such as the ones just mentioned, take a certain length of time: retraining of labour, the replacement of capital goods in one industry by those of another, and the replacement of obsolete capital goods by more modern, are all time-consuming processes. During such a process of adaptation it is no use letting labour remain unemployed, and so the problem arises of how to ensure high employment in a number of "compartments" of the labour markets. Evidently the general instruments of public expenditure and general taxes will not perform this. The simplest way to solve this problem is to differentiate between the taxes applied to the various compartments; this can only be done as far as indirect taxes are concerned. If one indirect tax rate is available for each compartment, it would be possible to regulate employment in each. If in addition a general instrument is also used (cf. problem 001), there is one instrument more than strictly needed, introducing one "degree of freedom". One instrument may be chosen arbitrarily, say the level of government expenditures; and the other (i.e. the indirect tax rates) then adapted to the targets of high employment in each industry. The higher the level of public expenditure, the higher also the tax rates have to be. The degree of freedom may be particularly useful if it is desired also to sustain employment in an industry for which demand is relatively weak, and not to do so by subsidizing that industry, i.e. not to do so by applying negative tax rates.

3.6. Main Problems of Development Policies

3.61   As a second set of examples we will consider some of the quantitative problems of long-term economic development and the policies needed to further it. Development policy, to be sure, is such a complex phenomenon, embracing not only the whole of economic life, but also important extra-economic phenomena, that it cannot, in its totality, be considered an example of quantitative policy. But some of the main interrelations are of a quantitative nature and they will be dealt with in this section. Other aspects will be considered elsewhere (cf. § 4.122, 5.7 and 6.4).

Development will be taken to mean the increase, over a prolonged period, of production per head of a given economy. It represents the most natural and the most reliable basis for a long-term increase in material well-being, a target that will be considered important by all peoples living at a low level and becoming aware of it. In recent times there has been an increasing awareness of the deficiencies in the standard of life of many Oriental, African and Latin American peoples, due partly to the ever increasing well-being of some Western countries, to the increasing contacts with the Western world, and to the growing interest in material well-being spread by socialists and communists.

There are various ways of raising production per head; the most important may be said to be an increase in capital per head, or in capital goods available per head, and improvements in the skill of a population and in the methods of production used. As a rise in capital per head is equivalent to investment and the improvements in skill and methods also require investments, to a certain extent, it may be said that investment is the key to increased production. For reasons to be discussed later, investment can only be made partly out of foreign savings and has, as a rule, to be obtained out of home savings therefore. The fundamental choice to be made here is between more consumption now and less development, or less consumption now and more development; the choice, in fact, as to what degree of development is wanted. It is difficult to indicate any definite criteria on which to base this choice; there are, however, certain limits which narrow down the range of figures that are practically feasible.

As a basis for discussing this problem we will, as before, consider a clear-cut example and continue the general discussion afterwards.

3.62   PROBLEM 091. MODEL 09.

Target: development of production at a rate of a per time unit.

Instrument: volume of investment

Comment: it is the intention of this example to show the interrelation between some fundamental variables in economic development, the fuller discussion of which will be given after this example. More particularly it introduces a scheme slightly different from the well-known Harrod-Domar model, which will, nevertheless, be taken up as the guide to the fuller discussion. The difference consists of a technically more specific representation of the process of production. As has been assumed in model 09, production is seen as technically related to the stock of equipment rather than to capital; i.e. to the number of machines available—whatever their age and hence their value, if only not worn out. It is recognized, of course, that the life time is not as precisely constant as has here been assumed; but on the other hand it is believed useful to introduce the distinction between stock of equipment, or capacity, and capital.

The solution of the system of dynamic equations of model 09 is possible along the following lines:

Writing δ for $1/T$ we have, from (4), (9), (2), (3) and (7):

$$j = v - c = \varphi w - (1 - \sigma) \ (\varphi - \delta)w = (\delta + \sigma\varphi - \sigma\delta)w \qquad (3601)$$

Since $\dfrac{dw}{dt} = j - j_{-T}$ it follows that

$$\frac{dj}{dt} = (\delta + \sigma\varphi - \sigma\delta) \ (j - j_{-T}) \qquad (3602)$$

This is a differential-difference equation, which is also valid for w and all variables proportional to w. It can be found that under certain conditions the solution of this equation can be:

$$j = j_0 e^{at} \qquad (3603)$$

The condition is that:

$$a = (\delta + \sigma\varphi - \sigma\delta)\,(1 - e^{-aT}) \tag{3604}$$

since this is the result of substituting (3603) into (3602) and happens to be a relation independent from t. If the initial situation of the economy considered satisfies certain further conditions this possible solution will at the same time be the only solution. The economic significance of these latter conditions may be vaguely indicated as conditions of equilibrium, as contrasted to cyclical disequilibrium. [1] It may therefore be stated that the rate of development likely to occur is the one defined by (3604).

A numerical example may clarify the formula. We choose $\sigma = 0.12$, $T = 20$ and hence $\delta = 0.05$, and $\varphi = 0.196$; this latter choice being based on the hypothesis that the "capital coefficient", i.e. the ratio of k/y should be 4. The resulting value of a is 0.03, i.e. the same value as would be found in the simpler approach used by Harrod and Domar.

With these constants the composition of production at the moment where $y = 1$ would be:

$$v = 1.34; \quad j = 0.46; \quad d = 0.34; \quad r = 0.26; \quad s = 0.12; \quad c = 0.88$$

The two stock figures would, in addition be:

$$k = 4 \qquad\qquad w = 6.58$$

Formula (3604) may now be used to calculate the necessary rate of savings for other values of a as well. The following results will be found:

a	σ
0.02	0.07
0.03	0.12
0.04	0.16
0.05	0.21

The results do not diverge much from the results that would have been found with the help of the Harrod-Domar formula

$$a = \frac{\sigma}{\varkappa} \tag{3605}$$

where $\varkappa$ represents the capital coefficient, which in our initial case was taken

---

[1] The general solution of (3602) is more complicated than (3603) and also contains fluctuating components. These will be absent only if their amplitude in the initial movement (the given values from j_{t-T} to j_t) is zero.

to be 4. The Harrod-Domar theory considers $\varkappa$ to be a constant, whereas our theory takes φ to be constant, leading to a dependency of the capital coefficient on the rate of development.

In the following analysis this will, however, be disregarded and a constant capital coefficient will be assumed to exist.

3.63   We will now introduce the important element of *population growth* in order to continue our general discussion of the fundamental choice of the degree of development. Let it be given that population grows at a rate of π (say 1% per annum); let the capital coefficient be $\varkappa$ (say 4) and the rate of development, i.e. the rate of increase in production per head needed be a' (say 2% per annum). What rate of savings will be needed? Since the total rate a of increase in production will now have to be $\pi + a'$ $(1 + 2 = 3\%)$ annually it will be necessary, according to the definition of the capital coefficient, for the rate of investment and (in the absence of foreign help) for savings to be $\varkappa\,(\pi + a')$ or, in our example, $4 \times 3 = 12\%$. Other figures could be easily calculated.

The rate of savings just found is already quite high in comparison to what is actually saved in most underdeveloped countries. A savings rate of 5 to 8% is the most frequent figure; and it is only in more developed countries that figures above 10% are found as a rule. Savings rates of 15% are exceptional, at least in free economies. It is in centrally regulated economies only that much higher rates have been obtained. And it will be clear that savings rates of this level imply an important sacrifice of a population with a low standard of life. The freedom of choice is therefore more restricted than it might seem at first sight.

3.64   In the present circumstances there are good reasons for advocating *foreign assistance* in order to step up the rate of development of under-developed countries. First of all, there are a number of developed countries able to supply such assistance. And secondly, it seems undesirable to let the divergence in living standards become larger and larger, as it actually has become during the last century. Such a divergence would, in the end, seriously threaten political stability. By a well-organized international effort important results might be obtained. [1] Nevertheless there are also here limitations to what can be done. Investment projects of any kind always contain important elements of local effort. A machine can be imported, but it also has to be installed. Roads, railways, irrigation dams, have to be constructed, to a very large extent, with the aid of local labour, partly skilled which is not usually abundant. It follows that there is a limit to the degree to which total investment can be stepped up. Suppose the ratio of foreign to home costs in the average investment project to be 1 : 1 (a rather favourable supposition), then, if the maximum savings rate for the country concerned is 8, the maximum investment rate (in terms of national income) will be 16; with a capital coefficient of 4, the maximum rate of increase in production will be 4 and, with a rate of population increase of 1, the maximum rate of development will be 3% per annum.

3.65   Apart from foreign assistance, the main short-term instruments for furthering investment activity will be *direct taxes* and *government investment*. Direct taxes will, of course, influence investment in a negative way; they can only, therefore, be used as an instrument if they, for some reason, have been high for some time and are then lowered. A reduction may be made possible by taking measures to decrease tax evasion. Such a reduction will be most effective if it is linked to actual increases in investment. In countries where private initiative is still weak, or where no important private capital formation takes place, government investment activity will have to play an important role. This is particularly true for countries where the type of investment needed is of the public utility or "social overhead" type, or where transportation is an important bottleneck. Some problems connected with public investments will be considered in section 5.73. There are, in addition, numerous other instruments that may be used incidentally, according to circumstances. It would lead us too far to discuss these other instruments.

As was already observed, capital is not the only bottleneck in underdeveloped countries; *skill* in its most diversified forms is another one.

---

[1] Cf. the calculations presented by H. Theil, Enige kwantitatieve aspecten van het probleem der hulpverlening aan onderontwikkelde landen, Haarlem 1953.

And there should be a certain proportion between the increase in both. The general feeling of those in touch with the problem is that the need for medium-level technicians and for all levels of managers is the most urgent need at the moment; and all efforts should be made to meet that need.

There is, finally, one main factor intervening that also has to be mentioned explicitly: population growth. As will be clear from our calculations, a *reduction in population growth* will also be of considerable help in stepping up production per capita for the simple reason that there will be more available per head if there are less "heads". In a country with a savings rate of 8%, with a capital coefficient of 4 and a rate of increase in population of 1%, half of the savings are needed only to maintain the standard of life of the growing population. The situation will be worse if the rate of increase in population is say 3%, as is the case in many Latin-American countries. It may even be stated that the problem of a rapid decrease in the divergence of standards of life is insoluble unless a check on the growth of population is one of the means used.

3.7. Example of Sector Policy in a Closed Economy: Transportation

3.71   Economic policy, by its nature, applies to the economy as a whole and it should not have any particular bearing on certain sectors: all sectors are, in principle, needed and no discrimination should exist. There may, however, be certain characteristics asking for acts of policy which are more pronounced in their effects on one sector than on the other. Since the execution of a policy requires familiarity with business life and this familiarity usually bears on a certain sector, it is understandable why economic policy is so often subdivided into sector policies. Sector policy will always be determined, to a large extent, by the particularities of the sector concerned. In addition it will have an element which is absent in general policy: it has to pay attention to the position of the sector with regard to other sectors. For these reasons we are going to discuss one or two examples of sector policy; the first being an example applying in a closed economy, i.e. where international aspects are not important. We have chosen transportation as the sector in this example.

3.72 We will discuss, in succession: (i) the characteristics of the transportation sector; (ii) the aims of transportation policy; (iii) the instruments that can be used and (iv) why and how these instruments gave to be used.

(i) The *characteristics* of transportation are, of course, many and not all of them are equally relevant to policy problems. The activity may be described as a relatively simple (and hence often highly mechanized) operation needed in many production processes and also for human beings, every time where physical distances have to be bridged. Simple though the operation in principle may be, each single unit is characterized by a large number of special features: route, time of leaving, velocity, degree of care in handling needed, frequency of connection, quantities transported. The typical performance of transportation industries is the way in which they group units with similar characteristics in order to apply the economies of scale which are very considerable. With a more or less given structure of demand for transportation a complicated structure of transportation services emerges, showing various types alongside each other: water, rail, road and air traffic along a number of fixed and a number of free routes, in large and in small units (ships, trains, trucks etc.) in frequent or infrequent services.

3.73 The economic and technical characteristics which matter most for transportation policy seem to be the following:

(*a*) The elasticity of demand for transportation is generally low since transportation costs are only a minor part of total production costs.

(*b*) Some of the investments needed for an efficient transportation system are of the "bulky" type, i.e. the minimum size of certain parts of the equipment is large. This is particularly true for railways, ships and aircrafts.

(*c*) On the other side, there are some types of investment which permit the use of very small units, thereby attracting small business men; this applies to river and canal shipping, and road traffic.

(*d*) Finally there is a large number of market compartments that are mutually non-competing or almost so: traffic is always traffic along some specified route at some specified time etc.

3.74   (ii) The *aims of transportation policy* have to be seen as part of the aims of general economic policy; the general aims discussed earlier therefore apply, but they should be modified in view of the limited area of interest. Instead of aiming at a maximum real national income transportation policy can only aim at a maximum contribution by the industry to national income as a whole. This implies the most efficient use of the factors at the industry's command and no command over factors that could better be applied in other sectors; it also implies a remuneration which is "reasonable", a term to be discussed, in another context, later on (cf. § 6.4), but provisionally to be interpreted as "according to the value of its contribution". Of the general aims discussed earlier that of continuity and stability is also of particular concern. It will be taken to mean here that transportation facilities have to be available to the rest of the economy continuously and at stable rates; the exact implications will be discussed under (iv).

3.75   (iii) The *instruments available* for transportation policy are in principle the same as those used for the economy as a whole, with some of them perhaps more needed or more easily applicable because of the special structure of the industry. It goes without saying that instruments that can only be applied in an indiscriminatory way to the economy as a whole are not particularly interesting, since they can hardly influence the position of the industry with respect to others. The more interesting instruments are those which by their nature do influence that position. First, price fixing may be mentioned, relatively easy to apply in some of the simpler types of traffic. A second instrument is that of quantitative restrictions, especially of investments; this usually takes the form of concessions on the one hand and the obligation to carry freight as a corollary. As a third example the formation as well as the control of monopolies has to be quoted.

3.76   (iv) The *use made of the instruments* is manifold and diversified. No policy can be a mechanical one and this is particularly true of transportation policy: it has continuously to be adapted to changing circumstances, because of the necessity for traffic to follow an inelastic demand. Because of the technical differences between the various types of transportation, policy has also to be different for these types. It cannot be the purpose of this section to give a complete and precise picture of this many-sided policy, but rather to indicate the general principles. These may be formulated so as to approach, as closely as possible, the ideal situation with respect to prices and supply of transportation services in all the compartments of the industry. This situation is the one described by the theory of free competition, where prices are equal to average unit cost. Because of the technical characteristics of the industry there is a permanently recurring tendency towards deviations between actual and ideal prices and supply. The bulky investments needed for railways and ships imply a tendency to over- or undercapacity; the small investments needed for road and inland waterway transportation imply a tendency to over-investment. If prices were left free, they would, as a consequence of the inelasticity of demand, tend to show heavy divergencies either upward or downward from equilibrium prices. In the branches with bulky investment the tendency to unreasonably low supply prices, only covering a little more than short-term marginal cost, will prevail in periods or in market compartments with over-capacity. This will, in turn, produce a tendency towards monopoly, leading to unreasonably high prices. The instruments of economic policy enumerated under (iii) have to be used in order to let prices and supply approach their ideal level as much as possible. Price setting may have the function of protecting the industry against cut-throat competition and protecting the customers against monopoly exploitation. Concessions will have to restrict investments to what can be reasonably expected to be needed; in cases of over-capacity the formation of an artificial monopoly may protect the industry. In cases of unreasonably restrictive practices the control of a monopoly may be necessary.

3.77   The policy pursued may be a looser one or a more rigorous one. A looser policy will only act in case of large deviations between the actual and the ideal situation; a more rigorous policy will begin to act with smaller deviations. The more rigorous the policy, the more need there will be for exact figures about what constitutes a reasonable price; and here the biggest practical difficulties arise. Cost calculations are difficult because, on the one hand, of certain theoretical problems involved and, on the other hand, of the lack of precise data. Cost calculations made by private enterprises are sometimes "falsified" by the existence of irrational taxes or by the absence of rational charges. Theoretical difficulties are, for example, those connected with the true costs of a road constructed in a low-price period, and those connected with the splitting up of joint costs between various types of freight. Precise data are not always available because of bad administration (small enterprises), secret administration (big enterprises) or because of theoretical difficulties about what types of data are relevant.

CHAPTER 4

QUANTITATIVE POLICY (II) IN AN OPEN ECONOMY, AND IN SETS OF ECONOMIES

4.1. Methods of Regulating Employment, Monetary Equilibrium and Balance of Payments Equilibrium in an Open Economy

4.111 We shall discuss problems of quantitative economic policy in open economies in the same manner as before, by first discussing the current adaptation of such economies to changing circumstances. This may generally be considered to be the main object of the policies encompassed within the title of the present section. For obvious reasons the emphasis will be laid on that which distinguishes an open economy from a closed one. In a general way this is, of course, the dependence on foreign countries, due to the fact that part of the product has to be sold abroad and part of the factors of production have to be bought from foreign countries. The latter is particularly true for countries whose imports consist, in a large part, of raw materials, semi-manufactured products or equipment, and this is by far the most frequent case. Even if imports consist largely of consumer goods they will almost never be completely finished goods and usually form an element in some further production or trading process.

4.112 The dependence on foreign countries, therefore, applies both to the volume of demand (in which export demand is an element directly dependent on foreign conditions) and to prices, the foreign influence being even more important in the latter case. Prices of imported materials, as well as prices of competing foreign products, tend to keep internal prices in line with international prices, and special measures are required to isolate a country's price structure.

4.113 Some of these fundamental features of an open economy are brought out even in the simplest models of such an economy. The influence of import prices on national prices is expressed by our supply or price setting equations. They therefore represent what we call the possibility of "importing inflation", meaning that an undesirable price rise due to inflationary policies abroad will make itself felt even if the economy under consideration is following a non-inflationary policy. It will also make itself felt in a rise in foreign demand.

The definition equation for national income

$$Y = X + E - I$$

expresses the dependence of Y on E; if written in the form

$$X - Y = I - E = D$$

it expresses a fundamental equality between a possible surplus of expenditure over income, on the one hand, and the deficit D on the current items of the balance of payments, on the other hand. This equality brings out the possibility of "exporting inflation". By this we mean the possibility of having expenditure in excess of income without causing changes in the national price level, so long as foreign credits or national reserves permit the financing of a deficit on the current items of the balance of payments.

4.114 The consequences of the "fundamental features", just discussed, for short-term economic policy will be considered in this §. We start this discussion by a somewhat more precise definition of the main targets usually involved in this policy of current adaptation. Instead of two, we will now consider three such targets, mentioned in the title of this section. Concerning the first, "full", or rather high and stable, employment, nothing needs to be added to the definition already given for a closed economy (cf. § 3.5). But the second, monetary equilibrium, certainly requires some further explanation. We have explained why we adhere to the definition of *"the realization of the most desirable price level"* and we have now to specify this definition for the case of an open economy. We do not now have the complete freedom in choosing the price level which existed in the case of a closed economy: the dependency of the open economy on other countries restricts our choice and it depends on the instruments we are willing (or permitted) to use, and their influence, whether we can divorce the national price level from the international one. Here another important feature of the economic policy of open countries comes in: *much depends on the policies followed by other countries.* Where policies can be internationally co-ordinated, more possibilities exist than when they cannot. An open country can pursue a constant price level as the most desirable one, if other countries are doing the same; it will be much more difficult to do so if other countries have a fluctuating price level. It may then be possible to counteract such fluctuations by fluctuating exchange rates, or by fluctuations in home prices[1]. A less ambitious "desirable price level" may also be aimed at, for example, a price level which does not show more fluctuations than those caused by foreign prices.

4.115   As a third target for current economic policy, in addition to the other two, *balance of payments equilibrium* needs to be introduced. This, again, may have several different meanings; it may refer to the balance of payments as a whole; or to the current items of the balance of payments, or to still other aspects. The obvious raison d'être of this target is the necessity, for the country, of financing its imports and its other possible financial obligations. It depends on the reserves and on the credits available to the economy, therefore, what exact form the target will assume. The essential thing is, however, that some level of the balance of payments deficit or surplus will be a datum, and we shall, for simplicity's sake, sometimes assume that it must be zero.

We shall discuss our subject matter, as before, against the background of a number of clear-cut separate "problems" and try to summarize our findings at the end of this §.

4.121   PROBLEM 111. MODEL 11.

Target: full employment
Instrument: government expenditure
Comment: This problem is similar to problem 011 and will be discussed to show some implications of the dependence on foreign economies.

In this simple model the employment target will again need to be inter-

---

[1] The first of these proposals was made by, among others, Lindahl, B. Hansen and Metelius; the second, for smaller variations in import and export prices, by Lindahl. I am grateful to Professor Hansen for this information.

preted as a specific value Y^F attributed to Y; from equations (1), (2) and (3) we have now to eliminate X and I and we obtain:

$$X_0 = Y^F (1 - \xi_1 + \iota) - E \qquad (4101)$$

The required increase in public expenditure will again be smaller than the increase needed in Y^F, since $1 - \xi_1 + \iota$ will usually be smaller than 1; but this is not necessarily the case any more. For very small countries imports may exceed national income and ι may then be > 1 even. In the inverted Keynesian form the formula is better known:

$$Y^F = \frac{X_0 + E}{1 - \xi_1 + \iota} \qquad (4102)$$

and the multiplier is now smaller than for a closed economy. Another feature of our result (4101) is that the increase needed in X_0 will be, for obvious reasons, the smaller, the higher the value E of exports is; national income and employment will be changing with changes in exports.

There is no guarantee at all that with X_0 equal to (4101) there will be balance of payments equilibrium. If exports E happen to be relatively small, the imports corresponding with Y^F, namely $I^F = \iota\, Y^F$, may well surpass E. If therefore the economy concerned wants to follow a policy of full employment it has to have ways of financing a balance of payments deficit. This is the well-known problem facing countries that wish to maintain a policy of full employment during an international depression.

4.122 PROBLEM 112. MODEL 11.

Target: balance of payments equilibrium
Instrument: government expenditure
Comment: If only one instrument of economic policy is used, for which government expenditure is here chosen, only one target can be attained; problem 112 is an alternative to problem 111 therefore. From the target $D = 0$ it follows that $Y = X$ or

$$X_0 = (1 - \xi_1)\, Y \qquad (4103)$$

and

$$E = \iota\, Y \qquad (4104)$$

Since Y is now an irrelevant variable, we have to eliminate it and we find that

$$X_0 = \frac{1 - \xi_1}{\iota}\, E \qquad (4105)$$

Both X_0 and Y will now have to be parallel to E; if E happens to show fluctuations, the economy has to follow these fluctuations. And Y need not coincide with full employment income Y^F; it is $\dfrac{E}{\iota}$, which may be quite different. The problem also illustrates some questions of development policies. If a country wants to expand its national income by, say, increasing public expenditure, but, because of lack of reserves or credits, is forced to maintain balance of payments equilibrium, it has to solve the problem just discussed. The amount X_0 it is able to spend without disequilibrating the balance of payments will also determine the extent to which deficit spending can be applied. The increase in monetary circulation must not exceed the amount which corresponds to the possible increase in national income; an amount that may be defined with the help of an equation of the type of equation (3526) in § 3.532.

4.123 PROBLEM 113. MODEL 11.

Target: the optimum combination between employment and the balance of payments situation
Instrument: public expenditure
Comment: As already stated, it is impossible to attain two quantitative targets with the aid of only one instrument. If no other instruments are admitted, the best that can be obtained is an optimum combination; presupposing that there is a way of evaluating the relative advantages of unit increases in employment and in balance of payments surplus. We are now dealing with a flexible target, according to our terminology. Assuming that the policy-maker (the government) is acting on the basis of a welfare function $\omega\,(Y, D)$ depending on the level of national income and the balance of payments surplus (represented, negatively, by D), it is possible to determine a maximum of ω, with the side condition that both Y and D can only be varied as a consequence of variations in X_0. In somewhat more practical terms we may say that an optimum situation can be found if the policy-maker has a scale of valuations for various combinations of Y and D.

Expressing Y and D in terms of X_0 we find (4102)

and
$$D = \frac{\iota X_0 - (1 - \xi_1)\,E}{1 - \xi_1 + \iota} \tag{4106}$$

from which it follows that a small increase $\varDelta X_0$ causes increases in Y and D given by the formulae:

$$\varDelta Y = \frac{\varDelta X_0}{1 - \xi_1 + \iota} \tag{4107}$$

$$\Delta D = \frac{\iota \Delta X_0}{1 - \xi_1 + \iota} \tag{4108}$$

The corresponding increase in welfare will be

$$\Delta \omega = \frac{\partial \omega}{\partial Y} \Delta Y + \frac{\partial \omega}{\partial D} \Delta D \tag{4109}$$

and, under normal conditions as to the shape of ω, the optimum will be reached if $\Delta \omega = 0$, i.e. if:

$$\frac{\dfrac{\partial \omega}{\partial Y}}{\dfrac{\partial \omega}{\partial D}} = -\frac{\Delta D}{\Delta Y} = -\iota \tag{4110}$$

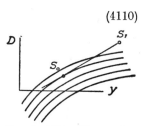

The increase in X_0 should therefore be stopped at the value of X_0 where the marginal value of a unit increase in national income Y is estimated to be ι times the marginal value of a unit increase in balance of payments surplus (being $-D$). In a practical way indifference curves with regard to Y and D may be constructed from interviews of the policy-maker; and (cf. graph 4.12) starting from the initial situation S_1 the optimum point will be found to be S_0, if $S_1 S_0$ is a straight line with a slope ι.

Graph 4.12. Illustration of a method to determine an optimum position with the aid of indifference curves of a social welfare function depending on two variables D and Y. Initial situation: S_1; optimum situation: S_0. Slope of straight line $S_1 S_0$ depends on nature of model.

4.131   PROBLEM 121. MODEL 12.

Target: "full" employment
Instrument: government expenditure
Comment: We give one more repetition of our simplest one-target-one-instrument problem for this somewhat more complicated model in order to show the complications in the field of prices arising in the case of an open economy. Since a general solution, i.e. one expressed in all the Greek coefficients, is difficult to interpret, we will discuss a number of numerical examples, as stated in the description of the model. (Cf. what is said about the numerical values of the coefficients at the end of the description of model 14.)

The general solution can be found with the aid of algebra applied to equations (1), (2) and (3), with the variables Y, X and v retained and the others eliminated with the aid of the other equations. The reader is invited to test the procedure.

4.132   The numerical result in case Csn, i.e. for a country of which imports are 50 % of national income, considering short-term reactions and a normal cyclical situation, are, for the most important variables:

$$v = 1.99\, X_0 - 1.06\, p^i + 1.39\, p^w \tag{4112}$$

$$Y = 1.57\, X_0 - 0.93\, p^i + 1.35\, p^w \tag{4113}$$

$$D = 0.71\, X_0 + 0.21\, p^i - 0.26\, p^w \tag{4114}$$

$$p^x = 0.20\, X_0 + 0.22\, p^i + 0.14\, p^w \tag{4115}$$

According to (4102) with $\xi_1 = 0.8$ and $\iota = 0.33$ the multiplier is 1.89; here it is 1.57 for nominal income and (since $v = 1.5$) $\dfrac{1.99}{1.5} = 1.3$ for the volume of production.

From (4113) and (4115) we may also calculate the change in real income:

$$Y - p^x = 1.37\, X_0 - 1.15\, p^i + 1.21\, p^w \tag{4116}$$

where approximately the same multiplier (1.37) appears to apply. As explained before (cf. § 3.522) the lower multiplier is due to the rise in prices, represented by (4115). At the same time there is an increase in the deficit D on the balance of payments (current items), which is considerable.

4.133   Our formulae also illustrate the influence exerted by foreign prices. As could be expected, a rise in import prices is unfavourable to production, income and the balance of payments and raises internal prices, though only by 22 % of the foreign price rise: the fall in internal demand being a counteracting force. The effects just indicated are usually described as the effects of the "terms of trade". This is not a very accurate terminology, since the terms of trade, if conceived of as the ratio of p^i to p^e, are not data, but partly dependent on the internal situation. Instead, p^w and p^i are data and it makes sense to speak of their influence on the national variables. Assuming for a while that the ratio $\bar{p}^i/\bar{p}^w$ is called terms of trade, it still appears that it is not exactly the ratio (whose variation would be $p^i - p^w$) which determines v, Y and D, but that in all three cases p^w's influence is relatively more important than p^i's.

4.134   Our results will be given some further perspective by comparing them with the results obtained for countries in different circumstances. Using the symbols explained in the description of model 14 (cf. Appendix 3) we have the following figures for Y:

Case	Formula
Asn	$Y = 5.35\, X_0$
Bsn	$Y = 2.40\, X_0 - 0.625\, p^i + 0.97\, p^w$
Csn	$Y = 1.58\, X_0 - 0.93\, p^i + 1.35\, p^w$
Dsn	$Y = 0.95\, X_0 - 1.34\, p^i + 1.82\, p^w$
Csb	$Y = 1.95\, X_0 - 1.13\, p^i + 1.62\, p^w$
$C'sn$	$Y = 1.85\, X_0 - 1.12\, p^i + 1.59\, p^w$
$C''sn$	$Y = 1.37\, X_0 - 1.00\, p^i + 1.18\, p^w$
Cln	$Y = 1.81\, X_0 - 1.74\, p^i + 3.62\, p^w$

$$(4117)$$

As might be expected, the multiplier falls and the influence of foreign prices rises with an increasing intensity of foreign trade. In case D the increase in income is even less already than the increase in X_0. Under boom conditions (Csb) the multiplier is larger than normally but this is a price effect. The multiplier again rises, but also in the physical sense, if the marginal propensity to spend is higher ($C'sn$); and it is lower for $\xi_1 = 0.7$ ($C''sn$). Long-term reactions (Cln) once more show a higher multiplier. In this case the influence of foreign prices is also considerably larger, evidently since the elasticity of demand for exports is now much higher. The influence would have been smaller if wage rates had been assumed to change. If they change, which is very probable in the case of rises in foreign prices, the resulting influence of the latter will be counteracted.

4.14   PROBLEM 131. MODEL 13.

Targets: "full" employment and balance of payments equilibrium
Instruments: public expenditure and the wage rate
Comments: Since some form of balance of payments equilibrium is a necessity for a number of countries, and full employment a very desirable target, and since, for two targets, two instruments are needed, a second instrument is now added. Preferably this should be an instrument from the price structure, since, evidently, the position of an open economy among the other economies is to a large extent dependent on its relative price level. In view of practical possibilities three instruments seem to stand out: indirect taxes, the wage rate and the exchange rate. Indirect taxes were already discussed in section 3.56. Model 13 has been constructed with a view to applying the wage rate.

4.142   The general solution to the analytical problem may be found in the same way as indicated for problem 121. It runs, for case Csn, i.e. for *short-term* reactions:

$$v = 1.99 \, X_0 - 0.27 \, l \tag{4118}$$

$$D = 0.71 \, X_0 - 0.01 \, l \tag{4119}$$

$$p^x = 0.20 \, X_0 + 0.30 \, l \tag{4120}$$

$$Y = 1.57 \, X_0 + 0.20 \, l \tag{4121}$$

The influence exerted by changes in wage rates appears to be quite modest. The influence on D is even negligible; the balance of payments situation will have to be regulated almost entirely with the help of public expenditure. If a reduction in expenditure would be required for this purpose, the only way of maintaining employment would be a fall in wage rates in order to attract foreign orders. The influence of wage rates on employment is somewhat more pronounced than in a closed economy (cf. § 3.5), but it is still very low: the elasticity being only $-\dfrac{0.27}{1.5} = -0.2$.

4.143 In the *long run*, however, this influence will be considerably larger, as the results for case *Cln* show:

$$v = 1.81 \, X_0 - 1.88 \, l \tag{4122}$$

$$D = 0.87 \, X_0 + 0.105 \, l \tag{4123}$$

$$p^x = 0.181 \, X_0 + 0.482 \, l \tag{4124}$$

$$Y = 1.48 \, X_0 - 0.568 \, l \tag{4125}$$

Again the influence of wage rates on the balance of payments situation is very modest: wage rates appear to be an inefficient regulator of the balance of payments; but now the influence on the volume of production is considerable: the elasticity being $-\dfrac{1.88}{1.5} = -1.25$. A closer analysis of the figures, based on the formulae obtained for the other variables, shows that this is due to (i) the greater influence now exerted by wage rates on the export price level and (ii) the larger elasticity of export demand. In the long run therefore the wage rate appears to be a fairly efficient regulator of employment.

4.144 This is illustrated by the solutions of the political problem listed below for the case where $e_0 = 0$:

Table 4.144   Some numerical solutions of problem 131 for $e_0 = 0$

Target values		Instrument values	
v	D	l	X_0
Case *Csn* (short-term reactions)			
0	0	0	0
0.1	0	—0.39	—0.004
0	—0.1	—1.18	—0.16
0.1	—0.1	—1.57	—0.16
Case *Cln* (long-term reactions)			
0	0	0	0
0.1	0	—0.05	+0.006
0	—0.1	—0.10	—0.103
0.1	—0.1	—0.15	—0.098

For a short-term increase of 0.1 in the volume of production a wage reduction of 39 %, for a short-term reduction of 0.1 in the balance of payments deficit a reduction of more than 100 %, would be necessary; figures which can only mean that no practical solution exists. In the long run the necessary reductions would be considerably more realistic, although even then not too easy.

4.151   PROBLEM 141. MODEL 14.

Targets: "full" employment and balance of payments equilibrium
Instruments: government expenditure and the wage rate
Comments: In order to make comparisons between the two instruments from the price structure, the wage rate and the exchange rate, we have constructed the somewhat more complicated model 14, which we are now going to apply in three problems, 141 to 143, inclusive; 141 and 142 show two instruments and 143 three. In problem 141 the wage rate is used to regulate the price structure, whereas in problem 142 the exchange rate is used. Comparisons between 141 and 142 will show the relative advantages and disadvantages of both. Problem 143 will be devoted to a three-target problem.

The formulae obtained here only differ from those of problem 131 in that foreign prices are included; therefore only the solutions of the policy problem may now be mentioned.

Table 4.151   Solutions to problem 141 for $e_0 = 0$

Target values		Instrument values	
v	D	l	X_0
		Case *Csn* (short-term reactions)	
0	0	$-6.9\,p^i + 8.8\,p^w$	$-0.39\,p^i + 0.49\,p^w$
0.1	0	$-0.39 -6.9\,p^i + 8.8\,p^w$	$-0.004 -0.39\,p^i + 0.49\,p^w$
0	-0.1	$-1.18 -6.9\,p^i + 8.8\,p^w$	$-0.16 -0.39\,p^i + 0.49\,p^w$
0.1	-0.1	$-1.57 -6.9\,p^i + 8.8\,p^w$	$-0.16 -0.39\,p^i + 0.49\,p^w$
		Case *Cln* (long-term reactions)	
0	0	$-0.99\,p^i + 1.99\,p^w$	$-0.067\,p^i + 0.067\,p^w$

The reader will understand why, in the first four lines, the terms with p^i and p^w are the same; for this reason the results for case *Cln* have only been given for $v = D = 0$; the solutions for the other values of v and D given in the upper half of the table may be obtained from this table and the previous one.

It is found, as a result, that the wage changes required to attain the targets set are heavily dependent on the simultaneous changes in foreign prices. One per cent rise in prices p^w without a change in p^i will permit a wage rise of 8.8%; or will make a wage fall of 8.8% superfluous; and one per cent rise in prices p^i without a change in p^w will, on the contrary, make things considerably more difficult. If account is taken of long-term reactions, more moderate changes in l will be needed; and usually parallel changes in p^w and p^i will occur, making the required changes in wages still less. If a rise of 5% in p^i is accompanied by a rise of 3% in p^w a wage rise of some 1% will be justified. Formulae of this nature will be called *"directives"*: they imply a directive for a current adjustment in wage rates required by changes in the world market situation. Similar conclusions are implied as to X_0 (cf. § 3.33).

4.152   PROBLEM 142. MODEL 14.

Targets: "full" employment and balance of payments equilibrium
Instruments: government expenditure and the exchange rate
Comments: See problem 141. First we will compare the size of the changes required in wage rates with those required in exchange rates in order to attain the same targets. For case C (country whose imports are 50% of its national income) in a normal cyclical position the following solutions can be found for short-term and long-term reactions, respectively:

Table 4.1521   *Some numerical solutions to problems 141 and 142 compared*

Wage policy (141)

Short-term reactions

$X_0 = 1.59\,D - 0.06\,v - 0.393\,p^i + 0.492\,p^w$
$l = 11.8\ \ D - 4.17\,v - 6.88\ \ p^i + 8.82\ \ p^w$

Long-term reactions

$X_0 = 1.03\,D + 0.056\,v - 0.067\,p^i + 0.067\,p^w$
$l = 1.00\,D - 0.478\,v - 0.99\ \ p^i + 1.99\ \ p^w$

Exchange-rate policy (142)

Short-term reactions

$X_0 = D\qquad\ + 0.149\,v - 0.05\ \ p^i + 0.05\ \ p^w$
$k\ = 6.06\,D - 2.15\ \ v - 3.55\ \ p^i + 4.55\ \ p^w$

Long-term reactions

$X_0 = 1.03\,D + 0.056\,v - 0.067\,p^i + 0.067\,p^w$
$k\ = 1.00\,D - 0.478\,v - 0.99\ \ p^i + 1.99\ \ p^w$

For our comparison it will also be useful to have the solutions to the analytical problem, i.e. the expression of the main variables in terms of the instruments and data. They are:

Table 4.1522   *Solutions to analytical problems 141 and 142*

Wage policy (141)

Short-term reactions

$v\ \ = 1.99\ X_0 - 0.27\ \ l - 1.06\ \ p^i + 1.39\ \ p^w$
$D\ = 0.71\ X_0 - 0.01\ \ l + 0.21\ \ p^i - 0.26\ \ p^w$
$p^x\ = 0.20\ X_0 + 0.30\ \ l + 0.22\ \ p^i + 0.14\ \ p^w$
$Y\ \ = 1.57\ X_0 + 0.20\ \ l - 0.93\ \ p^i + 1.35\ \ p^w$

Long-term reactions

$v\ \ = 1.81\ X_0 - 1.88\ \ l - 1.74\ \ p^i + 3.62\ \ p^w$
$D\ = 0.87\ X_0 + 0.103\,l + 0.16\ \ p^i - 0.26\ \ p^w$
$p^x\ = 0.181\,X_0 + 0.482\,l + 0.156\,p^i + 0.362\,p^w$
$Y\ \ = 1.48\ X_0 - 0.568\,l - 1.4\ \ \ p^i + 2.96\ \ p^w$

Exchange-rate policy (142)

Short-term reactions

$v\ \ = 1.99\ X_0 - 0.33\ \ k - 1.06\ \ p^i + 1.39\ \ p^w$
$D\ = 0.71\ X_0 + 0.049\,k + 0.21\ \ p^i - 0.26\ \ p^w$
$p^x\ = 0.20\ X_0 - 0.36\ \ k + 0.22\ \ p^i + 0.14\ \ p^w$
$Y\ \ = 1.57\ X_0 - 0.43\ \ k - 0.93\ \ p^i + 1.35\ \ p^w$

Long-term reactions

$v\ \ = 1.81\ X_0 - 1.88\ \ k - 1.74\ \ p^i + 3.62\ \ p^w$
$D\ = 0.87\ X_0 + 0.103\,k + 0.16\ \ p^i - 0.26\ \ p^w$
$p^x\ = 0.181\,X_0 - 0.518\,k + 0.156\,p^i + 0.362\,p^w$
$Y\ \ = 1.48\ X_0 - 1.54\ \ k - 1.4\ \ \ p^i + 2.96\ \ p^w$

4.153 From these equations we observe that, in *short-term reactions*, k exerts a slightly stronger influence on both D and v and that, as a result, less extreme changes in k are required to produce given changes in D or v: k might be called a more efficient instrument for regulating both the balance of payments and the level of production, comparing equal percentage changes in l and k as equally "difficult". Since, in fact, wage reductions are more difficult to obtain than exchange rate reductions of equal size, this conclusion stands firm for reductions. It is only natural, but very important for our comparison, that internal prices p^x are affected differently: a wage change affecting them positively and an exchange rate negatively. For all groups with fixed money incomes, i.e. especially those dependent on savings in bonds, this makes a big difference. Of course it also makes a big difference to wage earners; we are going to discuss its consequences in § 4.155.

Under boom conditions (case *b*) as defined in the description of model 14 (Appendix 3) the coefficient of v in the expression k in table 4.1521, upper half, is —2.76 instead of —2.15.

It needs hardly to be stressed that the numerical values of the coefficients shown will depend very much on the structure of the country considered. The reader may be able to derive similar equations for cases B and D.

4.154 Turning now to *long-term reactions* we observe that, at least with our interpretation of this phrase, the influence of equal percentage changes in l and k on D and on v is exactly equal. On closer investigation this appears to be the consequence of two assumptions involved, namely that: (i) incomes of independents move parallel to wages, and (ii) the coefficients ξ_1 and ξ_2 add up to unity, meaning that there is no money illusion. [1] On these conditions it can be proved that the changes in each physical variable (e, x, v, i) and in D brought about by equal percentage changes in l and k are equal.

4.155 So far we discussed wage rates and exchange rates as alternative instruments. Very often the choice to be made is different: if wages are not considered an instrument, they will have to be considered as a dependent variable in the system; and if there is a devaluation of money they will change also. Evidently the consequences depend on how wage rates react to a devaluation. Often they will tend to move proportionally to internal

---

[1] This may be proved in the following way: since $dX = \xi_1 dY + \xi_2 dp$ we have $dx = dX - dp = \xi_1 dY + (\xi_2 - 1) dp$; if $\xi_1 + \xi_2 = 1$ this may be written: $dx = \xi_1 (dY - dp) = \xi_1 dy$, meaning that real expenditure increases are only dependent on changes in real income and not, in addition, on price changes.

prices. We will make this assumption and recalculate the consequences of a change in k. Instead of putting $l = 0$ we add an equation

$$l = p^x \tag{4126}$$

The analytical problem now shows the following solutions (case Csn):

$$v = 1.91\, X_0 - 0.19\ k - 1.14\, p^i + 1.34\, p^w \tag{4127}$$

$$D = 0.71\, X_0 + 0.054\, k + 0.21\, p^i - 0.26\, p^w \tag{4128}$$

These equations have to be compared to formulae 9 and 10 of table 4.1522. It appears that the influence on v is now considerably less than in the case of "pure" exchange-rate policy (without a change in wage rates): the coefficient has gone down from 0.33 to 0.19. The efficiency of exchange rates with respect to the volume of production is now less even than that of wage rates, provided we compare equal percentage changes in both rates as equivalent. This clearly is not realistic, however, and certainly devaluation will be the easier way still.

4.156 PROBLEM 143. MODEL 14.

Targets: "full" employment, balance of payments equilibrium and monetary equilibrium

Instruments: government expenditure, the wage rate and the exchange rate

Comments: Since our definition of monetary equilibrium does not coincide with that of balance of payments equilibrium there is scope for introducing both, as two different targets, together with the target of full employment. Since three instruments are then required, both the wage rate and the rate of exchange have been introduced as such, in addition to public expenditure.

The solutions to the political and the analytical problem are given below, for short-term and for long-term reactions.

Table 4.156 Solutions to problem 143, cases Csn and Cln

I. Political problem;   (s) short-term reactions:

$$X_0 = \quad 0.1\ v + 1.2\ \ D + 0.1\, p^x - 0.2\ \ p^i + 0.2\ \ p^w$$
$$l\ \ = -1.6\ v + 4.0\ \ D + 2.0\, p^x - 3\ \ \ \ p^i + 3\ \ \ \ p^w$$
$$k\ \ = -1.3\ v + 4.0\ \ D - 1.0\, p^x - 2\ \ \ \ p^i + 3\ \ \ \ p^w$$

(l) long-term reactions:

$$X_0 = \quad 0.06\, v + 1.0\ \ D \qquad\qquad - 0.07\, p^i + 0.07\, p^w$$
$$l\ \ = -0.26\, v + 0.33\, D + 1.0\, p^x - 0.66\, p^i + 0.66\, p^w$$
$$k\ \ = -0.22\, v + 0.67\, D - 1.0\, p^x - 0.33\, p^i + 1.33\, p^w$$

II. Analytical problem; (s) short-term reactions

$$D = 0.71 X_0 - 0.01 l + 0.049 k + 0.21 p^i - 0.26 p^w$$
$$v = 1.99 X_0 - 0.27 l - 0.33 \ k - 1.06 p^i + 1.39 p^w$$
$$p^x = 0.20 X_0 + 0.30 l - 0.36 \ k + 0.22 p^i + 0.14 p^w$$

(l) long-term reactions

$$D = 0.87 X_0 + 0.10 l + 0.10 \ k + 0.16 p^i - 0.26 p^w$$
$$v = 1.81 X_0 - 1.88 l - 1.88 \ k - 1.74 p^i + 3.62 p^w$$
$$p^x = 0.18 X_0 + 0.48 l - 0.52 \ k + 0.16 p^i + 0.36 p^w$$

The reader will be able to compare the solutions of the analytical problems with those given before and to explain the resemblance. The solutions to the political problem show the characteristics that could be expected: less violent changes in l and k will be sufficient in order to restore either a certain volume of production or a certain balance of payments surplus. An increase in production by say 5 % will require a wage reduction by 12% and a devaluation by 10 %; an improvement in the balance of payments situation by 1 % of national income or 2 % of imports will require a reduction of both rates by 4 %. If it is desired, at the same time, to let internal prices fall by 1 % this requires an *extra* wage reduction by 2 % and 1 % *less* devaluation. Although these figures are indeed less considerable than the ones previously calculated, they are still high.

The long-run figures are much more acceptable from the practical point of view. Their application will not lead to the desired aim within the course of one or two years, but only after two or three years. The implication is that other instruments of economic policy will then have to be applied meanwhile, e.g. quantitative restrictions, or that the evils of unsatisfactory employment or balance of payments deficit or too high prices, when they occur, will have to be borne for some time.

4.161   PROBLEM 151. MODEL 15.

Targets: "full" employment and balance of payments equilibrium
Instruments: public expenditure and debt policy
Comments: In many countries wages are not considered an instrument of economic policy; and in accordance with the Bretton Woods agreement the exchange rate is not considered a current instrument either. On the other hand, the tendency to accept at least the two targets indicated requires more than one instrument. In this and the next problem two instruments from the sphere of credit policy are introduced as alternatives: government debt policy and discount policy. Their analysis requires a model which somewhat more explicitly deals with the monetary variables of the

economy; to this end model 15 has been constructed, of importance also in the purely statistical description of the economy. Unfortunately, the relations entering into this model have so far been neglected by statistical and econometric research; little is known about their true shape and hence our treatment can only be sketchy, and our conclusions tentative.

In this problem, ΔB_1 may be considered to be the second instrument. The values of E (exports) and of the two target variables Y and D are given, the former as a datum and the latter because they are targets. Unknowns are the instrument values X_0 and ΔB_1 and all the irrelevant variables; the total number of unknowns amounting to 25, for which model 15 supplies 25 equations. Some remarks on the probable results will be given together with those of problem 152.

The choice made implies that credit rationing is left out of consideration. Some remarks on it will be made in section 4.177.

4.162   PROBLEM 152. MODEL 15.

Targets: "full" employment and balance of payments equilibrium
Instruments: public expenditure and the rate of discount
Comments: The difference, as to logical structure, from the previous problem is only slight. In fact, in the simple version of model 15 there is no difference at all. In practice, however, there are several types of "bonds", that is, financial assets other than money, and among these are short-term debentures, whose creation the government may influence by a change in the discount rate of the Central Bank. A really satisfactory treatment of the problems considered requires the introduction of more types of assets and consequently more equations. The short-term interest rate m_M^1 will now be an instrument variable, and hence unknown, and the longterm rate m_B^1 will be given. The number of equations therefore will again be sufficient to solve for the unknowns.

Discussing, now, the possible solutions to both problems (151 and 152) we may state that there would be no solution if D were defined as before, namely as the deficit on current account: $D = I - E$. The reason is very simple: full employment requires a certain value of Y; from this a certain value for I follows; and with given E, D results and as a rule will not be zero. The cases where it is positive are the ones asking for a solution. A superficial solution will be possible if balance of payments equilibrium is understood in a different way, namely by including non-current items which are then required to offset any lack of equilibrium in the current items. By its nature such an equilibrium will, however, be a temporary one. Both debt management and discount policy can indeed attract a certain amount of capital from abroad, corresponding with the interest offered. When demand for assets reaches its equilibrium at the new interest rate, no further inflow of foreign investment will, however, occur unless a further rise in rates is effectuated. These policies therefore can only be recommended for temporary solutions. Little is known, as was already observed, about the extent to which a given interest differential with other countries attracts such a temporary flow of capital.

A lasting solution of the problem of balance of payments disequilibrium can only be obtained if E is adapted to the desired level of Y and I; which will require either price policy or policies of "sales promotion" on a national scale (cf. problems 131, 141, 142 and 143).

4.171   We may now summarize our findings in this §. The regulation of short-term equilibrium in an open economy is complicated by its international links. Economic development generally and economic policy in foreign countries both influence, and may disturb, the economy. Policy requirements depend very much on the degree of similarity between the targets set abroad and at home. They tend to become more difficult the larger the number of targets set. Even without any further targets it will be necessary, at least in the long run, to maintain balance of payments equilibrium. In modern societies the need will increasingly be felt to add the targets of "full" employment and of monetary equilibrium. One instrument will be sufficient in rare cases only: one or two other general instruments will usually be badly needed. Only if the country happens to be in favourable circumstances can it do without: if it commands ample reserves, or if its price level is highly competitive, there will be no balance of payments problem..

4.172   Again, the most effective instrument that may be used to regulate employment as well as balance of payments equilibrium or monetary equilibrium (but not simultaneously) is government expenditure (or more generally government surplus or deficit). The high efficiency of this instrument is due to the fact that it directly affects the volume of demand, whereas most other instruments do so only indirectly. The effectiveness of public expenditure is illustrated by its multiplier. This multiplier is lower in an open economy, however, than in a closed one, and is lower, the higher is the import quota of the country. It is also lower, in respect of the volume of production, in boom conditions than in a normal cyclical situation; and in the

long run as compared with short-run reactions. For nominal income
it is higher in a boom period and in the long run, but this is due to
a higher rise in prices.

4.173 If two targets are set it becomes necessary to add another
main instrument, preferably one taken from the price structure; for
technical reasons exchange rates and wage rates seem to be the best
ones. Both do influence the volume of production and hence employment, but their short-term influence is not strong. This means
that in the case of disturbances of some importance, intensive changes may be necessary. Both have their draw-backs. The Bretton
Woods agreement requires exchange rates to be as stable as possible.
Unions will oppose big reductions in wage rates. This situation illustrates
the importance of international coordination. Heavy disturbances are
less likely to occur if all countries adhere to a similar policy.

4.174 Wage policy is not a generally accepted main instrument of
economic policy; freedom of negotiation is very often felt to be of
great importance. The preceding analysis shows how necessary a
revision of this attitude is. The Netherlands have chosen in favour
of a centralized wage policy, making wage changes dependent on
government approval. Their experience in the ten-year period 1945–
1955 has been favourable. Holland regained its strong position in
international trade, vital to the country, by a policy of wage restraint
during the years 1951–1954.

4.175 Comparing the exchange-rate and wage-rate adjustments
required to meet a given disturbance we find that percentage changes
in exchange rates can be smaller than percentage changes in wage
rates. This, however, only applies to isolated changes in exchange
rates, that is changes not accompanied by wage adjustments. If wages
are adjusted so as to maintain real wages, the necessary exchange rate
changes will exceed those in wage rates. Neither isolated wage changes
nor wage-adjusted devaluations are very elegant: in the former case
wage earners bear the full burden, or more, and in the latter case they
do not share at all in the burden. Some sharing will usually be preferable.

4.176 In the long run the effects of exchange rate and wage rate changes are considerably larger and so the adjustments required to meet a given disturbance lie more within the limits of practical possibilities. This implies that such disturbances will have to be met temporarily either by drawing upon reserves or by quantitative restrictions (cf. § 5.2).

4.177 Credit policies, as a rule, do not form a powerful instrument in the maintenance of short-term equilibrium. The influence of a change in interest rates on activity is only weak; a rise in discount rates will attract short-term foreign capital, but this, by its nature, means only a temporary flow. Restrictive credit policy will, however, influence activity more directly and more effectively.

Credit restriction may be used to impose an upper limit to national expenditure and hence to national income. Thus, by credit restriction, it may be possible, if need be, to restrict the expansion of national income so as to avoid a balance of payments deficit: the level of income determined in problem 112, equation (4104). In other words, it is possible to restrict the growth of monetary circulation to the cash balances corresponding to that level of national income.

4.178 If three targets are set, three instruments are needed. This especially applies to a program of "full" employment, balance of payments equilibrium and monetary equilibrium in the sense of stable prices. If it is desired to carry out such a program in an unstable world, it will be necessary to accept exchange rates as a regular instrument of policy. This can only be avoided if the leading countries pursue a policy of stable prices.

4.2. Multiple-Target Policies for Open Economies

4.211 The general type of quantitative policy problems arising in most countries will pursue a number of different targets at the same time; among them will be short-term targets and the relevant phases of certain longer-term policies. Since most countries are definitely open economies, such "multiple-target policies for open economies" play an important role in practical life. We have collected, in the preceding chapter and the preceding section, sufficient elements of the problems involved in order to be able to face the design of such policies as a whole.

4.212   In an open economy the element of interdependency takes forms which are different from those which it takes in closed economies. We already discussed (cf. § 4.111–4.113) the reduction in freedom with respect to the price level, at least if exchange rates are not considered an instrument of current economic policy. We introduced the phrase of "imported inflation" as an illustration of this reduced freedom. On the other hand, an open economy can be helped by others in order to overcome certain difficulties of inflation; we used the expression "exportation of inflation" in order to illustrate that point. Another example of the change in economic interdependency is supplied by the consequences of changes in productivity. A rise in productivity with constant employment in a closed economy will increase the volume of production and hence the volume of consumption. In an open economy it may happen that such an increase in production does not result in an increase in consumption because of a deterioration in the terms of trade. The advantages of the increase in productivity have then been handed over to other countries; sometimes the circumstances will not permit any other attitude. And the country concerned may obtain a greater advantage from the increase in productivity elsewhere than from its own increases in productivity. The case is similar to the well-known fact that building workers have seen their wages rise during the last century more because of rises in productivity in other industries than because of rises in their own industry.

4.213   All these interdependencies have to be expressed in the models used, and it is because of the complicated interdependencies (especially in open economies) that these models render valuable services here. Models have to be designed so much with a view to the special problems to be solved that it is hardly possible to give a complete treatment in a general way. Again a number of examples will be discussed and some of the more general conclusions will be set out at the end of this section (cf. 4.27). These examples are intended to illustrate the formal as well as the material aspects of the problem of multiple-target policies. The author believes that, as far as the material aspect is concerned problem 162, in particular, is of practical relevance to present-day policies.

4.214   The examples to be discussed are still extremely simple in comparison to the problems of actual practice. As in earlier examples, they have been chosen to be simple for explanatory purposes. An additional reason for doing so is that the more complicated methods, including input-output analysis, are still in the experimental stage. Probably they will soon be available as supplementary methods, insofar as sufficient statistical data will have been collected meanwhile. For the time being it seems advisable to use a two-stage method. The main problems of economic policy for the economy as a whole may be provisionally solved with the aid of the methods to be described in this section. Sector problems may, as a second stage, be considered with the aid of these provisional solutions of the general problem, using the figures found concerning general activity, general price and wage level, etc., and applying methods similar to those of this section.

4.221   PROBLEM 161. MODEL 16 [EQUATIONS (1)—(17)].

Targets: "full" employment,
          balance of payments equilibrium,
          a given volume of investment,
          a given distribution of income between workers and independents;
meaning that the target variables are a, D, j and λ;
it depends on the initial situation which numerical values these variables have to assume.
Instruments: government expenditure C, wage rate l, indirect tax rate τ and direct tax rate θ.
Comments: this problem is chosen as an example of modern policy, with two targets of a short-run character and the two others representing long-term targets: a given volume of investment being a prerequisite for a certain rate of development and a given distribution being part of a policy of social equilibrium.

4.222   Evidently we have to solve the system of equations for the values of X_0, l, τ, and θ. Since this problem will be shown—for this model—to be insoluble, it is worth while to go into the process at some detail. using various methods of presentation.

   As a first method we use an "arrow system" constructed in an intuitive way: starting with data and given values of target variables we try to find out which of the irrelevant variables and of the instrument variables (forming, together, our unknowns) can be determined. And it appears that the structure is such as to permit us to go a long way with this "method".

Starting with equation (9) we see that the given value of a enables us to find v; equation (8) then yields i; equation (13) I; together with the given value for D, equation (15) then supplies E. According to (14) and (6)—here we have to combine two equations in order to find our way—then may be written:

$$E = (\bar{e} - \varepsilon_1)\, p \tag{4201}$$

from which we can find p, and with (6), e. Next, (7) now yields l, our first instrument variable. Also, we can now deduce Y, since equation (1) may be given a somewhat different form in this model, namely:

$$Y = v + \bar{v}p - I \tag{1'}$$

and all the right-hand side members are known.

Remembering now that j is also given, we find from equation (12) the value of J and from v, j and e, equation (16), the value of c. From (10) C^F can then be calculated. Taking up l again, and combining it with a, according to equation (2), we deduce L; Z can now be found with the help of equation (3).

4.223   Here our first important result emerges: now that we know both L and Z, *we cannot prescribe a ratio λ between them*, as equation (17) and our fourth target would require us to do: this social equilibrium target is not therefore compatible with the other targets so far used to find Z and L, i.e. only a and D. Of course this incompatibility only applies to the specific model now considered, including the choice of instruments. With one more instrument intervening in one of the relations so far used, it would be possible to reconcile the targets a, D and λ.

4.224   The second important result is the counterpart of the first one; it is that the two instruments not yet calculated, namely C_0 and τ, *cannot be calculated separately*. This is most easily seen if we eliminate C from our equations by substituting (11) into (4):

$$\bar{c}\,(p + \tau) + (1 + \bar{\tau})\, c = C_0 + \gamma\,(1 - \bar{\theta})\, Z - \gamma\, \bar{Z}\theta + L \tag{4'}$$

Having eliminated C we do not need equation (11) any more in our system and (4') is now the only equation left in which both the unknowns τ and C_0 appear. It follows that one of them can be chosen freely, and only then can the other be derived. The phenomena just discovered may also be formulated thus. If we had eliminated all the irrelevant variables and thus retained only four equations in the four unknown instruments, we would have found that in three of these four equations the values of the two instruments l and θ only would have occurred, whereas in the fourth equation only the two others, τ and C_0, would have occurred. This has the two consequences just stated; on the one hand the first three equations cannot be satisfied at the same time, meaning that the targets cannot all be reached at the same time, whereas the fourth equation is not sufficient to yield us the two remaining instruments.

4.225 The logical structure just discussed can be symbolized in the arrow scheme of graph 4.225. Here the symbols are those used in the equations;

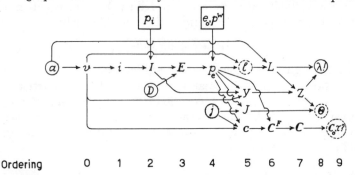

Ordering   0   1   2   3   4   5   6   7   8   9

Graph 4.225. Logical structure of problem 161. Symbols in fully-drawn squares indicate data; those in fully-drawn circles are targets and those in dotted circles (unknown) instrument values. Simon ordering is indicated below.

target variables are indicated by a fully drawn circle; data have been indicated by a square (these data do not occur in model 16, but might have easily been added in the same way as in model 12).

4.226 As another presentation of the same state of affairs we use Herbert Simon's causal ordering, which primarily comes down to writing the equations in another order: (see page 119).

4.227 From this presentation it is easily seen that the matrix of the system of equations is almost triangular; the exception being that in equation 14 a term $-e$ appears; and the implication being that, with that exception, every unknown can be calculated in succession from the others. This is, however, not possible with the unknowns τ and C_0, since these only occur in the last equation; they cannot be calculated separately. In revenge, the last but one equation (17) only contains variables (L and Z) that have already been determined and that will then satisfy equation (17) only by pure coincidence. Simon's "ordering" can be read from this list. Variables v, i, I, E are of orders 0, 1, 2 and 3, respectively; variables p and e of order

Table 4.225 Equations for problem 161

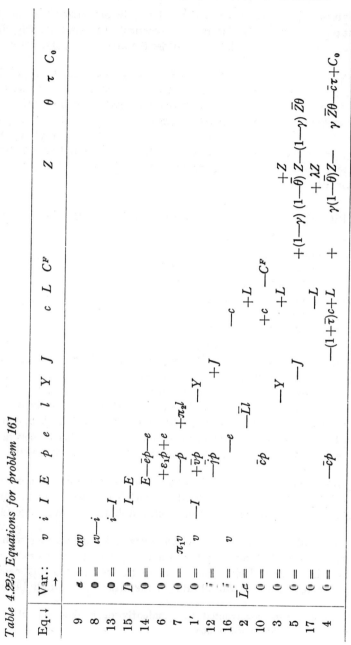

Eq.	Var.	v	i	I	E	p	e	l	Y	J	c	L	C^F	Z	θ	τ	C_0
9	$d=$	αv															
8	$0=$		$w-i$														
13	$0=$			$i-I$													
15	$D=$				$I-E$												
14	$0=$				E	$-\bar e p$	$-e$										
6	$0=$					$+\varepsilon_1 p$	$+e$										
7	$0=$	$\pi_1 v$				$-p$		$+\pi_2 l$									
1'	$0=$	v		$-I$		$+\bar v p$			$-Y$								
12	$0=$	v				$-ip$				$+J$							
16	$\bar L c=$	v					$-e$				$-c$						
2	$0=$					$\bar c p$		$-\bar L l$				$+L$					
10	$0=$										$+c$	$+L$	$-C^F$				
3	$0=$										$+c$	$+L$		$+Z$ $+(1-\gamma)(1-\bar\theta)Z$	$-(1-\gamma)\bar Z\theta$		
5	$0=$								$-Y$	$-J$		$+L$		$+Z$ $+\lambda Z$			
17	$0=$											$-L$					
4	$0=$					$-\bar c p$					$-(1+\bar\tau)c$	$+L$		$+\gamma(1-\bar\theta)Z$	$-\gamma\bar Z\theta$	$-\bar c\tau$	$+C_0$

4. Variables l, Y, J and c are of the order 5. In our arrow scheme this is brought out by their being placed in one (vertical) column. Similarly, L and C^F are of order 6, Z is of order 7, θ of order 8 and $-c\tau + C_0$ of order 9.

4.228   One last remark, one of *economic interpretation*, may be made. Upon closer consideration it will be clear that in this model and with the targets and instruments chosen, the instrument τ is irrelevant by itself; it only influences the internal price level for consumer goods; if it is raised, private consumption will fall but it may do so without changing anything else if only C_0, public consumption, is raised accordingly. It is only the two types of consumption together that matter for the balance of payments, for employment or for incomes.

4.231   PROBLEM 162. MODEL 16 [EQUATIONS (1)—(16) AND (17′)]

Targets: "full" employment,
　　　　balance of payments equilibrium,
　　　　a given volume of investment,
　　　　a given internal price level.
Instruments: public expenditure,
　　　　　the wage rate,
　　　　　the indirect tax rate,
　　　　　the direct tax rate.
Comments: by a slight change in the problem we have now presented a soluble problem. In addition, this problem may be considered a good example of modern economic policy, the emphasis now being laid on a somewhat different aspect of social policy: the protection of fixed incomes and of savings. (We already stated that the aim of a certain distribution of income between workers and independents might also have been brought in, but would have required the introduction of another instrument.)

4.232   After what has been said about the solution of problem 161 we may be brief here and only reproduce both the arrow scheme and the Simon arrangement of the equations. (cf. graph 4.232 [1]) and page 121).

4.233   We will now proceed to the *numerical solution* in order to be able to discuss the orders of magnitude of the changes in instruments necessary to attain the targets. Using the values of the coefficients and constants indicated in model 16 we will obtain, in the order of the table below, the

---

[1] This graph was constructed independently of B. Hansen (cf. Finans-politikens ekonomiska teori, p. 364).

Table 4.232 Equations for problem 162

Eq.↓	Var.→	v	i	I	E	p	e	l	Y	J	c	L	C^F	Z	θ	τ	C_0
9	$a=$	αv															
8	$0=$	vv	$-i$														
13	$0=$		i	$-I$													
15	$D=$			I	$-E$												
14	$0=$				E	$-\bar e p$	$-e$										
6	$0=$					$+\varepsilon_1 p$	$+e$										
7	$0=$	$\pi_1 v$				$-p$		$+\pi_2 l$									
1'	$0=$	v		$-I$		$+\bar v p$			$-Y$								
12	$j=$	v				$-\bar j p$				$+J$							
16	$j=$	v					$-e$				$-c$						
2	$\bar L a=$							$-\bar L l$				$+L$					
10	$0=$					$\bar c p$			$-Y$		$+c$		$-C^F$				
3	$0=$								$-Y$		$+c$	$+L$					
5	$0=$									$-J$							
17'	$p'=$					p											
4	$0=$					$-\bar c p$					$-(1+\bar\tau)c+L$			$+(1-\gamma)(1-\bar\theta)Z-(1-\gamma)\bar Z\theta$	$\gamma(1-\bar\theta)Z-\gamma\bar Z\theta$	$-\bar c\tau+\tau$	$+C_0$

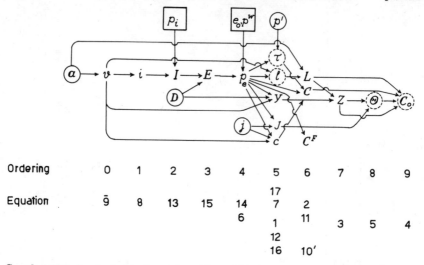

Ordering	0	1	2	3	4	5	6	7	8	9
						17				
Equation	$\bar{9}$	8	13	15	14	7	2			
					6	1	11	3	5	4
						12				
						16	10′			

Graph 4.232. Logical structure of problem 162. For explanation cf. graph 4.225.

expressions of the instrument and the irrelevant variables in terms of the targets:

Solutions of problem 162:

$$v = 2.5\ a \tag{4202}$$
$$i = 0.84\ a \tag{4203}$$
$$I = 0.84\ a \tag{4204}$$
$$E = 0.84\ a - D \tag{4205}$$
$$p = -1.68\ a + 2\ D \tag{4206}$$
$$e = 1.68\ a - 2\ D \tag{4207}$$
$${}^*l = -5.8\ a + 6\ D \tag{4208}$$
$$Y = -0.86\ a + 3\ D \tag{4209}$$
$$J = -0.16\ a + 0.2\ D + j \tag{4210}$$
$$c = 0.82\ a + 2\ D - j \tag{4211}$$
$$L = -2.41\ a + 3\ D \tag{4212}$$
$$C^F = -0.70\ a + 3.8\ D - j \tag{4213}$$
$$C = -0.90\ a + 2.2\ D - 1.1\ j + 0.9\ p' \tag{4214}$$
$$Z = 1.55\ a \tag{4215}$$
$${}^*\theta = 3.27\ a - 1.33\ D - 6.7\ j \tag{4216}$$
$${}^*\tau = +1.68\ a - 2\ D + p' \tag{4217}$$
$${}^*C_0 = 3.71\ a - 1.27\ D - 3.4\ j + 0.9\ p' \tag{4218}$$

4.234   The solutions with an asterisk refer to *instruments* and hence are of particular interest. They enable us to compute, for whatever change in targets we desire, the necessary values of the instrument variables. In order to illustrate their use let us suppose that a country finds itself faced with a deficit in the balance of payments of 10% of current items, i.e. $D = 0.05$; if it is desired to eliminate this deficit while maintaining employment, the rate of investment and the internal price level, our targets will be $D = -0.05$, $a = j = p' = 0$; and we easily deduce that: $l = -0.3$, $\theta = +0.07$, $\tau = 0.1$ and $C_0 = 0.06$, a very drastic programme indeed: the wage rate should be reduced by 30%, direct taxes increased from 0.3 to 0.37, i.e. by some 23%, indirect taxes from 0.1 to 0.2, i.e. doubled and public expenditure be increased from 0.25 to 0.31, i.e. by some 15%.

4.235   This program would, in most countries, be *politically impossible*; in our terminology, *boundary conditions* would be transgressed and a less ambitious programme should be accepted. Our formulae enable us to investigate a large number of possibilities. There are some remarkable further conclusions to be drawn: if, in particular, the huge reduction in wage rate should, rightly, be deemed impossible, the only change in targets that can help to overcome this difficulty is either a change in the balance of payments target or a change in the employment target: the other target variables do not enter into (4208). For each per cent less employment 6% less wage reduction could be "bought". Surely this statement does not apply to real wage rates; they can be easily calculated to be

$$l^R = l - p' = -5.8a + 6D - p'$$

and evidently depend on the internal price target as well; still not, however, on the investment target.

4.236   Suppose now we choose the targets: $D = -0.03$, $a = -0.01$, $j = 0$ and $p' = -0.05$; we find $l = -0.12$, $\theta = 0.01$, $\tau = -0.007$ and $C_0 = -0.044$; implying that real wage rates will now have to be down 7% "only". The striking feature is the very important place taken in these problems by the wage rate.

4.237   The reader should be aware of the simple structure of the solution now discussed; in particular it should be mentioned that for this same model the analytical method would be much more cumbersome: the matrix of the system of equations then becomes far from triangular and the causal ordering much less simple. This is not an incidental property of the example chosen; it is closely related to the role played by the two main targets, full employment and balance of payments equilibrium. Had a and D be among the variables, the interrelations between the variables would have been much more complicated.

4.241   PROBLEM 171. MODEL 17 [OMITTING EQUATION (4)].

Targets: "full" employment and conservation of a certain "desired" gold stock, to be represented by Y^F and Au^D respectively.

Instruments: the rate of discount m and the ratio ϱ of required reserves to deposits.

Comments: this problem illustrates some of the aspects of *monetary policy*, especially (i) the indirect guidance that can be given by the Central Bank to the credit market as a whole, and (ii) the narrow limits set to the effects on the general economy. In this field, especially, a careful distinction should be made between members of the endless variety of problems that may be considered. This will be illustrated by the choices that can be made as to targets and instruments, by the role boundary conditions may play and by a discussion of the difference between systematic and "trial-and-error" policy.

4.242   The targets chosen are indicative of the modern point of view that monetary policy should not only be directed towards the conservation of a certain desired gold stock (a target not essentially different from "balance of payments equilibrium", the phrase so far used) but also to the maintenance of "full" employment. It remains to be seen whether it will prove possible to do so under all circumstances, even under more or less normal circumstances.

The instruments have to be two, if we wish to pursue two targets. In some important countries there are the two instruments introduced in one model, the discount rate m and the reserve ratio ϱ. In some other important countries ϱ is not a regular instrument; in most countries open market policy would be another. This instrument works largely in the same way as the reserve ratio does, in that it influences the public's or the banks' need for central bank liquidities. [1]

Since m is considered an instrument variable, and so determined deliber-

---

[1] Model 17 might be adapted to this instrument of policy by adding a new item to the Central Bank assets: B^0, "open market holdings" by the Central Bank; this item also influences the public's demand for deposits and bank notes; hence equations (6) and (7) should have a third right-hand side item, $-\mu_3 B^0$ and $-\mu_3' B^0$, respectively.

ately in the light of its consequences, equation (4) has to be left out. It will be discussed when we consider "trial-and-error" policy.

4.243   The solution of our problem appears to be easy as far as the formal logic is concerned. Again the causal ordering is very differentiated. From (9) m will follow; from (8) m'; from (7) M', and from (6) M; from (3) B^R. Now R will follow from (1) and B^B from (2). Or in ordinary speech: the two interest rates will follow from the targets they have to fulfil; from them both the demand for bank notes and that for deposits will follow; and also the demand for rediscounts. This leaves only one item as the closing item in (our simplified version of) the Central Bank balance sheet, namely bankers balances (reserves); then, there remains one closing item in the private banks' balance sheet, namely their bills and advances. With deposits and reserves both determined, equation (5) will only lead the private banks to choose the correct private discount rate if the reserve ratio is chosen properly by the Central Bank. Graph 4.243 again illustrates, in the form of an arrow scheme, the logic of this solution.

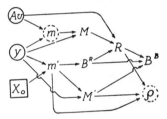

Graph 4.243. Logical structure of problem 171. For explanation cf. graph 4.225

It might seem as if this easy solution depends on our somewhat arbitrary assumptions that m only appears in the balance of payments equation and m' only in the national income (multiplier) equation. In fact, it does not matter whether this or a slightly different model is chosen, e.g. one where both rates occur in both equations.

4.244   So much for the qualitative logic; nothing yet has been said about the *numerical values* of the unknowns. These evidently depend very much on the numerical values of the coefficients in the equations. Here the difficulties about monetary policy come in. It is probable that the coefficient η_2 is rather small, meaning that not very much influence on the level of national income can be exerted by monetary policy (unless this takes the form of credit rationing, cf. below and § 3.532). Suppose, as an extreme case, that $\eta_2 = 0$. This would mean that m' is a consequence of, rather than a factor in, economic life; according to equation (5) it will reflect changes in demand for credit, but not itself influence that demand. It also means that the *only way to influence Y is to influence autonomous national expenditure X_0.* This may be an exaggeration, but it nevertheless gives a good first approximation. It means that the level of national income can hardly be influenced by monetary policy; and that only slight deviations from equilibrium will already require heavy changes in interest rates, with the possibility that certain boundary conditions will be violated. These we will discuss below.

4.245   There is not quite the same difficulty in relation to the *balance of payments*. The coefficient a' is not as low in an open economy: by a raising of its discount rate it may attract considerable short-term credits from abroad. Moderate discount variations will be able therefore, in the short run, to influence considerably the movements in the gold stock, as experience has shown. But this equilibrating influence is only a short-run one, as is illustrated by the occurrence, in equation (9), of the rate of change $m - m_{-1}$. If, for another time unit, another inflow of foreign capital is needed, the discount rate has to be raised again. And the influence is only superficial; it does not affect the fundamental economic variables E and Y in this equation very much. Even if it did, the difficulty, already discussed in § 4.121, would exist that the level of Y wanted for its own sake (Y^F) does not necessarily produce the balance of payments surplus we want; it produces $E - \iota Y^F$ on current account, which may be different from what we want in order to obtain Au^D.

In the light of these two difficulties it is not very important how the details of the other equations look; they determine the proportions within the monetary sphere but do not change the fundamental difficulties.

4.246   These equations will determine, however, whether certain *boundary conditions* will be reached and possibly violated. These we are now going to discuss. There are two which in more or less stringent form may play a role, both referring to a "reserve ratio": the Central Bank's and the private banks' reserve ratio. As soon as Au falls below a proportion a of notes in circulation (possibly corrected for some minor items) there will be concern about the gold stock (based or not on a legally prescribed ratio); and as soon as R would fall short of a certain proportion ϱ of deposits, there will be similar concern about the banks' reserves. The reaction to such an event will be, first, a raising of the discount rate concerned (official rate m in the former case and private rate m' in the latter). As far as the Central Bank is concerned, this reaction may be represented by a slight change in the setting of our problem. In stead of considering Au to be given we may assume that the ratio of Au to M is given: $Au = aM$. For private banks the reaction just mentioned has to be represented as follows. Although in equation (5) of model 17 some reaction of this kind is already expressed, it will not be sufficiently strong to prevent M', under all circumstances, to rise above $\dfrac{R}{\varrho}$. If this is desired, the interest rate m' will have to be raised to such an extent as to restrict demand to $\dfrac{R}{\varrho}$. This rise in m' will be found if a boundary condition for M' is assumed, namely

$$M' = \frac{R}{\varrho}$$

This equation will now replace the supply equation (5) and at the same time the problem will change its character. Equation (7) will now determine the level of national income attainable in these circumstances and equation (8) will determine the rate of discount m'.

4.247   Our present problem supplies a good example for discussing the *difference between systematic and trial-and-error policy*. The solution to our problem takes the form:

$$m = \mu_{11}Au^D + \mu_{12}Y^F + \mu_{10} \tag{4219}$$

$$\varrho = \mu_{21}Au^D + \mu_{22}Y^F + \mu_{20} \tag{4220}$$

where the coefficients $\mu_{11} \ldots \mu_{20}$ can be expressed in terms of the coefficients of model 17. If the model is exact, these values of m and ϱ are such that Au actually will assume the value Au^D and Y the value Y^F. This choice of m and ϱ we shall call *systematic policy*. For simplicity's sake we will forget about the target Y^F for a while and continue the discussion for the case of one target Au^D and one instrument m. Systematic policy will then be represented by a choice:

$$m = \mu_S Au^D$$

Trial-and-error policy has to be applied if the structure and the coefficients of the model are not exactly known. It will, in principle, consist of a succession of changes in the instrument values, as long as actual Au values do not coincide with desired values Au^D, and may take the form:

$$m - m_{-1} = \mu_S' (Au_{-1}^D - Au_{-1}) \tag{4221}$$

where suffixes —1 indicate a time lag; i.e. the discount rate will be raised as long as Au is below Au^D. Since a rise in the interest rate will attract foreign credits, it is possible that Au will rise, and if μ_S is sufficiently large and the time units sufficiently small, the target value will be reached after some time. But there will be values of μ_S' and the time lag applied which may not necessarily always bring Au closer to its target value. In a general way it depends on the dynamics of "the system" whether there will be convergency towards a limiting value of the variables or not. "The system" now means the system of equations of model 17, plus equation (4221). The methods of dynamic analysis, in this case of difference equations, have to be applied to find this out; and it is well known that, especially in the more complicated cases, rather unexpected movements may be the result of some seemingly "natural" reaction equation. With too high values of $\mu's$, e.g., fluctuations with ever increasing amplitudes may occur; with more than one difference equation, or more than one lag in the same equation, long swings may occur, not necessarily converging towards an equilibrium. This particularly applies to the cases where, again, more than one target and hence more than one instrument occur. An interesting illustration of the difficulties that may arise here is the question of the direction of the changes that should be brought about. Suppose we have again the two targets of problem 171, and suppose also that Au as well as Y are too low. In order to raise Y, a reduction in m has to be performed. What should the total reaction of the authorities be? Evidently here the knowledge of the formulae of systematic policy would be of great help. They tell us whether an increase in Au of a given extent, plus an increase in Y of another, given, extent requires a rise or a fall in m and a rise or fall in ϱ.

The essence of trial-and-error policy is that it introduces a dynamic feature into the system, leading to an adjusting movement of the system, which upon certain conditions (in our simplest example of one target, this condition is that $\mu's$ be below some limit) ends up with equilibrium values of the variables as desired for a systematic policy. The dynamic feature may take different forms. In stead of (4221) we might have chosen:

$$m = \mu\left(Au_{-1}{}^D - Au_{-1}\right) + \mu_0 \tag{4221'}$$

Here the conditions for convergence towards an equilibrium will be different.

4.248   So far we *did not specify* Au^D. In a number of situations it will be chosen so as to be at least the amount required by the reserve ratio to note circulation; i.e. aM. We may substitute this expression, adding perhaps an extra item for safety's sake or in order to build up an extra reserve, into equation (4219) and (4220). These would then indicate how m and ϱ should be regulated in order just to maintain the minimum gold reserve required. This same specification of Au^D would give (4221) the form

$$m - m_{-1} = \mu's\left(aM - Au\right) \tag{4222}$$

approaching equation (4) of model 17. It would completely cover equation (4) if we had given to the trial-and-error reaction the form (4221') and again specified Au^D to be aM.

This leads to:

$$m = \mu\,(aM_{-1} - Au_{-1}) + \mu_0 \tag{4223}$$

which, apart from timing, is identical to equation (4) of model (17), the equation we so far left out. Under conditions of convergency of the adjusting movement, this variant of trial-and-error policy therefore leads to the situation described by model (17), including equation (4).

Both (4221) and (4223) assume also that trial-and-error policy is in a way systematic, namely that there is a constant pattern of reaction of the monetary authorities, represented by the coefficients of these equations. Even this constancy need not be complete. There may be—and usually will be—a random component in such a reaction. Still the effect may also then be a gradual approach to Au^D.

4.249   The difference between systematic policy and trial-and-error policy should not be exaggerated. Systematic policy as here advocated will sometimes be able to reach the goal more quickly and with less waste of time and energy. But the conditions for an exact systematic policy are exact and complete knowledge of the functioning of the economy; and these conditions are not fulfilled. In addition, the continuous change of data causes the target values to move continuously also, requiring a succession of changes also with systematic policy. The difference between systematic and trial-and-error policy thus becomes less pronounced; still the chances are that even a policy that is only partly systematic will, on the average, make a better "hit" than a trial-and-error policy.

4.251   **PROBLEM 181. MODEL 18.**

Targets: "full" employment, balance of payments equilibrium
Instruments: increases in productivity in 2 industries
Comments: This problem has been chosen in order to illustrate as clearly as possible some of the drawbacks of international connections. Contrary to what is usually thought, isolated increases in productivity in a single country are as a rule not very appropriate for solving, in the short run, any employment or balance of payments problems. The model used is very simple in some respects but probably gives, if anything, a favourable bias, in that it assumes that cost reductions are passed on to the buyer by price reductions of the same magnitude.

4.252   The solution of the political problem appears, in this case, to run parallel with the solution of the analytical problem, and, since the latter may help to clarify certain of the conclusions, we will take up both at the same time. The two target variables D and a depend on the v's and the a's:

$$D = (\varepsilon_1 - \bar{e}^1)\, a_1 + (\varepsilon_1 - \bar{e}^2)\, a_2 + \iota_1 v^1 + \iota_2 v^2$$
$$a = \bar{v}^1\; a_1 + \bar{v}^2\, a_2 + \bar{a}_1 v^1 + \bar{a}_2 v^2$$

but the v's cannot be determined without the X's:

$$v^1 = X^1 - \bar{x}^1 a_1 - \varepsilon_1 a_1$$

and similar for v^2; and so we have to use equations (1)—(3) leading to:

$$Y = \frac{A}{1 - \xi_1 (1 - \iota_1) - \xi_2 (1 - \iota_2)} \tag{4225}$$

$$X^1 = \frac{\xi_1 A}{1 - \xi_1 (1 - \iota_1) - \xi_2 (1 - \iota_2)} \tag{4226}$$

$$D = \frac{-1 + \xi_1 + \xi_2}{1 - \xi_1 (1 - \iota_1) - \xi_2 (1 - \iota_2)} A \tag{4227}$$

where

$$A = (\bar{e}^1 - \varepsilon_1 + \iota_1 \varepsilon_1 + \iota_1 \bar{x}^1)\, a_1 + (\bar{e}^2 - \varepsilon_2 + \iota_2 \varepsilon_2 + \iota_2 \bar{x}^2)\, a_2 \tag{4228}$$

From the preceding equations we then find:

$$v^1 = \xi_1 Y - (\bar{x}^1 + \varepsilon_1)\, a_1 \tag{4229}$$

$$a^1 = \bar{a}_1 v^1 + \bar{v}^1 a_1 \tag{4230}$$

The discussion of the influence of a_1 and a_2 on the target variables may best be given in successive steps. The denominators of Y, X^h and D ($h = 1,2$) are evidently positive; and, almost always, ξ_1 and ξ_2 will also be positive; Y, X^1 and X^2 therefore have the same sign as A, and D has opposite sign. Since increases a_1 and a_2 must be negative in order to represent productivity increases, the sign of the contribution of each industry to A will be opposite to the sign of $\bar{e}^h - \varepsilon_h + \iota_h \varepsilon_h + \iota_h \bar{x}^h$ and this apparently depends to a large extent on ε_h. Writing η_h for the elasticity of export demand of industry h we have

$$\varepsilon_h = \bar{e}^h \eta_h \tag{4231}$$

and hence:

$$A = \Sigma^h \{\bar{e}_h (1 - \eta_h + \iota_h \eta_h) + \iota_h \bar{x}^h\} a_h \tag{4232}$$

Since ι_h is always <1, the expression between $\{\}$ becomes negative and hence A positive for "sufficiently" large η_h's. But for $\eta_h = 1$ we have

$$A = \Sigma^h \iota_h \left(\bar{e}^h + \bar{x}^h \right) a_h = \Sigma^h \iota_h \bar{v}^h a_h < 0 \qquad (4233)$$

Since the various η_h need not be equal there is a range of uncertain signs in between. For $\eta_h = 2$, a realistic approximation in many cases, we have

$$A = \Sigma^h \left\{ \bar{e}^h \left(-1 + 2\iota_h \right) + \iota_h \bar{x}^h \right\} a_h \qquad (4233')$$

where it depends on ι_h and the ratio between $\bar{e}^h$ and $\bar{x}^h$, whether $\{\}$ is positive or negative. In the case of one single industry (our usual macro-economic approach) and a "small" country (cf. model 14, Appendix 3) we had $\bar{e} = 0.5$, $\bar{x} = 1$ and $\iota_h = 0.33$, leading to $A = \{0.5 \left(-1 + 0.67 \right) + 0.33\} a = 0.17\, a < 0$. This is an indication for the probability that negative values of A and hence deterioration of the balance of payments may be very often a consequence of increased productivity and will only be avoided if elasticities are well above 1.

4.253   The second step in the analysis, to be based on (4229), shows us that v^h, apart from a component proportional to A, includes a component $- (\bar{x}^h + \varepsilon_h) a_h$, which will always be positive and, furthermore, the more so the higher is ε_h. The influence of A will be the more pronounced the higher is ξ_h, for obvious reasons. In the above case of only one industry with $\xi_1 = 0.9$ and $\eta_1 = 2$, we have:

$$v^1 = \frac{0.9\, A}{1 - 0.9\, (1 - 0.33)} - 2\, a_1 = -1.6\, a_1,$$

a clearly positive value.

4.254   The final step brings us to a with the aid of (4230) and shows that a negative component, the direct influence of the increase in labour productivity, is now added, which introduces the possibility for a to be negative. Combining the last two steps, we may express a in terms of Y:

$$a = \Sigma^h \bar{a}_h v^h + \Sigma^h \bar{v}^h a_h = Y \Sigma^h \bar{a}_h \xi_h + \Sigma^h \left(\bar{v}^h - \bar{a}_h \bar{x}^h - \bar{a}_h \varepsilon_h \right) a_h \quad (4234)$$

Of this expression the second sum will have a negative sign for an important range of ε_h-values, since $\bar{v}^h = \bar{x}^h + \bar{e}^h$ and hence:

$$\bar{v}^h - \bar{a}_h \bar{x}^h - \bar{a}_h \varepsilon_h = \bar{x}^h \left(1 - \bar{a}_h \right) + \bar{e}^h \left(1 - \bar{a}_h \eta_h \right).$$

Here the first term is positive, while, even for $\eta_h = 2$, the second term will usually also be positive. Remembering that even Y may, in many normal cases, be negative we deduce that over a wide range of values for the constants employment will have fallen. For the one-industry small-country case with $\eta_h = 2$, already quoted a few times, we again find

$$a = 1.0\, a$$

a clearly negative value.

4.255   This orientation may suffice to show that in many cases with realistic values of the coefficients the *effect of productivity increases on both the balance of payments and employment will be negative*. As already briefly indicated, this is largely due to the fact that the terms of trade will deteriorate; and this effect will be stronger the shorter the period considered: for longer periods the elasticity of demand for export products will be higher. In addition other adaptations will be possible.

4.256   Our formulae enable us to make more precise calculations, taking account of divergencies between the two industries as to all the characteristics considered. Evidently the contribution of each single industry will be influenced by its ε, ξ, ι, $\bar{x}$ and $\bar{e}$ and a large variety of possibilities exist. This opens up the possibility of a *"directed" increase in labour productivity*, i.e. directed towards the types of industries most suited to make positive contributions to either the balance of payments or employment. As far as the balance of payments is concerned we saw already [cf. equation (4227)] that the highest contributions will be made by the industries of which

$$\bar{e}^h \{\eta_h (1 - \iota_h) - 1\} - \iota_h \bar{x}^h$$

is as high as possible. Export volume $\bar{e}^h$ and elasticity η_h evidently are the favourable factors and import quota ι_h and home market sales volume $\bar{x}^h$ the unfavourable ones. The employment effect is more complicated. With the help of equations (4230), (4229), (4231) and equation (16) of model 18 we obtain:

$$a^h = \bar{a}_h \xi_h \, Y - \{\bar{x}^h (\bar{a}_h - 1) + \bar{e}^h (\bar{a}_h \eta_h - 1)\}\, a_h$$

where Y is due to the combined effect of the productivity increases in all industries, and the coefficient of Y as well as the whole second term on the right-hand side depend on the particular data of industry h. The reader is invited to discuss the influence exerted by the various coefficients $\bar{a}_h, \xi_h, \bar{x}^h, \bar{e}^h$ and η_h on a^h.

2.261   **PROBLEM 191. MODEL 19.**

Targets: "full" employment in all H industries; balance of payments equilibrium
Instruments: the wage rate and indirect tax rates in H industries.

Comments: This problem is chosen as an illustration of a possible treatment of problems with a large number of industries. Comparison with the previous problem will show that again the political problem is much simpler than the analytical problem if employment and balance of payments equilibrium are among the targets.

4.262   The solution will not be considered with the degree of detail given with the solution of problems 161 and 162, but the reader will be able to go into the relevant questions himself. This time the sketch only of a solution will be given.

Using equations (7), (8), (10), (3) and (5) we transform equation (11) into:

$$D = \sum_h \iota_h \, a^h \frac{}{a_h} - l \sum (\bar{e}^h - \varepsilon_h) \, \pi_h \tag{4235}$$

from which we can compute l and hence all p^h.

Next x^h $(h = 1 \ldots H)$ can be calculated from (12), (7) and (3):

$$x^h = \frac{a^h}{a_h} + \varepsilon_h \, \pi_h \, l \tag{4236}$$

With (8), (9) and (1) we then find Y:

$$Y = \sum_h \{x^h + \bar{x}^h \, p^h + (\bar{e}^h - \xi_h) \, p^h\} - \sum_h \iota_h \, a^h \frac{}{a_h} + X_0 \tag{4237}$$

Equations (2) can now be used to find the system of τ^h $(h = 1 \ldots H)$:

$$X^{Fh} (1 + \bar{\tau}^h) + \bar{X}^{Fh} \, \tau^h = \xi_h Y + \sum_k \xi_{hk} (p^k + \tau^k) \tag{4238}$$

Because of the presence of the "mixed" terms with ξ_{hk} the τ^h cannot now, as in problem 061 (§ 3.535) be found separately each of them, but only simultaneously.

4.271   We will now try to *summarize our findings* and to suggest some general conclusions. As stated earlier, we distinguish between the formal and the material aspects. We first discuss the *formal aspects*, i.e. the mathematical aspects that may present themselves whatever the material contents of the policy are. The relevant starting point to any problem of quantitative policy then is the set of target values, or the numerical combination of targets, e.g. 1% more employment, a surplus on current account of the balance of payments of say 1%

beforehand, and more hidden. Mathematically, such a situation arises if the targets are not contradictory to any one single equation of the model but to a combination, that is, to the result of the elimination of certain variables between a number of equations. Here our problem 161 yields an example. Our analysis has shown that in that problem, based on model 16, the target λ of a given ratio between the increase in labour and non-labour income will, as a rule, be contradictory to the targets of a given employment and a given balance of payments deficit (or surplus): the latter two already determine a certain ratio between labour and non-labour income and it could only be by mere coincidence that this ratio would be the desired one. The situation there appears to be that three of the four equations, from which the unknown values of the instruments have to be determined, contain only two of the unknown instruments and one contains the two remaining ones. The consequence is that the first three equations will as a rule be contradictory, whereas the fourth cannot yield us the values of both unknowns but only of a certain combination. In other words, the two latter instruments appear to be relevant to the targets in a fixed combination only, and in no other way. The two instruments meant here were indirect taxation and government spending. In the model discussed, and with the instruments proposed, indirect taxation would only affect total home expenditure, and so would government spending; and only the difference between government spending and indirect taxation revenue is therefore relevant. No matter at what level one of them were chosen, the other could always be chosen such as to let them, together, have the desired effect on the targets. On the other hand, the remaining two instruments, the wage rate and the direct tax rate, would have "to do three jobs", and this they cannot. One instrument can only "do one job" as a rule. Other examples can be given; they would, however, require a mathematical treatment which goes beyond the limits set to this book. The reader may be referred to some literature. [1]

4.275   Still another form of inconsistency manifests itself even if, mathematically speaking, the solution of the equations presents no

----

[1] J. Tinbergen, On the Theory of Economic Policy, Amsterdam 1952; id., Centralization and Decentralization in Economic Policy, Amsterdam 1954.

difficulties, namely if certain of the values found for the unknown instruments violate the *boundary conditions* that, for practical considerations, have to be set (cf. § 3.4). The problems just discussed contained some examples of this type of inconsistency, and other examples have already been given.

4.276   The use of more instruments of economic policy than strictly needed (i.e. dictated by the number of targets explicitly assumed) may be recommended. Not only will it be possible so to avoid some difficulties arising from boundary conditions, but also the "pressure" on the population may be more evenly distributed, that is, the temptation to evade taxes or otherwise to diverge from the behaviour required. Evidently these are other targets, implicitly assumed.

4.277   In practical discussions it is often asserted that there may be *inconsistency between short-term and long-term policies* or targets. A well-known example is the desirability, in a boom period, of raising taxes for short-run employment regulation, while it may be desirable, at the same time, to lower taxes with a view to stimulating long-term development. Similarly, for short-term considerations it may be desirable to maintain a certain industrial activity, whereas for long-term considerations it may be better to replace it by other activities. Such inconsistencies are not always real. It depends on the possibility of *sufficiently differentiating the set of instruments* chosen. If taxes are used as a general regulator of activity and, in addition, investment is treated in a special way by subsidies or tax exemptions, it may be possible to put a brake on general activity and yet, at the same time, to stimulate investment. This may be called a *reconciliation by instrument differentiation*. If, however, no such differentiation is possible, the only possibility is a "weighing of targets" or, in practical terms, a compromise. This impossibility of differentiating may be due to a lack of administrative possibilities or to a lack of imagination on the part of policy-makers. If they are not permitted, or not willing, in our first example, to introduce subsidies or tax exemptions for stimulating investment, and taxes remain the only instrument, then the advantages and disadvantages have to be valued and an optimum level has to be found, leaving both targets only partly realized. The impossibility of differentiating may, however, also be in the nature of things. It may be, in principle, one and the same target variable which has to be subject to both long-term and short-term influences. A certain type of government expenditure may have to be falling in the long run since it covers a need which diminishes over time; but as part of an anti-cyclic policy it may have to rise during the development of a depression. In such a case it is necessary to add both components and this may yield a rise in some time periods, and a fall in others as the most desirable outcome.

4.278   A final point on the formal side of quantitative policy refers to the *relation between "systematic" and "trial-and-error" policy*, exemplified in some technical detail in problem 171. The aim of this book is to indicate methods for making policy more systematic, meaning that the values to be given to certain instrument variables are those required to reach the target at once, if possible. In the absence of the different types of knowledge needed for the execution of such a systematic policy we shall often have to follow trial and error methods. These will only lead immediately to the desired values of the target variables by coincidence. They may do so after several consecutive steps but will not always necessarily do so. If they consist of steps taken sufficiently close together and related in magnitude to the divergence still prevailing between the desired and the actual value of the target variable, then they may be successful. Even so, their success depends on the satisfaction of certain numerical conditions by the magnitudes of the steps. Clearly, therefore, systematic policy is at an advantage; this advantage is, however, somewhat reduced by the fact that the continuous changes in data necessitate, for both types of policy, a continuous revision, or that we have a bad model only.

4.281   Turning now to the *material side* of the problem, it should be made clear at once that it is impossible to make statements of general validity. The state of our knowledge about economic models is still too primitive to make this possible, and it may be that, even were our knowledge better, general statements of practical importance would be very difficult to arrive at. It can only be, therefore, in a provisional and tentative way that some of our findings are summarized here. Part of the problem has already been dealt with in §§ 3.5 and 4.1 and we will only try to complete the findings presented there. The relevance of problem 162 to practical policy, already stressed, may be taken as an excuse for emphasising some of the conclusions derived from it. The *important role of the wage rate as a supplementary instrument in an open economy* is confirmed. An equally important instrument may be found in *indirect tax rates*, because of their immediate influence on consumer prices and hence on national expenditure. In many countries wage rates are not considered a feasible instrument of economic policy in that government intervention in wage negociations is not considered desirable; it may be questioned whether this attitude is wise in the long run. With an increasing desire to consider full employment and a constant price level as important targets of economic policy the need for these instruments will have to be recognized.

4.282   *Monetary policy*, on the contrary, looks less promising. There are important arguments to be given in favour of constant or almost constant *rates of exchange*. Once they are recognized as an instrument of current economic policy there will be a tendency to use them for everything. It seems better to have them in reserve for emergencies. *Discount policy* has a very restricted influence; its influence on general activity is very limited and its influence on the balance of payments of a small country, though more important, is only temporary. The only monetary influence of importance is *credit rationing*, which, from its nature, only works one way.

4.283   Finally, as an instrument of economic policy *productivity* has some considerable peculiarities. Although it represents, without any doubt, a vital factor in the long-term world-wide development of wellbeing, it can evidently work in a paradoxical way, in the short run, in isolated countries and accordingly should be handled with some care. From our example we showed the usefulness of *"directed productivity increases"*.

4.3. Example of Sector Policy in an Open Economy: Agriculture

4.31   An example of sector policy in a closed economy was discussed in § 3.7, where the features specific to sector policy were mentioned. These will also be found in the present example. In addition it will show some features characteristic of an open economy. Agriculture provides a good example of a sector in an open economy since most agricultural products have international markets. Foreign policies will, as a consequence, exert a considerable influence on national agriculture. An independent price policy for agricultural products will only be possible if trade impediments are accepted as one of the instruments. An important question for the design of a national agricultural policy is whether the aims of that policy coincide or do not coincide with those of international policies, if these exist, or with the combined outcome of foreign policies as far as they are relevant to the market concerned.

4.32   Our example, agriculture, is a very specific one, itself characterized by a number of features that are decisive for the policy being devised. They are:

(a) the existence of random fluctuations in production, that cannot be foreseen and usually create a deviation between intended and actual production;

(b) a low elasticity of supply: prices cannot exert a short-term influence on the volume of product available, especially of crop products;

(c) a low elasticity of demand: prices cannot, in the short run, exert much influence on the quantity demanded, particularly of primary food;

(d) a time-consuming production process: crop products often take more than half a year, some even much more, whereas meat and dairy products, as far as dependent on the numbers of livestock also require years, sometimes many years;

(e) the existence of seasonal fluctuations of different types;

(f) in many western countries agriculture is a well-organized industry, able to carry out a number of measures of regulation, either of prices or of production or trade;

(g) usually land is in short supply, at least in the densily populated areas; and in particular in the country taken as an example here, the Netherlands, there is the additional characteristic

(h) of high fertility of the soil.

4.33   As our example we not only take the situation prevailing in

Dutch agriculture but also the agricultural policies of the Netherlands government. Its aims may be said to be, loosely speaking [1]:

(1) agriculture should make a maximum contribution to national income, under the following conditions:
(2) agricultural income should at the same time be as stable as possible;
(3) it should be reasonable in comparison to the incomes earned in other industries;
(4) it should be regionally well distributed, and
(5) the seasonal pattern in labour demand should not show too wide fluctuations.

A more precise formulation will only be possible if certain of the rather loose terms have been given an exact meaning; evidently there is, in the minds of the policy-makers, a system of preference scales with regard to the degree of stability, the ratio of agricultural to other incomes, the regional distribution and the amplitude of seasonal fluctuations in labour demand, each of which have to be defined. These preferences should be given numerically if any precise and consistent policy is to be designed; in practice the relative weights are, of course, a question of feeling. They provide good examples of the target variables that may be chosen in a more elaborate economic policy.

4.34   The instruments needed in order to carry out a policy with so many aims must, of course, be numerous. Nevertheless there would seem to be quite a variety of possibilities. Historically there has been, during the period the policy was carried out, some shift in emphasis, in line with the general trend of preferences. Immediately after World War II a larger number of instruments was used than in later years and gradually a considerable extent of freedom was introduced. This was partly due to the fact that, in the beginning, a detailed intervention in consumption was also considered necessary. The instruments

---

[1] The terminology is loose in that the following expressions are of doubtful clarity: (a) the contribution to national income made by agriculture; (b) it should be a maximum and (c) agricultural income should be reasonable. Probably a better formulation of the aims would be that total real income for the country should be a maximum (account taken of the sacrifices made) and that the distribution of benefits and efforts over the various sectors should be reasonable; but, even then, much remains to be explained (cf. §§ 1.4 and 1.5).

that were used are the following: import duties or subsidies, export duties or subsidies, price subsidies to the consumer, quantitative restrictions in imports and exports, the regulation of production, periodic stock accumulation and liquidation, and rent and wage control. With liberalization of trade developing in Europe, several of these instruments have been given up, in particular, quantitative restrictions on trade and price subsidies to the consumer. Accordingly, some of the aims have had to be given up or to be interpreted more loosely. Regional distribution of agricultural income, to quote one example, may be influenced in a very precise way as long as the prices of all separate products are regulated; if only a few prices are regulated, however, only a loose influence on regional distribution can be exerted.

4.35   The use made of some of the instruments in order to attain the set aims may be illustrated by a few examples. It goes without saying that a complete and thorough discussion would require a rather more complicated mathematical treatment than it is intended to offer. The policy obviously has to be flexible, since world market conditions change rapidly; in principle the production pattern has to be adapted to the profitability of world market prices. A complete adaptation in this sense would, however, mean that absolute priority would be given to the first of the aims mentioned before; corrections will be needed in order to satisfy the other aims. The extent of these corrections must depend on the relative weight given to the other aims as well as on the influence the corrections exert on the target variables. In view of aim (5), rather less of products with very wide fluctuations in labour demand and rather more of products with small fluctuations will have to be chosen. World market prices may be considered to be abnormal because of exceptional crop conditions; either too low or too high. Accordingly it may be thought better [cf. aim (2)] not to let national prices follow world prices for this would yield either too low or too high incomes to farmers, and place consumers in either a too favourable or a too unfavourable condition; and it would perhaps induce farmers to production patterns which, in the following year, when the products become available, would no longer be considered attractive. In order to regulate internal prices, then, duties or subsidies will be needed. For products of which the country has a deficit and so is importing, these duties or subsidies will have to be applied on the import side, while for products of which there is a surplus in the country, export duties or subsidies may be necessary.

Stabilization of farm income may also require direct regulation of production; this applies particularly to time-consuming processes, such as pork production. Here the well-known endogenous cycle, which does not serve any useful purpose, may be eliminated by such regulation.

To the extent that agricultural incomes are high in comparison to other industries with due account taken of differences in the quality of labour required [cf. aim (3)]—a fact that may be due, for example, to the high fertility of the soil—prices to consumers may be fixed at a lower level than world market prices. These again will have to be accompanied by certain regulations at the frontier. In addition there may be need for rent control, the more so if the supply of land is very restricted. On the other hand aim (3) or (4) may sometimes require price regulations in favour of farmers as well. This may be possible if incomes in certain regions depend largely on one product and there are no other possibilities of assisting the regions concerned in the short run. In the long run shifts in production will be the better solution.

4.4. Quantitative Economic Policy Where Policy-Makers are Many: (1) International Quantitative Policy

4.41   So far we have assumed that the responsibility for the design of economic policy is the concern of one single unit or at least of a group of agencies and persons acting as one unit: in brief, that there is only one "policy-maker". We will now consider cases where there are a larger number of policy-makers, that is, of centres of action in the field of economic policy. Evidently, the assumption of the existence of only one policy-maker applies approximately if one single country is considered.[1] It certainly does not apply to the international community, and even in one nation there may be, in reality, more than one centre of action. In this §, some attention will be given to international economic policy. In accordance with the subject matter of this chapter we restrict ourselves to quantitative policy.

[1] Cf., however, §§ 8.3 and 8.4.

4.42   Each of the policy-makers will handle a certain number of instruments. If there is no doubt as to the policy-maker's sovereignty in handling the instruments, the problem remains relatively simple. It becomes more complicated if certain instruments can only be handled after agreement has been reached with other policy-makers. Here the negotiating process should be considered part of the problem. We will not go into this complication.

Again, as in the case of the single policy-maker, the instruments will be handled in order to attain certain targets. An important complication, due to the larger number of policy-makers, is the uncertainty on the part of any one of them as to what the others will do with the instruments under their command. These instruments will, as a rule, also influence the target variables of the other policy-makers. Any one of them who has to decide on the numerical value to be given to his instruments has to make an assumption about the level of the other policy-makers' instrument variables. The simplest assumption he can make is that the other instruments will not be changed. In certain cases this may be erroneous, however; it is well possible that an act on the part of one policy-maker will evoke a reaction from some of the others. This is especially true for instruments in the nature of trade impediments, and in the field of currency policy.

The problems emerging from this state of affairs are more complicated, therefore, than in the case of a single policy-maker; they are comparable to the problems of duopoly or polipoly in the theory of imperfect competition. They will be illustrated by a problem of employment policy in a group of ten countries.

4.43   PROBLEM 211. MODEL 21.

Targets: for each of the ten countries, balance of payments equilibrium and full employment.

Instruments: public expenditure (represented by $x_0{}^h$) and national component in price level $p_0{}^h$.

Comments: The problem is the international analogue of problems 131 and 141, or 142, since $p_0{}^h$ may either be changed by a change in wage rates or by a change in rates of exchange, or both. It has been simplified in order to make it easily manageable: there is complete "symmetry" between the countries in that they all have the same value of the coefficients ξ, μ and ε. It would not be impossible to introduce diverging values for these coefficients, but it would be a cumbersome process of algebra, whereas some of the fundamental features of the problem are to be found even in this simplified version.

For the solution of our problem the reader will be referred to a previous publication [1] where it is shown that:

$$dx^h = 3.7 \, dx_0{}^h + 4.7 \, dx_0{}^{h''} - 7.5 \, (dp_0{}^h - dp_0{}^{h''}) \qquad (4431)$$

$$dD^h = 0.7 \, (dx_0{}^h - dx_0{}^{h''}) + 2.5 \, (dp_0{}^h - dp_0{}^{h''}) \qquad (4432)$$

where $x_0{}^{h''}$ and $p_0{}^{h''}$ are averages for all values of $h' \neq h$.

These formulae illustrate the fact that the target variables x^h and D^h of country h depend not only on the instruments $x_0{}^h$ and $p_0{}^h$ of the same country but also on the instruments $x_0{}^{h'}$ and $p_0{}^{h'}$ of the other countries. Evidently the values to be given to $x_0{}^h$ and $p_0{}^h$ have to depend on the values assumed to be given, by the policy-makers h', to their instruments.

We may apply the formulae to a situation of general depression in the ten countries. The targets to be set will then be an increase of x^h, say $dx^h = 1$, while maintaining balance of payments equilibrium, which we assume to exist already; hence $dD^h = 0$. If country h policy-maker assumes that the other countries will not follow the same policy, but rather be inactive, i.e. $dx_0{}^{h''} = dp_0{}^{h''} = 0$, equations (4431) and (4432) will become:

$$1 = 3.7 \, dx_0{}^h - 7.5 \, dp_0{}^h \qquad (4433)$$

$$0 = 0.7 \, dx_0{}^h + 2.5 \, dp_0{}^h \qquad (4434)$$

leading to $dx_0{}^h = 0.17$, $dp_0{}^h = -0.048$, i.e. an increase in national expenditure of some 2 % (since $\bar{x}^h = 8.3$) and a reduction in income scales of some 5 % (since $p_0{}^h = 1$).

If, however, country h's policy-maker assumes that the other countries will act the same way as he will, i.e. if $dx_0{}^{h''} = dx_0$ and $dp_0{}^{h''} = dp_0$, the solution becomes:

$$1 = 8.4 \, dx_0{}^h \text{ or } dx_0{}^h = 0.12; \; dp_0{}^h \text{ arbitrary}$$

making it possible to attain the same targets without any change in income scales and by an increase in national expenditure of only 1.4 %.

4.44   The problem just discussed illustrates the fact that the policy-maker's decisions will vary with different assumptions about the

[1] J. Tinbergen, Centralization and Decentralization in Economic Policy, Amsterdam 1954, pp. 30–34.

attitudes of his colleagues. This uncertainty is inherent in the situation. It can be removed only by some kind of co-operation or co-ordination between the policy-makers. A more important argument for such co-operation can also be seen in our example. The solution obtained in the second version of the problem, where it is assumed that the ten countries would behave in the same way, is essentially more attractive to all concerned. The same objective of full employment and balance of payments equilibrium is obtained without reduction in income scales and with the help of less additional expenditure. This situation may again be compared with the situation in problems of polipoly. It is well known that the situation where all competitors act as if they were members of one monopolistic coalition yields higher profits than any other situation. This raises the question whether not a change in organization would be in place. This represents a problem of qualitative policy which will be considered more systematically in Chapter 5 (§ 5.6).

4.5. Quantitative Economic Policy Where Policy-Makers are Many: (2) Pressure Groups

4.51   As was observed in § 4.41, the assumption of one policy-maker only is an approximation, even for one nation. Usually, upon closer consideration, there are other centres of action which are relevant for the shaping of economic policy. On the one hand, government does not represent one single unit. In most countries there is a certain autonomy in the various ministries and examples of a certain amount of competition between them are only too well known. Even if the government acted as a unit, there are more or less important fields sometimes left to other agencies. In various countries the Central Bank has a certain autonomy, if only in the short run. On the other hand, important parameters of economic life are sometimes fixed by non-governmental organizations. Wage rates are determined, in most countries, by negotiations between employers' and workers' unions. Prices of certain monopolized products may be fixed by private groups. Sometimes such groups have their channels for influencing certain government agencies. This brings the matter back to our first example. In a general way non-governmental centres of action relevant to the

design of economic policy may be called pressure groups. The picture
of the mechanism of economic policy derived from recognition of the
existence of pressure groups is again one of imperfect competition, or,
more generally and in more modern terms, one of a game between
various persons. As in the theory of games, the number of possible
situations, each of them to be described by the rules of the game, is
very large; and many more data would have to be available for a
practical application of any such theory. In this study we can only
illustrate, and by no means try to treat systematically, the type of
problems which emerge. We will do so in a very simple example.

4.52   The example has been treated in full elsewhere.[1] Let it be
assumed that both workers and employers are organized, each in a
monopolistic union. The workers' union dictates wage rates, with a
view to maximizing the real wage bill of all workers taken together.
The employers' union dictates prices, with a view to maximizing total
real profits. Together they include all citizens of the economy, which
is supposed to be an open economy of the type described in models
12–14 (cf. Appendix 3). Both unions are aware of the fact that higher
prices mean a smaller volume of exports; in addition, the workers'
union is also aware of the influence wage rates exert on prices.

With these assumptions it is possible to compute the wage and price
level as well as the resulting levels of production, employment and
both types of incomes that will result from the two pressure groups'
policies. It appears that wage rates would be pushed up by 44% of
the level they had in the situation actually observed in 1949 in the
Netherlands (for which the data were estimated); prices would be
raised by 29%; leading to a volume of production of 73% and to
real profits of 70% and total real wages of 90%.

If, on the other hand [2] the two unions had co-operated and acted
as a single monopolist, the level of prices would have been 90 %, and
total real income 102% of the figures of 1949. It would have depended
on the nature of the agreement how this income was distributed.

4.53   The example exaggerates, of course, the influence of pressure

[1] J. Tinbergen, Centralization and Decentralization in Economic Policy,
Amsterdam 1954, pp. 25–28 and 41.
[2] Loc. cit. p. 65.

groups because of the oversimplification it implies. It seems to illustrate tendencies, however, and it should not be overlooked that it is based on coefficients that are not contradicted by observation. The example suggests that these "states within the state", as one might call pressure groups, may behave in a way which is distinctly counter to the general interest. As in the case of international policy, the conclusion should be that forms of co-operation and co-ordination are needed in order to avoid these adverse tendencies, as well as to eliminate the uncertainties in economic policy arising from the existence of more than one centre of action. The conclusions to be reached in § 5.6 may also apply to the problems created by the existence of pressure groups.

CHAPTER 5

QUALITATIVE POLICY: CHANGING THE STRUCTURE WITHIN GIVEN FOUNDATIONS

5.1. Qualitative Policy

5.11 After having discussed the problems of quantitative policy we are now going to discuss those of qualitative policy, that is, problems in which the structure of the economy is changed. We restrict our definition of this type of policy, however, as the reader will remember (cf. § 1.3), to changes in the less fundamental elements of social organization—those not affecting spiritual aspects or essential relations between individuals. In other words, qualitative policy refers, in our terminology, to changing the details of social organization rather than the foundations, even if such changes seem more than mere details to those immediately concerned. Changes in social organization, even if they refer to less important aspects only, will, as a rule, be less frequent than quantitative changes in the values of existing instruments of economic policy. By and large therefore the policies now to be discussed have to be seen as long-term policies. There are a few exceptions, however; among them is the application of quantitative restrictions.

5.12 Changes in organization may be *"induced"* or *"spontaneous"*. They will be induced if changes in quantitative data bring about circumstances that require another type of organization. Bad crops, war or other disasters may, for example, reduce the supply of certain primary commodities to such an extent that the free price mechanism will not work satisfactorily, and some type of rationing and price regulation will do better. Changing cost structures may also lead to situations in which the free pricing mechanism does not work and where monopoly will be the only solution. Better administrative techniques may develop, making it possible to carry out complicated

measures in the field of rationing, taxation or planning, which were
not possible beforehand, but do function more satisfactorily. Changes
in organization may also be the result of spontaneous new ideas. Certain types of modern retail distribution are examples: department
stores, moving stores, supermarkets; manufacturing industry shows a
continuous succession of such new ideas carried out. In the social
field certain new taxes may be quoted, as well as newer wage systems
or the ideas about business cycle policy or international economic
integration.

5.13　The characteristic difference between quantitative and qualitative policy problems is of a methodological nature. In the case of
quantitative policy the alternatives are of a quantitative character:
between high and low taxes of a given type, or high and low exchange
rates; and the search for the most attractive alternative can be made
in a systematic way, best illustrated by our algebraic methods. In the
case of qualitative policy even the enumeration of all alternatives
would be hardly possible according to any system; and a choice still
less therefore. [1] Social organization may be changed in so many
different ways that it would be virtually impossible to give a complete
list. The best that can be done, therefore, is to collect the proposals
so far made or tried out, to add other possibilities discovered by
chance, and to investigate their consequences one by one. In principle

---

[1] An attempt at a systematic solution of the problem of social organization
might be undertaken along the following lines. Of course it has to be assumed
that, in some way, a social welfare function is given; the very difficulty of the
problem is that such a function will at least have to be very complicated and,
according to many economists cannot even be determined on objective grounds.
Apart from the social welfare function all indispensable technical relations
between the economic and social variables have to be known. The most important of these relations are the production functions. A priori relations with
regard to income distribution and spending should not be included: they
represent the "unknowns" of this problem. The conditions for the welfare
function to be a maximum subject to the indispensable technical relations
will then have to be expressed. They may take the form of first derivatives of
the welfare function with regard to the free variables of the system being
required to be zero. They may also be expressed in other ways. If such conditions can, then, be interpreted as "rules of behaviour", the optimum organization
consisting of these rules would lead to the desired maximum. There would be
no need for any supplementary rules.

this investigation will mean that each time a comparison is made between two states of the economy: the original state and the situation created by the structural change considered. More precisely still, and by way of example: if the structural change consists of the intro-

A very simple example may be given. Let there be two groups of individuals, workers and organizers. Let all workers be identical and all organizers too. The workers are each supplying, a number a of hours of work, which may be distributed over a_1 hours of unskilled and a_2 hours of skilled work;

$$a_1 + a_2 = a \tag{1}$$

The organizers are owners of a quantity of capital k; there is one organizer for every n workers. The product obtained from the quantities na_1, na_2 and k of the three factors of production is written u, and

$$u = (na_1)^{\lambda_1} (na_2)^{\lambda_2} k^\mu \tag{2}$$

which is a production function of the Douglas type. The product is distributed between workers and organizer:

$$u = nu_a + u_k \tag{3}$$

where u_a is a worker's income in kind and u_k an organizer's. This is another necessary relation. The social welfare function Ω is supposed to be:

$$\Omega = n\omega_a (a_1, a_2, u_a) + \omega_k (k, u_k) \tag{4}$$

The problem to solve is to find a maximum of Ω with (1), (2) and (3) as side conditions. We may combine (2) and (3) to:

$$(na_1)^{\lambda_1} (na_2)^{\lambda_2} k^\mu = nu_a + u_k$$

Using Lagrange multipliers α and β the conditions for this maximum are:

$$\frac{\partial \Omega}{\partial a_i} + \alpha \frac{\partial}{\partial a_i} (a_1 + a_2 - a) + \beta \frac{\partial}{\partial a_i} \{nu_a + u_k - (na_1)^{\lambda_1} (na_2)^{\lambda_2} k^\mu\} = 0$$

$$\frac{\partial \Omega}{\partial u_a} + \alpha \frac{\partial}{\partial u_a} (a_1 + a_2 - a) + \beta \frac{\partial}{\partial u_a} \{ \qquad\qquad \} = 0$$

$$\frac{\partial \Omega}{\partial u_k} + \alpha \frac{\partial}{\partial u_k} (a_1 + a_2 - a) + \beta \frac{\partial}{\partial u_k} \{ \qquad\qquad \} = 0$$

These conditions appear to be:

duction of a monopoly instead of free competition in a certain industry, what we have to do is to find out what level the economic variables will assume in each state of affairs, and then to appraise, with the aid of a welfare function, which of the two produces the highest level of welfare.

$$n \frac{\partial \omega_a}{\partial a_1} + a - \beta \frac{\partial u}{\partial a_1} = 0 \tag{5}$$

$$n \frac{\partial \omega_a}{\partial a_2} + a - \beta \frac{\partial u}{\partial a_2} = 0 \tag{6}$$

$$n \frac{\partial \omega_a}{\partial u_a} + n\beta = 0 \tag{7}$$

$$\frac{\partial \omega_k}{\partial u_k} + \beta = 0 \tag{8}$$

They may indeed be interpreted as rules of behaviour, namely, first of all from (5), (6) and (7):

$$\frac{\partial \omega_a}{\partial a_1} + \frac{\partial \omega_a}{\partial u_a} \frac{\partial u}{\partial a_1} = \frac{\partial \omega_a}{\partial a_2} + \frac{\partial \omega_a}{\partial u_a} \frac{\partial u}{\partial a_2} \tag{9}$$

Here, $\frac{\partial u}{\partial a_1}$ and $\frac{\partial u}{\partial a_2}$ represent the marginal productivities of the two types of labour. Under free competition between the organizers these two expressions would be the wage rates l_1 and l_2 the organizers would offer. Workers have to supply their two types of labour in such a ratio as if they were paid these rates; in the sphere of production they have to follow the course that would be followed under free competition. Equations (7) and (8), however, may be said to represent a rule of behaviour as to income distribution; this should be such that

$$\frac{\partial \omega_a}{\partial u_a} = \frac{\partial \omega_k}{\partial u_k} \tag{10}$$

meaning that marginal utilities of income would be equal between a worker and an organizer. This rule, to be sure, can only be executed if we have a method of comparing utilities, a subject discussed in § 1.6.

Needless to say that the author does not think this example to be a realistic picture of society; for this question the reader may be referred to § 6.4 in particular.

5.14   Such an investigation will only be possible if we know how the economy behaves in the new situation and if we know the welfare function—either the one of the actual policy-makers, if we have to do the appraisal for them, or our own welfare function if we are going to judge for ourselves. Both types of knowledge are defective, even more so than our knowledge concerning quantitative changes and the economy's reactions to them; and this lack of knowledge sets a narrow limit to the precision of the statements that can be made. The reader will therefore find that this precision is gradually tapering off and that our statements will become less and less definite. The author hopes that this attempt at bringing some system into the main ideas so far put forward will at least induce the formulation of new and better ideas and knowledge.

5.15   The characteristics of qualitative policy, just discussed, make it somewhat premature to deal with the problems of such policy in the way chosen for the treatment of quantitative policy. This synthetic treatment, with the aims considered to be given and the means unknown, presupposes knowledge of the "model", i.e. the set of reactions to be expected to each conceivable measure of policy; it also presupposes knowledge of the alternative policies. With this knowledge lacking in so many respects the author preferred to give short sketches only of the possible consequences of a number of policies proposed, enabling the reader to make his own combinations. The same is true, even to a larger extent, for the more fundamental changes in social organization called reforms; and the same method will therefore be followed in Chapter 6. The attempt at a synthesis at the end of that chapter cannot but have a provisional and personal character, therefore.

5.2. Quantitative Restrictions

5.21   As a first example of qualitative policy we shall deal with a type of measures that has been applied, usually only temporarily, with the purpose of restoring equilibrium between demand and supply in a direct way: by so-called quantitative restrictions (Q.R.). Well-known examples are the rationing of consumer goods, the allocation of raw materials to industrial enterprises, building permits, or foreign exchange regulations. Their common characteristic is that a buyer is not permitted to buy the quantity of a certain, extremely scarce, good which he would be willing to buy at the income-price situation of the moment. We use the term *extreme scarcity* to indicate that the supply of a good is so small as to endanger the general socio-economic equilibrium. If under conditions of extreme scarcity prices and quantities bought would be permitted to move freely, the increase in prices and, as a consequence, in money incomes of productive groups, would become so pronounced that the financial structure as well as social equilibrium would be threatened. The real value of savings would go down considerably and the income derived from them (of special importance to old-aged and other handicapped persons) would be reduced very much in real terms. The incomes of workers, although probably adjusted by frequent wage increases, might tend to lag behind and the frequency of the wage changes would bring unrest.

5.22   All this is largely due, in the situation of extreme scarcity, to inability of the price mechanism to stimulate supply or to reduce demand. This is particularly true if the supply of a considerable number of essential commodities—i.e. commodities with a low demand elasticity—is lower than usual for some general political or technical reason, to be called a "disaster". Low elasticities of both supply and demand are, in fact, the conditions under which the "efficiency" of the price system as a regulator of equilibrium is low. This is why, under circumstances of extreme scarcity, attempts are being made to replace the price mechanism by a direct relation between supply and demand: certain upper limits are set to the quantities that people are permitted to buy. If such a system of Q.R. is to work in a complicated modern society it has to be fairly *complicated*. Certain reasonable discriminations have to be made. In the field of food rationing, for example, higher rations for heavy work, and special rations for certain types of illness or for babies and their mothers will have to be introduced. Some more flexibility may also be brought in by admitting certain personal choices, e.g. between coffee and tea, or between various qualities of meat, etc. Allocations of raw materials, of equipment and of foreign goods to enterprises will have to be much more complicated: there are numerous important reasons why one enterprise has to receive much more than the other. The best criterion in theory would be the contribution to national welfare that can be made by the enterprise; but upon trying to apply such criterion governments have experienced all the complications involved. In emergency situations there is, at least in the beginning, hardly any time to go into details and often therefore only a freezing of the existing proportions has been the solution chosen. The longer the period of Q.R. lasts, the more is the need for, and also the greater is the possibility of, investigating certain details; but the general experience is that this competition between need and possibility is lost by the possibilities: no system of control can do justice to all the details and a certain freedom for producers to reach their own decisions seems to be more efficient than complete centralization of all decisions (cf. §§ 5.7 and 6.6).

5.23   Complicated systems of Q.R. will also often result from a succession of attempts, not fully co-ordinated, to meet a succession of difficulties; and the chances of such series of difficulties occurring are large because of the general interdependence between economic phenomena. Regulations in some markets entail disruptions elsewhere and will have to be followed by regulations in other markets. If bread is rationed, everybody will buy more potatoes and soon the necessity for also rationing potatoes will come up. If all primary food is rationed, there will remain more buying power in the hands of consumers for buying non-essentials and the necessity of further rationing may arise. If the large items in the balance of payments are subject to Q.R., there will remain unused income in the hands of households or enterprises and balance of payments equilibrium may again be threatened.

Often external payments are regulated in bilateral arrangements with each of the partners. A set of bilateral arrangements has a tendency to create inconsistencies in many respects. The equalization of demand and supply of any two currencies on a bilateral basis leads to mutually inconsistent exchange rates and hence to tendencies for deviation from such rates. Here again, it may be better that Q.R. be applied by a group of countries as a whole to outside groups (European countries in EPU e.g. against the dollar area) and to admit deviations from bilateral equilibrium inside the group.

5.24   Rationing, even if a number of reasonable discriminations have been introduced, remains a rigid system tending to eliminate some of the stimulating forces in social organization. In fact, it introduces a greater equality in real income, by reducing the possibilities of enjoying a higher income. Or, to put it another way, it adds to money income an income in rationing points, the money value of which becomes higher and higher the more pronounced scarcity becomes. The sum total of money income and rationing points-income, or complete income, is distributed much more evenly than money incomes, and accordingly the stimulus to increase productivity is reduced. As long as dissatisfaction with the usual income distribution is not itself a force of some importance, the elimination of such a stimulus will, after some time, reduce welfare by reducing production.

5.25   The foregoing analysis may be summarized by stating that Q.R., in other than the short term, will have to be complicated in order not to disturb the functioning of a complex society too much, but yet can scarcely be complicated enough to meet all requirements of differentiation and stimulation, even though, as a consequence, it becomes more and more costly. Where possible it should be avoided; and this will often be the case if the proper financial measures are taken. This is particularly true for war and post-war economies where a surplus of money in circulation maintains a level of demand that cannot be met with by the lower supply characteristic for such periods (cf. § 3.53).

Professor M. Allais has worked out a complete set of such measures of taxation and subsidy, as could replace the whole of rationing and allocation measures taken in France after World War II. [1] The only general criticism one could make on his proposals is that at certain points they require such high taxes that the temptation to evasion must be very high.

The case for Q.R. remains strong, therefore, for temporary situations of extreme scarcity and, in particular, for markets where supply and demand show a low elasticity. This does not only apply to certain essential commodities, as already mentioned, under special circumstances, but it does also apply to the market for foreign exchange in

[1] M. Allais, Abondance ou misère, Paris 1947.

certain types of countries in certain circumstances: for both supply of, and demand for, foreign currency may show a low elasticity. In other terms, it may happen that in the short run both exports and imports can slightly only be influenced by a reduction in exchange rate and that, therefore, equilibrium in the balance of payments, when disrupted, can be restored only by either a large reduction in exchange rates or by Q.R. If the prospect is that in the longer run equilibrium may be obtained at the prevailing rate there are good reasons for a temporary application of Q.R.

5.3. Built-in Stabilizers

5.31 A second example of structural changes meant to improve the efficiency of social organization will be taken from the proposals to change certain attitudes of business, and, above all, of public authorities, so that cyclic movements will be less intensive. This type of change may be illustrated by a change in government spending behaviour. For a long period governments would spend more when their tax revenues were higher and less when these receipts were lower. This implied that governments would usually spend relatively much in times when private incomes were also high and less when private incomes were less, thus reinforcing the general cycle. If, instead, governments followed a "compensatory" pattern, spending less when private spending was already high and spending more in times of slack business or depression, total demand would be more stable. Such a pattern of spending would, if properly carried out, be represented by a lower marginal propensity to spend for the economy as a whole. Its influence on the nature of economic fluctuations will be illustrated by problem 101.

5.32: PROBLEM 101. MODEL 10.

Aim: stabilization of cycle
Means: compensatory public expenditure as a built-in stabilizer
Comments: The effect of this structural change will be studied in the way announced in § 5.1: by comparing economic movements in the absence of such policy with the movements in its presence.

According to the equations of model 10 endogenous movements (i.e.

movements in the absence of changes in data) will be determined by the difference equation:

$$X_{t+1} - \{\xi_1 + (\xi_1\eta + \xi_2)\,\pi\}\,X_t + \pi\,(\xi_1\eta + \xi_2)\,X_{t-1} = 0 \qquad (5321)$$

This equation is obtained from equations (1), (2) and (3) of model 10 by eliminating the variables Y and p; the same equation would have been obtained for Y and for p if, each time, the two other variables had been eliminated.

In the absence of a compensatory cyclic policy the marginal propensity to spend ξ_1 will be close to 1. We will, in addition, assume that $\eta = 2$, meaning that the habit of including paper profits on inventories is general; $\pi = 0.5$, representing the usual reaction of prices on changes in activity and implying that price fluctuations and volume fluctuations are of about equal percentage amplitude; $\xi_2 = -0.4$, meaning that paper profits may be spent only for 60 %.

With these coefficients equation (5321) becomes:

$$X_{t+1} = 1.8\,X_t - 0.8\,X_{t-1} = X_t + 0.8\,(X_t - X_{t-1}) \qquad (5322)$$

This equation expresses the fact that, so long as no changes in data occur, an increase or decrease in X_t will continue, be it at a decreased rate: the increase of X_{t+1} over X_t will be $0.8 \times$ the increase of X_t over X_{t-1}. The movement will therefore continue, as long as not a ceiling or a bottom is reached. If the original movement was a powerful one, the movement will be rapid, if it was weak, there will be a chance that, before a ceiling (or bottom) is reached, the movement has already become negligible. Since the increases form a geometric series (with a ratio 0.8), there will be a maximum (or minimum) level

$$\frac{1}{1-0.8}\,(X_t - X_{t-1}) + X_{t-1} = 5\,X_t - 4\,X_{t-1}.$$

Such a maximum (minimum) will be an equilibrium as long as no fresh changes in data occur [1]. Introducing now, as is usual in modern theory of the cycle, the existence of a ceiling, a bottom and numerous irregular changes in data which either increase or decrease X_t at irregular intervals and to a changing extent ("shocks"), the following picture of the economy's movements is obtained. Any strong upward change will cause X to go up

---

[1] Such an equilibrium would not even exist and the cumulative character of the endogenous movements would be even more pronounced for slightly different values of π and ξ_2, namely $\pi = 0.6$ and $\xi_2 = -0.3$; which would yield an equation $X_{t-1} = X_t + (X_t - X_{t-1})$.

in a cumulative way, and any strong downward change will cause it to go down cumulatively. Cumulative upward or downward movements will be interrupted if (i) the ceiling or the bottom is reached, (ii) if fresh shocks occur of sufficient strength to invert the movement or (iii) if an equilibrium position will have been reached. Neither of the states in which the economy can find itself will last very long, because of the shocks. This picture seems to be a fair representation of "the cycle".

In the presence now of a compensatory government policy the change in structure will be a reduction of ξ_1, say to 0.5. The endogenous movements will now be determined by:

$$X_{t+1} = 0.8\ X_t - 0.3\ X_{t-1} \tag{5323}$$

The nature of these movements is different from what they were in the previous case. The characteristic equation being

$$z^2 - 0.8\ z + 0.3 = 0 \tag{5324}$$

it follows that $z = 0.4 + 0.37\ i$, meaning that X will show cyclic movements of a period of a little more than 8 time units, i.e. 2 years, and with a high damping ratio: after half a year (2 time units) the amplitude will have been reduced to 30 %, after a year to 9 %. This means that cumulative movements will hardly occur any more; after one year any movement will reverse itself. The cycle as we know it, and as it is possible with the previous choice of coefficients in equation (5321), cannot occur anymore.

5.33   It appears that the change in behaviour just indicated will succeed in changing the character of economic fluctuations. The change in behaviour may be facilitated by creating a legal obligation to make certain types of expenditure in times of depression; a good example being unemployment benefits. It is these kinds of regulations, in particular, that are called built-in stabilizers. We will discuss another example of such structural changes in section 6.5, where we discuss the raw material standard. In a general way it may be stated that we can influence the type of movement an economy is able to perform by influencing the structural constants of that economy. And here we even have a possible method of dealing systematically with part, at least, of the problem of structural change: we may formulate certain criteria regarding the type of movement we prefer (and hence set as an aim of policy) and then try to find out which values of the coefficients will satisfy these criteria in the best way. It may, for example, be asked, for what values of the structural coefficients is the average damping degree of all components of the fluctuations a maximum. And this question may then be posed concerning those far more complicated models of the cycle which have been constructed as a closer approximation to reality than is our model 09. We will not go into details, since we believe that the two most important aspects of this type of structural change are the two examples given in this book; but it should be clear to the reader that, in this field of investigation, much could still be added to our knowledge.

5.34 It will also be clear that the subject dealt with is the same as the one treated in §§ 3.5 and 4.1 under the heading "alternative methods of regulating employment", the difference in treatment being that, in those sections, ad hoc changes in government expenditure were discussed as being applied year by year, taking account, in each year, of both the systematic cyclic situation and the incidental "shocks", whereas in the present section the relation of government expenditure to the systematic factors over the succession of years is the focus. If public expenditure is determined according to the new structural coefficient considered, there would still remain erratic shocks in general activity, but their influence would be small and quickly dampening down. If public expenditure is considered anew each year it is also possible to compensate for some of these erratic shocks, although not all of them; and not those which occur after the decisions have been taken.

5.4. Changes in Pricing and Taxation Schemes

5.41 Each economy is regulated by a large number of schemes used in the pricing of products as well as of factors of production, and in taxation. Such schemes may sometimes be changed and these changes will influence the economic situation. They are examples, therefore, of qualitative policy. There are numerous possibilities, many of them different as to their effects. Sometimes, these effects may be estimated fairly accurately on the basis on known patterns of reaction; sometimes, if new patterns of reaction are possible, it will be difficult to estimate them. A general treatment does not seem promising, so that a number of examples will be considered one by one.

5.42 Starting with pricing schemes for products, the well-known example of non-flat rates may first be discussed. Instead of being charged an amount proportionate to the quantity bought the consumer of e.g. electricity pays a fixed amount (which may depend on his income) and a much smaller proportionate amount. This means that the marginal amount paid per unit is much lower; when comparing the advantages and the costs of buying one more unit the consumer, once he has paid his fixed amount, finds the costs reduced considerably and buys units he would not otherwise have bought. The reaction of the consumer to the introduction of this pricing scheme may be said to be the combination of two reactions, namely (a) a reduction of his income by the "fixed amount" and (b) a price reduction. Both reactions are known from statistical studies and can be predicted relatively accurately. The probable result is a considerable increase in quantities sold. Looked at from the side of the producer the scheme is also attractive: the fixed amounts are contributions to his fixed costs and as long as he is able to produce additional units at relatively low extra costs per unit he will make a profit even if his additional receipts are less than the average price so far obtained. The social advantages may perhaps best be illustrated by the fact that, in certain circumstances, the production of a commodity if sold at "proportionate charge" may not even be profitable at all and therefore not be undertaken, whereas at a non-flat rate it would be profitable and so be organized. In a general way the argument in favour of non-flat rates may be given the following form. Non-flat rates represent an organization of the distribution which adds an instrument to those already existing: in addition to the amount proportional to the quantity taken there is the fixed amount to be paid. The introduction of a new instrument, including as a special case the old situation (i.e. where the fixed amount equals zero), always opens the way to higher welfare. This, as a limiting case, is not true (i.e. the zero value for the new instrument is to be preferred), if that instrument is not relevant to welfare or to production, since the costs of production do not contain an important fixed element. Put in a different way: the organization of distribution should add as few autonomous elements as possible to the phenomena relevant to welfare and production relations. The more the sacrifice asked from the consumer corresponds to the sacrifice made by the producer, the less chance is there that the optimum of welfare will be barred by artificial rules of conduct.

5.43 As a next example a pricing scheme for a factor of production may be discussed; we choose the so-called *sliding scale for wage rates*. As with so many structural changes the introduction of sliding scales for wages can also be explained by the occurrence of circumstances in which free wage rates were an inefficient institution for either employers or employees. An old example is the sliding scale payment to miners that was correlated with coal prices; employers suffered from the heavy fluctuations in coal prices as compared with relatively sticky wages. Newer examples, in accordance with changed conditions of power, are sliding scales where wages are linked up with cost of living indices, or farmers' incomes with prices of farm appliances and cost of living. In quite recent proposals old-age pensions are also linked to cost of living indices. We will discuss the far-reaching device of a complete proportionality between wage rates and cost of living indices. Clearly such a sliding scale reduces the adaptability of an economy, in particular if it is an open economy. In situations where the demand for the economy's products decreases, and hence unemployment threatens, it will not be wise to maintain wage rates; and it will not be wise, either, in situations where that demand is increasing. In a situation where the country's product is in unchanged demand but certain imported foods or stimulants are increasing in price, it is again unwise to let wages go up, and, when import prices are going down, to let wages fall. These, then, are certain disadvantages of an a-priori link between the wage rate and the cost of living. There are certain advantages also; workers will be protected against easy inflationary policies and inflationary policies will be less attractive to the monetary and central authorities. The choice will have to depend on how high up these various aspects rank in the general welfare function. In a country where financial policies are not sufficiently sound a sliding scale may be just the type of warning certain other organized groups or the authorities need; our preference would be for sound financial policies without a sliding scale.

5.44 Our third example will be chosen from the field of *taxation*. In some sense, every detail of taxation policy provides an example of this kind; we do not intend, however, to give a full discussion of taxation policy in this section. Some important aspects have already been or will be discussed elsewhere (§§ 3.5, 3.6, 3.7, 4.1, 4.2, 6.4, 6.5). As our special topic in this section we take the choice between indirect and direct taxes. In order to make our discussion as precise as possible we assume a closed country and a given amount of total tax receipts; the problem to be discussed being first, whether the changing of a certain share of indirect taxes into direct taxes should be recommended.

Clearly there will be no difference at all if the indirect as well as the direct tax considered are both proportional and general taxes paid on all goods (including investment goods) or all incomes. In the case of the higher indirect taxes, prices will be higher, but disposable income will be equally higher for everybody. As soon as these conditions are not fulfilled there will be differences in effect, resulting in advantages to some and disadvantages to others; and also resulting in differences as to long-term effects to all. The most important practical deviation from the assumptions made is that direct taxes are progressive: low incomes are exempted and high incomes more hardly hit. The shift towards direct taxes will therefore equalize disposable incomes to some extent. At the same time it will somewhat reduce the attractiveness of higher incomes, and, in the first instance, therefore reduce the stimulus to training and increasing of productivity. [1] It will also tend to lower the savings ratio of the economy and thereby possibly its rate of development. [2] Some of these effects may, however, be counteracted by other, further effects: income scales may be readjusted to some extent and savings may be made by government. It is not probable, however, that these secondary effects will completely compensate the primary ones. Enterprises may increase incomes of high officials in order to "pay part of their income tax for them", but they have to charge their accounts with the higher income and there is a limit, although not a very sharp one, to what these accounts can bear. If government is to increase its savings, it will, on our hypothesis

---

[1] Such effects may be avoided, to a certain extent, by direct taxes based on assets or on expenditures. cf. N. Kaldor, An Expenditure Tax, Allen and Unwin, London 1955.

[2] Risk bearing becomes less attractive since losses are not treated symmetrically with profits.

of unchanged total tax receipts, have to reduce some other items and this will meet with resistance. In one respect higher taxes may, however, stimulate investment. Increased investment by an existing company will only be paid partly by the company if profit taxes are high; and hence may be stimulated by tax increases. [1]

It is not easy to test our reasoning with the aid of factual developments; many other factors have changed at the same time. No clear evidence exists, however, of a pronounced slowing down of general development during the era of high direct taxation. Our conclusion is that the main consequences of a shift from indirect to direct taxes are an equalizing tendency in disposable income and a possible slowing down of development. If inequality is very pronouced and becomes a threat to social stability, the former aspect may be the most important one; if it is less pronounced the latter may be the more relevant.

In the case of an open economy the consequences will be more complicated. Reduction of indirect taxes may then adversely influence the balance of payments situation. This complication will not be too important, however, if a group of open economies more or less simultaneously undertakes the same shift.

The shift presupposes one important technical fact, namely that the economy concerned is sufficiently well equipped with tax administrators and that the population is sufficiently co-operative in these matters. Both questions are matters of education.

5.45   Our final example in this § refers to *import duties,* an example covering, to some extent, all three preceding: it influences the pricing of products as well as the factor raw materials and may also be considered a tax.

One of the original purposes of import duties was to protect home industries against the increasing competition caused by continuous decreases in transportation costs. The free-trade doctrine taught policy-makers to consider the interest of a nation as a whole and, under certain assumptions, proved that import duties were against the national interest. The proof had to be based on three assumptions, namely:

---

[1] This is also mainly true because of the asymmetry argument. Cf., however, B. Hansen, op. cit. p. 193 ff.

i) that all factors of production are fully used
ii) that their productivities in various industries are not influenced by import duties, and
iii) that the prices at which the country buys its import goods are not influenced by such duties.
On these assumptions it can be proved that free admittance of all imports leads to a maximum product if
iv) that product is valued at free-trade world-market prices.

Accordingly the question may be put whether not import duties are still an instrument to increase an economy's welfare if by their application:
(a) unemployment can be reduced;
(b) industries can be developed of which the productivity will increase as a consequence of their development (so-called "infant industries") or
(c) imports can be obtained at prices that are more advantageous to the country.

The *doctrine of "optimum tariffs"* has been developed in various forms in order to show how welfare can be increased along each of these lines; more particularly along line (c) .The argument behind (b) is known as the "infant-industry argument".

Optimum tariffs advocated on the basis of argument (c) take the national interest as their criterion and not the international interest. As long as free-trade world market prices are accepted as a "true" valuation of commodities, total world production will be highest if no duties are imposed. By measures of *redistribution of income*—international redistribution—it would then be possible to let any one country have the advantages it could have had from optimum tariffs and still leave the others with more than they could have had if the first country had imposed its optimum tariff. It is not sufficient, to be sure, to make this statement: the method of redistribution should be indicated and carried out before one can expect that country to abandon its intentions as to the introduction of its optimum tariff. As long as we accept the world market free-trade prices as the true valuation of commodities, therefore, there is a case to be made for free trade if certain measures of redistribution of incomes between countries are taken, namely those which we deem equitable. Whether it will be possible to reach agreement on what is equitable is still another matter; but each expert should, for himself, have that one optimum in mind according to his own preference and should be aware of its being better, according to his own preferences, then any other solution implying duties. A solution with duties remains a second best solution.

This is no longer necessarily so when we do not accept world market free-trade prices as the best valuation of goods. Then it might be that a production pattern under protection would lead to a higher value of world market production than one under free trade. Still, it may be questioned then whether that same pattern cannot also be obtained, and a better one even, with the help of other means, primarily, again, certain subsidies. The present author believes this to be the case, mainly because it is difficult to understand why the national frontiers should have anything to do with the issues at stake. It should be recognized, however, that in a number of practical cases import duties are a relatively cheap instrument and for that reason may be preferred to subsidies.

5.5. Monopolies

5.51   In recent political discussion there has been a tendency to either oppose or support the existence of monopoly without making a distinction between the cases where monopoly may be wholesome and those where it does harm. A closer consideration of the consequences of monopolies under various circumstances shows that in fact these consequences may vary. The well-known statements about a monopoly in one single industry do not also apply in toto, if monopolies are more widespread. To the extent that certain changes in prices and quantities handled are brought about by the introduction of a monopoly it should also be asked whether the initial situation did, or did not, satisfy certain welfare standards. An increase in prices may be correct if prices were "too" low. This is why an appraisal of the creation of monopolies or their dissolution need not invariably be the same in all cases, but has to depend on a closer analysis.[1] According to the method

[1] This has been long understood in the Netherlands, where since 1937 one and the same law empowers the government to declare illegal or to impose on outsiders certain monopolistic regulations.

followed earlier in this book we will deal with the problems by discussing a few clear-cut cases and by trying to draw some more general
conclusions against the background of these cases.

5.52   PROBLEMS 071–074. MODEL 07.

Given: change from a competitive system to a system of monopolies
Problem: to find consequences for welfare
Comments: The problem has to be specified further; and several alternatives will be considered. One general specification we will make is that the
total volume of production will be maintained; this will be so, if full
employment is maintained. We make this assumption. We will now first
consider:

PROBLEM 071. FREE COMPETITION IN ALL INDUSTRIES

In this case the model is simplified in that all goods are now supplied at
their marginal cost, which is 1; hence $p^h = p = 1$; we choose the money
unit such as to make also the total value of production (national income) $= 1$
and it follows, since $y = 1$, that:

$$x^h = \xi_0{}^h \tag{5501}$$

5.53   PROBLEM 072. A MONOPOLY FOR ONE FINAL PRODUCT H

(comprising all vertical stages of that final product; i.e. production is
assumed to be *vertically integrated*). Assuming that the number of products
is large, we may conclude that neither the price level p^h of the non-monopolized products nor the level of total production y will be affected; for all
non-monopolized products we still have $p^h = 1$ ($h = 1 \ldots H - 1$). For the
monopolized product we have:

$$\frac{dZ^H}{dp^H} = 0, \text{ whereas } p = \frac{\Sigma \xi_1{}^h p^h}{\Sigma \xi_1{}^h} = \frac{\Sigma \xi_1{}^h}{\Sigma \xi_1{}^h} + \frac{\xi_1{}^H (p^H - 1)}{\Sigma \xi_1{}^h} =$$

$$= 1 + \frac{\xi_1{}^H (p^H - 1)}{\Sigma \xi_1{}^h} \tag{5502}$$

It will further be assumed, although the influence of this assumption is
only very small, that the monopolist does not consider p in the demand
function to depend on p^H.

$$\frac{dZ^H}{dp^H} = x^H - (p^H - 1) \xi_1{}^H = \xi_0{}^H - \xi_1{}^H (p^H - p) - \xi_1{}^H p^H + \xi_1{}^H$$

from which it follows that

$$p^H = \frac{\xi_0{}^H + \xi_1{}^H + p\xi_1{}^H}{2\,\xi_1{}^H} = \frac{\xi_0{}^H}{2\,\xi_1{}^H} + \tfrac{1}{2} + \frac{p}{2} \tag{5503}$$

and hence

$$x^H = \tfrac{1}{2}\xi_0{}^H - \tfrac{1}{2}\xi_1{}^H + \tfrac{1}{2}p\xi_1{}^H \tag{5504}$$

From these three equations we see that

$$p^H = 1 + \frac{\xi_0{}^H}{2\,(\Sigma + \Sigma')} \tag{5505}$$

$$x^H = \xi_0{}^H \frac{\Sigma}{\Sigma + \Sigma'} \tag{5506}$$

where $\Sigma = \Sigma_1{}^H \xi_1{}^h$ and Σ' means a summation excluding H.

From these equations we see that the price of the monopolized product will always be higher than under competition, whereas the quantity handled will be almost halved: normally Σ and Σ' will not differ very much. This is the well-known restrictive tendency of monopoly.

5.54 PROBLEM 073. VERTICALLY INTEGRATED MONOPOLIES FOR ALL FINAL PRODUCTS.

This is the problem where model 07 fully applies. Assuming again that the monopolists disregard the influence of their own price on the general price level and hence the indirect influence on the demand for their product, we have:

$$\frac{dZ^h}{dp^h} = x^h - (p^h - 1)\,\xi_1{}^h = 0 \tag{5507}$$

from which we deduce:

$$p^h = \frac{\xi_0{}^h}{2\xi_1{}^h} + \frac{p+1}{2} \tag{5508}$$

$$x^h = \tfrac{1}{2}\xi_0{}^h + \tfrac{1}{2}\xi_1{}^h p - \tfrac{1}{2}\xi_1{}^h \tag{5509}$$

From the definition of p [model 07 equation (5)] we also derive:

$$p = 1 + \frac{\Sigma\xi_0{}^h}{\Sigma\xi_1{}^h} \tag{5510}$$

and consequently:

$$p^h = 1 + \frac{\xi_0{}^h}{2\xi_1{}^h} + \frac{\Sigma \xi_0{}^h}{2\ \xi_1{}^h} > 1 \tag{5511}$$

and

$$x^h = \tfrac{1}{2}\xi_0{}^h + \tfrac{1}{2}\xi_1{}^h \frac{\Sigma\xi_0{}^h}{\Sigma\xi_1{}^h} \tag{5512}$$

We see that now all prices are higher than under competition; and that the quantities, as they should, add up to 1; some of them will be larger, others smaller than with competition. This evidently depends on the value of $\xi_1{}^h$; if

$$\frac{\xi_1{}^h}{\xi_0{}^h} > \frac{\Sigma\xi_1{}^h}{\Sigma\xi_0{}^h} = \frac{\bar\xi_1}{\bar\xi_0} \tag{5513}$$

the corresponding x^h will be larger than before; (5513) is valid for products with a high elasticity of demand. The situation has to be interpreted such that the factors of production (labour, land and capital) are now exploited by the entrepreneurs: nominal factor incomes do not rise, since we simply took costs of production to have remained the same, but the prices of products have risen and so real factor incomes have fallen. There is no reason for total demand to fall since the introduction of monopolies has changed the distribution of income, but has not necessarily changed total incomes. This could happen if there were a systematically lower propensity to spend with the incomes of the entrepreneurs.

5.55 PROBLEM 074. CUMULATIVE MONOPOLIES FOR ONE OR ALL FINAL PRODUCTS.

We finally assume that each stage in the production of each final product is itself monopolized; i.e. that each industry—not vertically integrated now—is conducted by a monopolistic group aiming at maximum profit. More specifically, it is assumed that each industry considers the price at which it buys as given but manipulates its selling price so as to obtain maximum profit. We will not describe this case in all detail but only indicate the method of analysis. Numbering the stages of production leading to one final product from the raw material state as 1 up till the final stage I, and indicating the number in a general way by i, we have the profits of stage i of product h:

$$Z^{hi} = (p^{hi} - c^{hi} - p^{h,\,i-1})\, x^h$$

Assuming c^{hi} as given, $p^{h,\,i-1}$ as given to the industry hi and x^h as a function of p^{hi} (and other factors such as y and the general price level p, also considered as given by the industry) the process of making Z^{hi} a maximum leads to a formula $\dfrac{dZ^{hi}}{dp^{hi}} = 0$ by which p^{hi} can be expressed as a function of all the "data" to this industry; and consequently also x^h. This then represents the demand function for industry h, $i - 1$; i.e. we have a "recurrent formula" to find the demand function for h, $i - 1$, as soon as the demand function for h, i is known. Since we know the demand function for the final product [see model 07, equation (3)], we are able to deduce all the "lower" demand functions. It will appear [1] that the coefficient before income and price is halved each time we pass on to a lower stage. This has two consequences. In the case where only one final product is "cumulatively monopolized", the tendency of integrated monopoly will be reinforced and the volume handled of this product will, instead of being halved, be reduced to about $\dfrac{1}{2^i}$, i.e. e.g. for a production in three stages, reduced to about $\dfrac{1}{8}$. In the case of general cumulative monopolization this will not happen in a general way, for the reasons discussed under problem 073; but the tendencies found with problem 073, vertically integrated monopolies, will be reinforced also here: i.e. the deviations from the state of competition will be greater and especially for those products for which ξ_1^h is relatively large or small in comparison to ξ_0^h.

5.56 Trying now to summarize our findings and somewhat to generalize them, we have found that a monopoly in one single industry, itself vertically integrated, tends to raise the price of the product and to restrict the quantity produced. Of these two consequences the one of the higher price remains true, if not only one, but all, industries are monopolized; but the one about the quantities no longer necessarily applies. It is possible to maintain total real income: our assumption that it be maintained appears not to be inconsistent with the other equilibrium conditions. To be sure, certain conditions as to the spending of income or with regard to monetary policy will have to be fulfilled during the period of transition from a competitive to a monopolistic system in order that total real demand actually be maintained. But this maintenance is not contradictory to the essence of monopolism: its essence being a certain distribution of income rather than a certain level of (total) income. Monopolies tend to redistribute income in favour of the monopolized factors; in our example these factors are those of entrepreneurship or "organization". The other factors: labour, capital

---

[1] Cf. J. Tinbergen, Beperkte Concurrentie, Leiden 1946, p. 82 ff. (Dutch).

and land will pay higher prices for finished products and thus be exploited. It is conceivable that the owners of these factors would in their turn try to pursue a monopolistic policy and thus exert a counterbalancing force. Or it is conceivable that organizers' monopolies are created in response to already existing monopolies or semi-monopolies of certain factors.

5.57   The interesting further conclusion that may be drawn from our "problems" refers to what have been called cumulative monopolies: i.e. a succession of separate monopolies in each of a series of consecutive stages of production, where the demand side of each consecutive market is assumed to be competitive. If such cumulative monopolies are created the intensity of the phenomena discussed will increase. Prices will be raised more than with a vertically integrated monopoly for each product. The meaning of this conclusion is that "vertical" co-operation is completely different from "horizontal" co-operation between producers. Whereas the latter introduces the typical features of monopolism, the former represents a counteracting tendency. To the extent that monopolism is harmful to welfare, vertical integration is wholesome. This conclusion is of great importance for the appraisal of attempts at "organizing" society in "corporations" or "industry-ships".

Whether the effects on welfare to be expected from the various types of monopolistic co-operation are favourable or unfavourable depends, as we already observed, on the initial situation. To the extent that, in that situation, certain prices were too low, an increase with the aid of monopolistic or semi-monopolistic practices will raise welfare. Whether the prices considered were too low or not depends on the criteria applied by the policy-maker. An important criterion is to be found in the question whether these prices yield a profit rate equal to profits in other industries; and whether profits generally are sufficient to attract capital and people needed for the desired rate of expansion of production. Other criteria may be derived from what is considered the most desirable distribution of incomes between the large classes of the population. It follows from our analysis that prices may be raised either by one monopoly for all stages of production of the product considered or by a vertical succession of monopolies for each stage; in the latter case the rise will be more considerable than in the former. For products whose prices are not too low, monopolization is not to be recommended, and, if it cannot be avoided, vertical integration is to be preferred to cumulative monopolization. For similar reasons organization of industries in corporations or industry-ships should be entrusted to one vertical corporation rather than to a number of corporations for the successive stages.

If, however, the initial situation is one of full employment of all factors, there will be little scope for a monopolistic organization of any of the markets.

5.6. Decentralization or Centralization in Administration

5.61 The next example of qualitative policy consists of acts of centralization or decentralization in administration. We will consider these acts in their pure form, meaning by centralization not merely a change in administrative technique but, in our terminology, the substitution of one single policy-maker for what before were two or more independent policy-makers. Conversely, decentralization will mean, in this context, the substitution of two or more autonomous policy-makers for one single one, and not merely the execution by a larger number of agencies of a centrally-designed policy. As in the other examples discussed, decentralization or centralization may occur as a consequence of changed circumstances. Decentralization in a geographical sense may mean the granting of independence to a certain territory; and centralization an act of "integration" of a number of countries. Both may be an expression of new ideas and power conditions; and part of a reshuffling of political forces. Decentralization or centralization may also, however, refer to institutions rather than to geographical areas; and then they are equivalent to the creation of new institutions or the amalgamation of existing ones.

A distinction may be made between weaker and stronger forms of centralization. The weaker forms will often be called co-ordination and may differ among themselves; they range from mere information via consultation towards common decisions. In the case of information, the policy-makers inform each other about their policies; in the case of consultation they ask each other's opinion but still take their decisions in isolation; in the case of a common decision, the decision may be taken in a meeting, where an attempt is made to arrive at one generally accepted point of view. The stronger forms of centralization will be those where a decision by one body is taken and accepted by all concerned, even if some of the co-operating policy-makers are opposed. One form may be a decision by a majority vote of the policy-makers concerned. The strongest form is obtained if one single policy-maker is substituted for the co-operating group.

5.62   For a *comparative analysis* let us discuss two situations, to be called C and D, of which the former is characterized by a centralized policy, i.e. the existence of only one policy-maker, and the latter by a decentralized policy, i.e. the existence of several policy-makers.

The fundamental feature, from our point of view, of D, is the existence of several policy-makers with their own aims and means. Each policy-maker when manipulating his means will now influence not only the welfare of his own realm but, as a rule, that of the other policy-makers' realms also. The question to be answered is whether there will be a systematic difference in the way the means of economic policy will be handled in C and D. For the purpose of this analysis it appears to be useful to distinguish between four categories of means; the criterion being their effect in situation D on the welfare functions of the other policy-makers. It may be taken for granted that a change in a means of policy will always positively affect the welfare of the policy-maker's own field of action. If it also affects all the other welfare functions favourably, we call it a *supporting* means. If it affects all the other welfare functions unfavourably, we call it *conflicting*; if it does not affect the other realms' welfare it will be called *neutral*; and if the effects on other welfare functions are of mixed signs we call it a *mixed* means of policy. It will depend not only on the nature of the means but also on several other factors whether a certain means is of one type or of the other. As an example consider a group of countries, each of them with one policy-maker, in the situation D. Suppose they are all in a state of economic depression. Government expenditures are a means of economic policy and, in our terminology more particularly an instrument of quantitative policy. In these circumstances they are a supporting instrument: their increase in any one country will not only improve the economic situation in that country but also in the other countries. If all the countries are not in a depression, but some are in a state of over-employment, government expenditure will be an instrument of mixed character. The character of some means of economic policy will also depend on the size of the areas or sectors considered. For large areas a larger number of means will be neutral or almost neutral, since the influence exerted on the outside world is generally smaller.

5.63   The *consequences* of any act of decentralization can now be formulated if we realize what determines the policy-makers' choices. When making their decisions they will compare the advantages and the disadvantages involved, from the standpoint of their own sphere of activity. Since, in situation D, their own realm is restricted to only a part of the total, they will consider part, only, of the effects on welfare. In the case of a supporting means they will, therefore, underestimate the advantages to be obtained: they will not count, or will not fully count, the advantages accruing to the other policy-makers' realms. In the case of a conflicting means they will, on the contrary, overestimate the advantages to be obtained, since they will not fully count the disadvantages accruing to others. If the problem is that of manipulating a neutral means, such a miscalculation will not occur; and, in the case of a mixed means, a closer investigation will be necessary to decide whether an overestimation or an underestimation of the advantages is likely to occur.

So far we have only discussed the influence that a manipulation of means of economic policy will exert on the welfare functions of the various realms involved, via the aims or target variables. In addition there is the "cost side", that is, the disutility connected with the use of the means of economic policy. Here the chances of miscalculation are far less; most of the trouble involved will be borne by the policy-makers' own realm.

Accordingly, we may conclude that there will be, in a situation D of decentralization, as compared with C, a tendency to make less use, or a less intensive use, of supporting means and to make more use, or a more intensive use, of conflicting means. The use made of neutral means will not be influenced, in sofar as the costs involved are the same; and in the case of mixed means, what will happen will depend on further data; in certain cases there will be a less intensive, in other cases a more intensive, use made of such means in a state D of decentralization.

5.64   Having pointed out the consequences of decentralization, we need to *appraise* it as a policy. Our appraisal will evidently depend on the welfare function we apply ourselves. The simplest situation presents itself if *all welfare functions involved are similar* (cf. § 1.44); if those of the separate policy-makers in state D are similar, there is good reason to assume that the single policy-maker in situation C has a similar welfare function, and there is good reason, too, to apply that same welfare function for the appraisal of both situations. Divergencies of taste are then excluded beforehand. Our appraisal will have to depend on the two elements already mentioned, namely the "cost side", or disutility involved in the use of means, and the "effect side", or the utility obtained from the changes brought about in target variables or in aims. We shall discuss the category of neutral means first; on the effect side, there is no difference here between C and D. It will depend on the disutility side whether C or D is to be preferred. We think it is correct to say that there is, usually, a strong argument in favour of decentralization arising from this disutility side. All the arguments in favour of self-determination, and all the friction caused by centralized treatment of matters of local, provincial, or regional importance, may be quoted. In addition, the possibility of erroneous decisions may be noted as an argument in favour of decentralization: for these will be less harmful in a state of D than in one of C. We may call this complex of arguments the general argument in favour of decentralization. It will obviously apply, not only to purely neutral means of policy, but also to nearly neutral means. It can only be compensated (and even over-compensated) by the effects of clearly supporting and clearly conflicting means, concerning which we have seen that decentralization may lead to under-, or over-, use, respectively, in comparison to what a unique policy-maker would judge to be optimal. And since there are no differences in tastes between that unique policy-maker and ourselves we will agree with him as long as the similarity assumption applies. Summarizing, therefore, we may say that *decentralization is to be preferred for nearly neutral means and centralization for clearly supporting or conflicting means.*

One implication of our conclusion should be stressed explicitly: it may be that in a state of centralization (in the sense of the presence of only one policy-maker) decentralization of certain means is preferred by that policy-maker himself, and that there is not, therefore, a state of centralization in the sense of a necessarily centralized handling of all means.

5.65 The situation is less simple if there is *no general similarity of welfare functions*. It may be that there are reasons why the appraisal of the situation should be based on another welfare function than the unique policymaker's in state C. Such a difference of taste may occur, but is not directly relevant to the question of centralization as such, and will therefore be disregarded.

But there may also be dissimilarity between the welfare functions of the separate policy-makers in state D, and then some problems typical of centralization may arise: to what extent will it be possible to take account of differences in taste between different territories if policy is going to be centralized? If country A prefers 1% extra employment at the expense of 1% more taxes and country B does not desire this extra employment at such a price, then it is certainly possible to use different standards of "full employment" for various parts of an integrated territory. This is an example of the possibility of a synthesis; in other cases a compromise, only, will be possible, namely in those cases where the difference of opinion refers to one and the same decision. If, in the centralized state, only one tax rate on a certain product will be permitted to exist for an integrated territory, that one rate will have to be a compromise between those who want a higher and those who want a lower rate.

5.66 Some examples may illustrate our analysis of this type of qualitative policy. Applying our analysis to the special case of *international integration* we conclude that such integration should imply the centralization of the use of instruments of a clearly supporting, or a clearly conflicting, character. Taking account of the possibility that one and the same instrument may change its character under changing circumstances, we would recommend centralization for instruments that are generally supporting or conflicting. We already mentioned the instrument of *government expenditure* as an example;

some form of central decisions seems very desirable indeed and is essential for a reliable international employment policy. National autonomy in these matters creates an undesirable element of uncertainty in international economic development. No doubt, resistance against such centralization is strong; the weakest forms of centralization i.e. mutual consultation about the surplus or deficit only in public finance as a whole, might be applied to begin with. Stronger forms of centralization will be better from the purely economic point of view; they will only gradually be accepted.

Trade impediments are another important example. Some difference of opinion may exist on their true nature. The popular feeling that they are a conflicting instrument, or means, of economic policy will not always be accepted by the economist. To the extent that the classical theory of international trade applies (i.e., among other things, in a state of perfect competition between a larger number of small countries) it may be maintained that trade impediments are adverse to every country's interest and so of a supporting character. The establishment of such impediments would simply be an act of stupidity, even from the country's own point of view. If the modern theory of optimum tariffs is accepted, tariffs below the optimum would be conflicting instruments, and those above it supporting ones. Their centralization would follow in both cases, but their optimum level may be a matter of dispute. The author wants to defend their abolition, anyhow, under the conviction that there are better instruments: subsidies and income transfers. It should be recognized, however, that subsidies to an industry comprising a large number of units may be more costly, even to the community, than import duties.

As a last example exchange rates will be quoted. They are usually of the conflicting type; if one currency is clearly overvalued or undervalued, exchange rate correction is a supporting instrument of policy. The centralized manipulation of such corrections has been accepted, in principle, as the basis of the competence of the International Monetary Fund. Exchange rates may be considered an instrument for adjusting national price structures to the competitive situation of the countries concerned. This function is also exerted, to some extent, by wage rates, which might be used for this purpose as an alternative, and which may even have to play their own role in a policy with several aims (cf. section 4.1.). The arguments in favour of centralization of exchange rates also apply therefore, to wage rates; but the willingness to accept their centralization is almost completely absent.

5.67   International integration constitutes an important example of the centralization of administration. Our analysis enabled us to formulate some recommendations as to which means of economic policy should, and which should not, be made an object of centralized policy, that is, of integration. The analysis suggests that there is, in particular, a case for centralization with clearly supporting, and with clearly conflicting, instruments of policy. We saw that the same instrument will sometimes be supporting and sometimes conflicting, but it may be added that some instruments will usually be of one type and others usually of another type. To the extent that this is true we may add a further conclusion. Supporting means or instruments will have to be used more intensively in a state of centralization than they are being used in a state of decentralization. This may be called *positive integration*. Conflicting means will have to be used less, or even not at all, in a centralized state; this may be called *negative integration*. The extreme form of negative integration consists of the abolition of certain means of economic policy; such an abolition has been advocated with respect to import duties and quantitative import restrictions. It should not be forgotten that this type of integration only represents a very special case, essentially that of negative integration. Positive integration may be even more important.

One other instrument may be quoted as an example of positive integration: income transfers from one country to another. Such transfers are very rare in a state of decentralization; they may be important, and are possible, in a state of centralization.

5.7. Appraisal of Investment Projects

5.71   A choice between different economic structures has also to be made in development policy when a selection has to be made between a number of alternative projects. Such a choice represents, therefore, another example of qualitative economic policy, to be dealt with in this chapter. The choice will be based, as a rule, on certain ideas as to the results to be obtained by the execution of each of the projects;

and these results will be of a qualitative as well as of a quantitative character. Qualitative results are involved if, for example, a hospital or a school is to be built; they will be less clearly involved if purely productive projects are considered. In these latter projects, quantitative aspects prevail; and they may be complicated. Because of their complexity, quantitative results can also often be considered only in a more or less intuitive way. Priority tests are attempts at a more systematic calculation of the attractiveness of projects in which qualitative factors are not decisive. Private investors will take future profits as a test; but there are various reasons why, for the economy as a whole, private profits are not the best measure of a project's attractiveness. We have discussed this subject already in § 1.4, dealing with the aims of economic policy. Private profits represent only part of the effects on the economy, since other incomes may also be involved. A better test for application by policy-makers would be the increase in total national income instead of the increase in profits. We will discuss this "national income test" at some length in the following sections. Before doing so we wish to state at once that such a test does not make a consideration of other aspects, not implied in it, superfluous. Qualitative aspects, as well as, for example, the influence exerted on the distribution of income, regionally or socially, are points in case. Mechanical tests, however accurately calculated, should be regarded as information for use by the responsible policy-maker together with information on these other aspects.

5.72   The importance of the national income test or similar tests springs from the fact that total national income is the material source of the economy's welfare and that the contribution made to national income by a project may be very much more important than private profits of the investors might indicate. Incidentally, the reverse is also sometimes true, in particular, if such profits are obtained at the expense of some competing firm or industry. Moreover, the estimation of a project's contribution is a rather complicated matter, better handled by experts. It consists of a technical part, concerning the product obtained as a result of the investment, and an economic part, concerning the repercussions on other sectors. The technical part will very often be of an agronomical, geological or engineering character and will not be discussed here at all. Its results are assumed to be available to the economist in the form of data. In the economic part, a distinction has to be drawn between (i) *direct* and *indirect* effects, often summarized as *primary* effects and (ii) *secondary* effects. Direct effects are the contributions made by the production process to be created. Indirect effects are the effects on the industries vertically connected with that production process, including the industry to which it itself belongs. They may consist of an increased production of raw materials or of investment goods needed, or of an increased production of finished products. They may also consist, however, of a decreased production in a competing industry or enterprise. Secondary effects are effects created by the increase in income. In a situation of unemployment the well-known multiplier effect is an example. Whether secondary effects will occur depends on the precise setting of the problem. As is so often the case, this is a vital point in priority test calculations. It may be stated thus: a project's contribution to national income has, in principle, to be derived from a comparison between two well-defined alternative developments of the economy, one where the project is carried out, the other where it is not carried out. Even when the problem is stated as precisely as possible, there may, of course, remain difference of opinion as to whether certain events to be expected for the future are or are not a consequence of the execution of the project. The statement just given illustrates the desirability to have a certain idea of the economy's *development potentialities*. This part of the problem will be given attention to in a simplified example (cf. § 5.73). An essential point here is the inter-relation between the selection to be made and the general problem of economic policy of the country, a point usually somewhat neglected.

One other aspect of the economic part of the analysis refers to the consequences of disequilibria that may exist in the economy. These may result in prices which do not reflect the "true value" of a certain product or factor to the country. In a country with heavy structural unemployment the market wage rate may be higher than the true cost to the country (i.e. the product foregone) of an hour's labour. In a country with a balance of payments deficit the official exchange rate may not be a true measure of the value of foreign currency to the country. The contributions to be made to national income should be estimated, as far as possible, on the basis of "true prices", to be called *"accounting prices"*.

The essence of the solution consists of a trial and error process; a set of "accounting prices" will have to be assumed from which values for the contribution to discounted future national income $\tilde{Y}_0^h$ for all projects follow; those showing positive $\tilde{Y}_0^h$ will be selected; the equations expressing equilibrium in the scarce factor markets will have to be tested and, if they are not satisfied, another set of prices will have to be tried until the equations are satisfied. Of all sets of projects satisfying the equations the set showing the highest value of $\Sigma^h \tilde{Y}_0^h = \tilde{Y}_0$ should finally be taken. In principle boundary conditions (e.g. for taxes) can be added. The method may be made plausible in the following way. Since projects for which $\tilde{Y}_0^h$ is zero, will be on the margin of being rejected, it may be said that the marginal product to be obtained from a unit of a factor is equal to its accounting price. $\tilde{Y}_0^h$ therefore truly represents the net addition to discounted future national product $\tilde{Y}_0$ to be obtained from the execution of project h. By selecting the set of projects showing a maximum $\tilde{Y}_0$ we obtain the maximum possible addition to national product.

The question may be posed whether not, among the means of policy to be used, the manipulation of the prices of scarce factors should also have been included. The question is the more interesting since one might expect that the optimum value that would then be found for these instruments would be equal to the accounting price. In other words: is not the best policy to be followed a policy by which, first of all, the difference between market (or official) prices and accounting prices is eliminated, and is not the use of accounting prices to be avoided at all? To the author the answer seems to be that this is correct, according to the central proposition of free exchange, but only for markets where those conditions are fulfilled under which free exchange can work and can exert its favourable influence. There are some notable exceptions to be expected. The most important one is that land and capital may be so scarce as not to permit full employment of unskilled labour, even in the least capital-intensive production processes; and that the resulting accounting price of zero cannot, for obvious reasons, be accepted as a market price. Another exception is that disequilibria which may be considered to be only temporary, sometimes occur, and that, for reasons of social coherence, a stable market price, and hence a temporary deviation between equilibrium price and market price, is to be preferred.

5.73 PROBLEM 201. MODEL 20.

Aims: (a) fixed (or side conditions): full use of scarce resources, illustrated by equation (12) of model 20, referring to capital and by a condition on the use of foreign currency;

(b) flexible: maximum present value (at time 0) of discounted future income $\tilde{Y}_0$.

Means: (a) optimum values of instrument variables T^d and T;

(b) a proper choice of investment projects h.

Comments: The problem is intended to illustrate the logical background of so-called "priority figures" attributed to projects of which a certain number has to be selected as a program of development. Usually techniques will have to be used which are somewhat, or even much, simpler than those implied in this problem and this model; these simplified techniques will be discussed later (cf. § 5.74). Correct techniques must, however, be derived from a proper setting out of the problem in hand. Essential features are the following: (i) the availability of a number of scarce factors of production, exemplified in this model by capital and foreign exchange [1]; (ii) an economic development dependent on and interrelated with the choice of the program; (iii) but also dependent on other means of policy, exemplified in our model by two types of taxes. More particularly it has been assumed that foreign capital will be made available in an amount equal to the import requirements of the program; that in particular the influence on future savings exerted by the program may vary according to the projects chosen and that an optimum rate of development is sought by the use of a "policymaker's interest rate" representative of the valuation of future goods in comparison to present goods.

The problem, in the degree of generality chosen here, is a problem of dynamic programming with somewhat more complicated side conditions than usual, and the solution will not be treated fully but only sketched out.

---

[1] For foreign currency a condition may have to be added, of the type:

$$D = p^i \left(\Sigma i^h + i^0 \right) - pe + \frac{1}{\tau} \Sigma K^{ih} + m^i \, \Sigma K^{ih} = -c$$

In principle, this equation has to determine the "accounting exchange rate" $\tilde{k}$, which in its turn determines the choice of projects. Since the left-hand side of this condition may be a discontinuous function of $\tilde{k}$, it may have to be read "$|D + c|$ a minimum".

There may be scope for making it more general still, for example, by increasing the number of scarce factors or the number of products; or by introducing non-linear relationships, especially in the production functions of the private sector [i.e. equations (8) and (9)]; or by introducing trends in some technical coefficients. Some other possible generalizations are those where the effects of one project are supposed to be dependent on the execution of another.

The solution will be found by the introduction of "accounting prices" for the scarce factors which may but need not coincide with actual prices, and application of the trial-and-error process described in § 5.72.

5.74   The method outlined in § 5.73 (problem 201) has not so far, to the author's knowledge, been applied, but it may be applied in the near future. Usually the data available for the private sector are not integrated with those for the projects into one coherent model. Often the data will be insufficient for so doing. In addition the year by year specification of future development meets with considerable difficulties or requires many arbitrary guesses. The model may be used, however, and is indispensable, in fact, for understanding the nature of the interrelations. Practical work has to be based on a number of simplifications; whether these are not inconsistent can only be judged with the aid of a model of this type.

If the "rest of the economy" is not explicitly introduced it will, nevertheless, be taken into account by corrections to the computed effects of the projects for the changes they cause in that sector. One method, rather frequently applied, of doing so, is to deduct from the contribution $\tilde{Y}_0{}^h$ project h makes to discounted future national income the value, at accounting prices, of the scarce factors of production which the project is supposed to withdraw from the rest of the economy. If a quantity $a_t{}^h$ is being used of factor a and if the accounting price is $\tilde{l}_t$, we will then correct our equation (14) by adding a term $-\tilde{l}a^h$ and not include $\tilde{Y}_0{}^0$ in equation (16). Sometimes we will also take account of the effect of changes in product prices on the income of the rest of the economy; denoting prices before the operation of the program by p_0 and after the operation by p, this effect will be $(p - p_0)v^0$ and may be important if Σv^h is large or its composition one-sided, and Σe^h is large in comparison to the world market of the products involved. Another way of taking account of the rest of the economy consists of introducing so-called secondary effects, already discussed in § 5.71. This should not be done, however, in a state of full employment of the relevant factors of productions, for then no secondary effects will be possible.

Further simplifications may be introduced with regard to the projects themselves. It may be assumed, first, that accounting prices do not depend on the choice of projects but can be estimated independently of the precise program drawn up. The justification for this may be that the technical coefficients of the projects do not differ very much among themselves and that more or less the same use will be made of the scarce factors whatever the composition of the program, provided the program is of a given "total size".

Even if the accounting prices are determined by the process of trial and error described in § 5.72, and still more if the preceding simplification is applied, one may give up using different prices for each future year and assume constant accounting prices. In view of the many uncertainties involved this may often be the only practical method.

Again one may go one step further and refrain from introducing accounting prices at all. This may mean that market prices are used instead, in the assumption that they are a sufficiently accurate indication of the "true values" of the products and factors considered. It may, in rare cases, also mean that they are not needed in order to determine priorities. Such will be the case if only one factor is scarce; the criterion which may then be used for selecting projects being, instead of $\tilde{Y}_0{}^h$, the gross product obtained per unit of this scarce factor. Those projects showing the highest values for this ratio should then be selected in such a number that the supply of the scarce factor is fully used.

5.75   A few remarks may be added about the *accounting prices* to be used. From the nature of the part they play in the process of selection it will be clear that the best method of estimating them is the trial and error method described in § 5.72. Often this will not be possible, as has already been observed. For some factors, a priori values for accounting prices may be estimated, however. For unskilled labour and other non-scarce factors the price may readily be taken as zero, plus the cost necessary to move the factor to the project. For foreign currency it will sometimes be possible to make estimates on an econometric basis. If there is a deficit in the balance of payments, apart from the capital imports earmarked for development, and if some knowledge of the elasticities of demand for and supply of imports and exports can be derived from econometric research, calculations may be made as to the equilibrium level of the balance of payments under various hypotheses. One of the hypotheses may be that only the public sector uses accounting prices; the other that by a system of subsidies and taxes, the private sector can also be induced to use these prices in their calculations.

It is particularly important for development policy that the accounting price used for capital (i.e. the accounting interest rate), be based on a correct understanding of its function and meaning. The interest rate used in equation (17) will exert a considerable influence on the volume of investment chosen and hence on the rate of development. It has to represent, at the same time, the policy-maker's "marginal discount rate for future products", the maginal yield to be obtained from additional investment, and the marginal rate at which capital can be obtained. The latter cannot be represented by the low rates at which certain international loans can be obtained, but should rather be taken equal to the rate to be paid for additional capital if desired. The marginal yield of (additional) investment can be estimated from the projects and on this basis it may be possible to get some impression of the accounting interest rate.

5.76   The probable result of a correct use of accounting prices will be that, for countries with little capital and abundance of labour, labour-intensive industries will be particularly attractive and capital-intensive industries unattractive. In this context it should be noted, however, that the phrase "industry" stands for a combination of technically inseparable complementary activities. One cannot, for example, establish a textile industry without also creating a certain minimum of energy and transportation supplies. The construction of the necessary plants, as well as their operation, should also be included in the calculations. The construction process may sometimes be more labour-intensive than the operation process. It is the complete combination that matters.

"Labour", in addition, should be understood to mean unskilled labour; skilled labour in a way implies, to some extent, an element of capital in that the training and education requires resources.

CHAPTER 6

REFORMS: CHANGES IN FOUNDATIONS

6.1. Reforms

6.11 We defined reforms as changes in the more fundamental features of social organization: those affecting spiritual aspects of society and essential relations between individuals. The changes we call qualitative policy are more superficial: quantitative restrictions, changes in taxes or in pricing schemes, changes in the organization of marketing, and even international integration, have no immediate importance for spiritual values such as the access to education or the change in conditions of employees by social security schemes or institutions of industrial democracy. Nor do these more superficial changes affect the essential relations between men, such as the relation of employee to employer, or the relation between citizen and government official. The changes to be discussed in this chapter do all affect spiritual values and essential relations to a greater or lesser extent. They are all somewhat concerned with attempts to eliminate fears that have governed the outlook and the attitudes of millions of people for long periods: fears of want, fears of lack of freedom; fears which have led to tensions and to opposition which cannot lead to an attractive pattern of social organization. In the minds of very many, these tensions have centered around the feeling of social injustice, a concept so far scarcely used in official welfare economics but, however vague it be, very important for the understanding of social policy. This feeling is a corollary of the fact that people's happiness is not only determined by the absolute level of their own physical situation, but also by the relative level in comparison to other individuals, a fact gradually recognized by economists but not yet given its full place in welfare economics.

6.12 The reforms to be discussed should be seen as attempts to weaken the social tensions existing in most economies. These reforms very often have both quantitative and qualitative aspects, and their aims are to be found equally in the quantitative as well as the qualitative elements of welfare. Social security schemes, for example, affect the quantitative distribution of income but, at the same time, also affect the degree of freedom of individuals and the feeling of social justice. Much the same is true of improved access to education, of industrial democracy and of nationalization. All of these and various other proposed reforms should be considered as experiments—actual and theoretical—for approaching, by trial and error, a more satisfactory social organization. "More satisfactory" either in the sense of increasing welfare as seen by large numbers of citizens and as seen by a number of policy-makers—mostly the representatives of these citizens—or in the sense of some more objective criterion still to be discovered. The problem before us is, in its widest version, thus the central problem of long-run economic policy, the problem, par excellence, of welfare economics. As already stated in Chapter 1, economic analysis is able, in principle, to make various contributions to the solution of this central problem. It may judge the degree of inconsistency in the set of aims and means proposed by certain politicians or political groups. It may also indicate the optimum policy for attaining given aims. And it may make fresh suggestions as to aims, based on the consistency analysis. Some attempts in each of these directions will be made in this chapter. For reasons to be set out below, these attempts will have to be very modest, however.

6.13   The economist needs, in order to make the contributions just mentioned, a large number of behavioural data. In order to determine the consequences of certain reforms he needs to know how people will react, not only to the quantitative changes involved, but also to the qualitative changes. This knowledge has to be taken from experience or from inquiries about expected behaviour; both sources of information are scarce, however. They will be replaced, to some extent, by deduction which, unfortunately, is a less reliable source. It will be clear that this state of affairs is a considerable handicap to economic analysis in making the contribution that it can to this important subject. Nothing more than rather sketchy (and in many respects subjective) contributions can therefore be expected. The author has tried to round off in a more or less harmonious picture the elements of contributions derived from discussions in which he participated and from experiences known to him.

As previously announced in § 5.1, the method to be followed in this chapter will be the analytical rather than the synthetic method followed in Chapters 3 and 4. The reforms selected will be discussed one by one and a provisional appraisal will be given. In a final section an attempt is made to test the consistency of certain policies, to indicate an optimum policy and to make some suggestions as to aims.

6.2. Social Security Schemes

6.21   The essential feature of social security schemes is that part of the national income is distributed to categories of citizens who have not contributed to the productive effort made during the time period considered. Benefits are being paid to the sick, the unemployed, to old people, and so on. These benefits are financed out of contributions made by the other groups, either by premiums paid by employers and employees or by government contributions themselves collected out of indirect or out of direct taxes. They may also be financed partly out of "funds", meaning that they are again financed out of contributions to such funds, or out of interest collected. Interest itself will as a rule be obtained from government securities and then is financed out of general public revenue; or it may be obtained on mortgage loans or private bonds and then also originates, in one way or another, from the general production process, as part of overhead cost. The questions to be considered are, which are the consequences of the imposition of such schemes and how far should they be extented?

6.22   Of course, the outstanding consequence which needs first mention is the improvement in the situation of many of the "handicapped" mentioned above. As a rule, they will not be able to take care of themselves, even if they try to do so by saving in more fortunate periods or circumstances; and it should be borne in mind that the distribution of these handicaps over different groups is very unequal. Some might, therefore, have taken care of themselves, others definitely not. The elimination of much fear and risk of this kind not only makes a direct contribution to material welfare of those concerned, but also an indirect contribution to welfare in that it may favourably affect people's attitude towards the society in which they are living.

6.23   On the other hand, there will be consequences for those who are paying. They will receive a smaller income, implying, among other things, that the relation between effort and income will be a weaker one than would be the case without social insurance. Both aspects, a redistribution of income and a redistribution of stimuli to produce, are important for an appraisal of social insurance schemes.

In order to appraise the redistribution involved we need to know from whose income the contributions are made. It would be an error to assume that those who formally pay the contribution also pay it in fact. In order to determine the true contributors we have to ask ourselves, what would incomes be without the insurance scheme. In fact, the introduction of such a scheme produces shifts in incomes which will be more important the longer the time period that has elapsed since the initiation of the scheme.

Immediately after introducing the scheme, the formal contributors will coincide with the true ones. But soon there will be shifts. A distinction should be made between (i) contributions, to be called "premiums", which are proportional to the wage rate paid, (ii) contributions to be paid out of profit taxes and (iii) contributions to be paid out of general public revenue.

6.24   Premiums will directly affect marginal costs whereas the other types of contributions will only do so indirectly. Premiums will therefore affect prices; to what extent, depends on the elasticities of demand and supply. If prices are increased by the full amount of the premium, it is the consumer who, at that stage of development, pays the contribution. If prices are only increased by a small portion of the premium, it is the producer who pays. Since consumers are, at the same time, either employees or employers, it will be clear that these two groups will, in an unknown proportion to each other, be the true contributors. This part of the analysis holds as long as no new wage negotiations occur. When such negotiations enter the picture, the burden may be shifted again. There is a general argument in favour of the idea that most of the burden of premiums will, in the long run, rest on the employees. The argument is that the subject negotiated in this bargain, and finally determined by the market and power position of the two parties, is the total amount to be paid to the marginal worker; this total amount includes direct (disposable) wage rate as well as premiums and other proportional additions. If a higher premium is established by legal provisions this can only mean, therefore, that the direct wage rate will be lowered. It is only to the extent that the market and power position are themselves influenced by the insurance scheme that this argument does not apply.

6.25   A different conclusion applies in the case of contributions made out of taxes on profits. These do not directly influence marginal cost, since the marginal producer is not affected. It is only to the extent that the changed position of intra-marginal employers or taxpayers affects income requirements of marginal employers that marginal costs are affected. Prices are therefore virtually unaffected and, in this stage, employers and taxpayers are the true contributors. Since, in possible wage negotiations, the payment made to the marginal wage earner is not affected either, the conclusion is that the present type of contributions is paid by the intra-marginal employer and the taxpayer.

6.26   Contributions made out of general public revenue will be of an intermediate type, the exact nature depending on how revenue is increased. If it is increased by an increase in profit or income taxes, more or less the same conclusions apply as in the case of contributions made out of profit taxes. If public revenue is increased by an increase in indirect taxes, the effects will be about the same as for premiums: marginal cost will be affected.

6.27   The redistribution of income caused by an insurance scheme therefore boils down to a redistribution of labour income only in the case of premiums and of financing out of indirect taxes; in the other cases it is a redistribution beween labour and non-labour income. In the former case, stimuli to workers' productivity will be somewhat lowered and in the latter cases stimuli to employers' productivity and to capital formation may be involved. Our knowledge concerning these matters is restricted, and it would be difficult to draw clear-cut conclusions. The present author feels that certain handicapped groups are still neglected, even in Western European countries, and that some expansion of social insurance in these directions is justified (old age pensions, widows' and orphans' benefits). Some of the usual types of social insurance (sickness, unemployment, accidents) are, in his opinion, at their optimum levels and caution is called for with regard to their expansion. In many other countries much remains to be done in this field, however.

6.3. Minimum Incomes; Guaranteed Minimum Employment

6.31   Various other proposals have been made to reduce the feeling of social insecurity caused by low wages, unemployment and the other risks of life. They have in common that some "bottom" is provided for, either as to income or as to the opportunity to earn an income.

A well-known first proposal, already carried through in a number of countries, is the institution of *minimum wages* for a number of low-wage occupations. They may be compared to price regulations; and in principle they have the same consequences, namely to disturb the equilibrium between demand and supply unless further measures are taken. If the wage rates of the lowest-wage jobs are regulated, that is, fixed at a level above their equilibrium level, demand will decline somewhat and supply increase. At the same time demand for and supply of jobs in the "neighbourhood" (i.e. slightly better paid jobs) will be affected in the opposite way and hence tend to raise wages there also. Minimum wages will therefore support the lower part of the wage structure as a whole: but, at the same time, they will create some unemployment. As long as minimum wages apply to a small portion of the labour market they will not do much harm of the latter type and therefore probably cause more good than bad effects. They cannot, however, be applied to large portions of the labour market without causing considerable unemployment. Other, and more complicated measures will be required if a general increase in wages in the low-wage sectors is aimed at (cf. § 6.4).

6.32   A second proposal of this type refers to the establishment of a "basic income" to certain groups of the population especially exposed to risks of poverty. Such a basic income should not necessarily be a sufficient income, but it might be a contribution to it, to be supplemented by other incomes dependent on the individual's activity or savings, or on other provisons of a less general character. A good example is offered by the Dutch proposal to establish an old age pension to everybody who reaches the age of 65; the level of the pension being about $400 for a married couple. Groups other than the old might be treated similarly, for example, certain sick or disabled. The proposals are not very different from social insurance proposals; but the link between contributors and recipients is a looser one. Economically speaking, the proposals are the same; and, in accordance with our analysis of § 6.2, the conclusion might be that such measures are to be recommended if they refer to recipients who otherwise would be very badly off in comparison with other groups of the population. At the same time it will be clear that a basic income of any importance (say 50 % of normal wages), and given to an important part of the population, would meet with unsurmountable difficulties of the kind set out in § 6.27: stimuli to productivity and saving would be reduced to an appreciable extent.

6.33 Proposals have also been made to create a guarantee to a certain minimum employment. They are, in principle, equivalent to creating a "right to employment". Such proposals are related to the ideas incorporated in the "ateliers nationaux" a century ago in Paris. The necessary corollary would be either the creation of an obligation for employers to engage a certain number of workers, or the creation of government plants with such an obligation. The difficulties involved are serious: the volume of employment required would probably vary, making it difficult to organize production in an efficient way. In addition, the quality and the qualifications of the workers offering themselves would probably vary considerably and not necessarily fit the requirements. A modern production process has to be so complicated in order to be efficient that considerable freedom has to be left to its organizers. If the requirement of efficiency were neglected only poor wages could be paid which was probably not the intention of those who made the proposal. The author's conclusion is that in matters of employment a policy of high and stable employment as discussed in Chapters 3 and 4 is all that can be done; something, to be sure, of the utmost importance. The nature of the modern production process,

however, makes it difficult to impose—except for short periods of
emergency—on its organizers an obligation to engage workers.

6.4. Equalization of Opportunities

6.41   The reforms so far discussed have all been proposed as a reaction
to the widespread feelings, already referred to in § 6.1, that the distribution of individual welfare in the nineteenth century was very
unsatisfactory and that many in the low-income groups suffered badly
as a result of their economic handicaps. Various well-known theories
have been put forward to prove that the distribution of income was
largely a question of power and that once power was attained by the
suppressed groups, incomes could be made more equal, so to speak,
"by decree". Experience since has shown (cf. § 7.6), and theory explained, why this is so much less simple than it seems to many at first
sight. Income distribution cannot easily be detached from a complicated and refined system of stimuli to production which are vital
to present-day economies. The theory of income distribution has been,
it is true, a neglected part of economic science; but many elements are
present. The author believes that they could and should be integrated
into another "econometric model" outlined in model 08 (cf. Appendix
3). The essence of the mechanism of income formation is to be found
in the supply of jobs offered by the organizers of production and
depends, in a large degree, on the capital available, the state of technology and that of organization. This supply may be regarded as a long
list of numbers of people wanted to fill the jobs created, each job
characterized by a number of "required qualifications". On the other
hand there is the demand on the part of citizens, for jobs, which, in
their turn, may be characterized by the qualifications actually present.
These qualifications should be interpreted in a wide sense, so as to
include not only physical and mental characteristics, but also the
individuals' wealth, their family size and other factors influencing
their willingness to accept a certain job. Income formation has the
economic function to fit supply and demand. If, for certain difficult
jobs, there are few persons willing to accept, incomes connected with
those jobs will have to rise in order to attract them; this is the only
way if freedom of occupation is required. Incomes may be said, in this

sense, to be the expression of the tension between supply and demand. And if we want to equalize incomes we will have to influence the factors behind them so as to change supply or demand without disturbing their balance. One of the most promising approaches then seems to be—our knowledge on these matters unfortunately is very restricted—to increase the possibilities for those who want more training and eduction, of being educated or trained according to their abilities. The problems connected with this well-known device of equalization of opportunities are presented in schematic form in problem 081.

6.42 PROBLEM 081. MODEL 08.

Aims: the general aims, described in Chapter 1. These may be symbolized by a welfare function

$$\Omega\left(\frac{P}{M}, \sigma_{log\ l}, \ldots; \gamma, L_1, \psi \ldots)\right) \text{ where}$$

P/M is production per head,

$\sigma_{log\ l}$ a measure for income inequality,

γ the rate of taxation,

L_1 the piece rate coefficient in general wage policy,

ψ the family allowance level. For more detailed definitions model 08 should be consulted.

Means: the instruments of policy have already been included in the list of arguments of the welfare function. The tax rate is intended to finance education and thereby to influence the average degrees t_i of "changeable" properties; the rate L_1 is intended to influence the intensity of work t_1, whereas ψ represents a redistribution device in favour of "handicapped".

Comments: The intention of model 08 and problem 081 is to present a clear-cut and therefore precise treatment of some of the problems of influencing the income distribution. A more general and therefore necessarily more vague treatment will be given in the general text. The numerous simplifications introduced into model 08, which are, in many respects, artificial, are necessary to obtain a model that can be used for explicit calculations about the income distribution. Even then, the full treatment of our policy problem cannot be given in an explicit way. All this is illustrative of the complicated nature of these problems. An additional feature is that very little is known about many of the coefficients of the functions that play an integral part in the process, including the coefficients of the welfare function.

We will assume e.g. that $\varrho_{log\ l}$ has a negative coefficient, meaning that an equalization of income distribution will be appreciated; but this may not be so in certain economies. The velocity with which the average degrees $\bar{t}_i$ of the changeable properties can be increased, if a given amount is spent on education, is not known either, and is illustrative of further difficulties.

From formulae (19) and (20) of model 08 some conclusions can nevertheless be drawn.

1. An increase in $\bar{t}_1$ without a change in τ_1 will raise $\dfrac{P}{M}$ without changing $\sigma_{log\,t}$ and hence increase Ω. We should be careful, however, not to overlook two points. An increase in t_1, while raising production also raises disutility as represented by φ in formula (2). It is not, therefore, correct, to conclude that every increase in t_1 is an advantage. We will not go into the details; they could be dealt with on the basis of our assumptions. The other point is that piece rates should reflect the real increase in product obtained by an increase in t_1; i.e. the most natural form for piece rates to take would be $l\,(t_1) = p\,(t_1)$.

2. Increases in $\bar{t}_i$, the average degree of properties i present with the population will both increase P and decrease $\sigma_{log\,t}$; and hence increase Ω. The reasons are that an improvement in average skill will increase production of the individual and at the same time make it less necessary to have wage differentials between less skilled and more skilled jobs.

3. While increases in ψ do not influence total production, they do influence distribution. It might seem that $\psi = 0$ would correspond to the smallest dispersion in incomes, but this would only be true for the dispersion in family income, not for income per head. The best measure for distribution evidently would be the dispersion in satisfaction ω; leaving apart the other factors influencing ω we have, according to (1) and (10):

$$\omega = \log \bar{t}_0 - \log t_0 + \psi\,(\log t_0 - \log \bar{t}_0) \ldots$$
$$= (\psi - 1)\,(\log t_0 - \log \bar{t}_0) \ldots$$

This component of the dispersion of incomes will therefore be least for $\psi = 1$, i.e. for family allowances just covering the disutility of the size of the family.

Having thus considered the simplified model we will now summarize and at the same time generalize our argument without the use of formulae.

6.43   Starting again from the interpretation of incomes as the expression of the tensions between supply of jobs and demand for them, we have to ask whether we can influence the supply or demand factors, or both, with a view to allowing supply and demand to approach each other. Generally speaking there appears to be a relative scarcity of qualified people; relative in comparison to what is required by the organizers of production. It would not be very attractive, even if possible, to clamp down on the requirements, since our general level of well-being is directly connected with the capital-intensity of production and the technology used. The better approach therefore seems to be to change people's qualifications. There is scope for making a distinction here between qualifications that can be changed and qualifications that cannot be changed at all; and between those that can be changed easily or rapidly, and those that can be changed only slowly. A good example of an easily changeable qualification is a man's speed of work which can be influenced by such simple devices as the introduction of piece rates. Training and general education are lengthier processes that may change some of his more fundamental qualifications; and some of these, say innate intuition, may hardly be changed at all, or only be changed from one generation to the other. Our problem then becomes: is it possible to find modes of changing some of the qualifications of the population in such a way as to maximize general welfare? The problem can only be solved if (i) general welfare is specified and (ii) if a large number of data are available, exemplified by the data in our simplified model. If we take general welfare to depend positively on the two broad aims, size of national income on the one hand and the degree of equality in income distribution on the other, we will find that some means of economic policy will affect one of the aims positively but affect the other negatively. This applies, for example, to changes in income or inheritance tax. Increases in these taxes, or increases in the progression of their rates, will increase equality but may damage productivity as well as the rate of investment. A number of "social measures", as previously discussed (§§ 6.2 and 6.3), have the same consequences. As long as we do not know the relative weight given to the two aims and the relative effect of these means on the two aims, it will be difficult to indicate where the optimum level of the intensities of the means is to be found. Measures, however, which lead to improved education and training, will have a tendency to further both aims at the same time. Increased supplies of qualified workers, in all ranges, will tend to increase productivity as well as equality. Again, it will depend on many more

numerical data which of the many conceivable measures of education
and training will be the most attractive, and in what intensity they
should be applied. Extensive research programs may have to be
developed in order to answer these important questions.

6.5. Monetary Reforms

6.51   Among those proposals for changing the social structure which
have been launched and discussed in the past century, monetary
reforms form a separate class. Many social and economic philosophers
have looked at our monetary system as the root of many evils. The
quality of the philosophies, as well as of the proposed reforms, has
varied widely. They range from the superficial and naive to penetrating
and practical theories and proposals. Some of the superficial proposals
either fail to look behind the outer form of social phenomena or neglect
some fundamental psychological truth. Those who hold money responsible for the large power that one group of society can exert over
other groups and hence want to "do away with money" seem to
confuse the outer form of wealth with its deeper causes. Those who,
in other proposals, wish to abolish bank secrecy and to concentrate
all transactions in one centralized administration seem to underestimate the significance of that secrecy.

6.52   Among the less radical and ambitious proposals are several
more promising ones. The sponsors of these proposals seem to have
understood well that money, although only an auxiliary instrument
of economic activity, occupies a strategic place in the organization of
the economy and may be the medium of important policies provided
that its character is not changed too much. In fact, during the last
century, a number of changes have already been made and have been
proved to work well. We still do consider changes in the monetary
system as "reforms" since the features of the monetary system are
felt, by many citizens, to be fundamental. Often these reforms were
changes in the relation between the circulating medium and its "cover".
The introduction of paper money and of bank debits, implying a
loosening of the tie between medium and cover have been an important
means of enlarging circulation and simplifying its technique. No doubt

they have also led to abuse in isolated cases, but nobody would advocate their elimination in order to prevent these abuses. The suggestion of requiring a 100% gold cover ("100% money") has been made in order to avoid excessive expansion of monetary circulation. The same effect may be obtained by a wise monetary policy as discussed in previous chapters and the 100% money proposal would seem to be too rigid.

6.53   In fact, the necessary improvement should not be looked for in such a rigid quantitative tie between circulation and the existing traditional reserve material. A more promising approach would seem to be contained in the proposed "raw material standard", where the nature of the reserve material would be changed. Instead of only gold, a combination of gold and a certain raw material "cocktail" would be accepted as legal cover. The cocktail should have a fixed composition, which might be gradually changed according to the changing significance of certain raw materials. A unit would consist of a given quantity of wheat, another quantity of rye, given quantities of barley, corn, rice, steel, copper, lead, zinc, and so on. Such units should be bought and sold by the Central Bank at fixed prices, the selling price some 5 or 10% higher than the purchasing price, which would have the effect of virtually stabilizing a certain average price of raw materials. The stabilization would be subject to certain conditions, to be sure: it would not work when the demand for some of the raw materials was so large as to deprive the Central Bank of its entire stock. Such a situation would call for some of the other means of restricting demand. Generally the establishment of a raw material standard would not imply that other means of economic policy, and particularly of stabilization policy, would be excluded.

The effect of a stabilization of raw material prices may now be considered with the aid of our simplified model 10.

6.54   PROBLEM 102. MODEL 10.

Aim: stabilization of general cycle
Means: stabilization of raw material price level
Comments: As in problem 101, § 5.32, the effect of this structural change will be studied by comparing cyclical movements that would occur without this change with those to be expected in its presence. The method has in

fact been demonstrated already in section 5.32, where we found that the movements of national expenditure X, in the absence of changes in data, will be determined by equation (5322). The resulting movements appeared to be the well-known cumulative movements characteristic of both the upturn and the recession in business cycles.

The change that will be introduced by the raw material standard consists of a considerable reduction in the coefficient π, indicating the change in general price level caused by a unit change in national expenditure. The reduction will be considerable since most of the price changes in finished products are due to changes in raw material prices, which are by far the most flexible component. Assuming that π will be reduced to one tenth of its original value, i.e. to 0.05, equation (5322) now becomes:

$$X_{t+1} = X_t + 0.08 \, (X_t - X_{t-1}) \qquad (6541)$$

This equation expresses that a rise in X between $t - 1$ and t will be almost stopped the next time unit, when the further rise will only be 0.08 times as large. This comes to saying that incidental movements in national expenditure, caused by changes in data, will almost immediately be "nipped in the bud": a perfect method of stabilizing cyclical movements. The main reason, evidently, is that a stabilization of raw material prices will considerably reduce the occurrence of any paper profits, which, according to several writers, played an important part in historical business cycles.

6.55   It should be added that our model 10 somewhat overstresses this phenomenon perhaps; and that problem 102, therefore, may also overstress the importance of stable raw material prices for the general cycle. This latter may be considerably damped down by other measures also, in particular by compensatory public expenditures in leading countries. The question arises whether the raw material standard is not superfluous.

The best answer to this question would seem to refer to two principles: the technological principle of two- or threefold security and the principle, recommended for economic policy (cf. § 4.2), of "distributing pressure". Put more directly, it would seem wise to have a separate and direct regulator in the sector of raw material prices because of the vital importance of these prices to a number of under-developed countries. Such a regulator would eliminate one source of instability which continuously threatens these economies and makes the difficult problem of their monetary policy still more difficult.

The necessity of introducing some such direct regulator has been stressed by large numbers of experts and several other forms have been advocated which, from an economic point of view, are far less attractive. The best known proposals are those on commodity agreements. These are meant to regulate individual prices by contracting minimum and maximum prices. It is evident that they can only work if supply is regulated in order to smooth out excessively violent fluctuations. The regulation of the supplies of a number of individual raw materials is, however, a far more cumbersome affair than anything like a raw material standard, where only the average or total supply is regulated by the purchases or sales of units by the Central Bank. The decision as to which of the two types of regulation should be chosen should not be made by authorities with a vested interest counter to the introduction of the raw material standard, but by authorities who must compare the troubles involved with the alternative troubles of establishing and maintaining a set of some twenty commodity agreements.

6.6. Centralization of Production Decisions

6.61   One of the far-reaching reforms that have been applied by the communists may be formulated as centralization of production decisions. An often used phrase is "planning" in its widest sense, including both the preparatory calculations about the most desirable levels of production and the decisions themselves, with control of their execution. The reform means that such planning should not be applied in a decentralized way of planning firm by firm, but in a completely centralized way, as it is done in the communist countries. The figures computed should be based on the "real needs" of the economy, defined in some way or another, and not to be left to the "anarchy" of the individualistic system of production.

6.62   What could no doubt be avoided would be typical "over-production", that is a volume of production larger than can be sold at reasonable prices. Such over-production may occur and has occurred as a consequence of a lack of co-ordination between producers in those industries where the process of production either takes a long time or the outcome of the process is fluctuating. Examples of the former are all construction processes, in building as well as in metal trade (houses, other buildings, ships, machinery etc.) and some processes in the cattle industry: raising of hogs or beef cattle. The difficulty only faces those producers whose production is "for the market" and not "to order". Indeed, the size of the market may change considerably during the period of construction or animal raising, and one producer will not know the others' supply until the end of the process. Serious overproduction may be the consequence, as has been usual on hog raising, and it could only be avoided by centralized decisions about the volume of production. Examples of production processes with fluctuating outcomes include almost all agricultural processes and fishery; here centralization of the production decisions could not help very much but centralized selling could.

6.63   A complete centralization would mean, of course, a considerable concentration of power at the same time. The disadvantages for political and spiritual freedom are evident and are a major factor in the appraisal of the proposal.

Another disadvantage is the loss of efficiency which results. The processes involved are very complicated. The demand for a large number of products, particularly intermediate products in manufacturing industry, depends on technical factors which change continuously as a consequence of technical development. In countries with a high standard of living, further complications are created by rapid changes in the tastes of the consumers, particularly in the field of textiles, and so on. Decisions about changing production programmes will need to be very frequent, and no one decision is of great importance to the economy as a whole. There is little scope for taking these decisions in a centralized way, and, if centralization is nevertheless maintained, there will be an unavoidable loss of time and energy. The alternative is that production fails to fit demand; this is no serious problem as long as there is a shortage of most goods—but in a wealthy community this is not likely to be the case.

6.64   We met a similar problem, but on a smaller scale, when discussing quantitative restrictions (§ 5.2). We then tried to enumerate the conditions under which such restrictions are efficient. Similar conditions might be formulated as to centralized production decisions. From the preceding argument it follows that for a few industries they will be efficient, namely where market production takes places, and requires time; also trade in agricultural products may sometimes be better based on centralized decisions. Complete centralization of all decisions could only be efficient in poor communities with simple patterns of production, and implies a danger to political and spiritual freedom. It is, moreover, scarcely necessary in industries where the period of production is short.

6.7. Industrial Democracy

6.71   By industrial democracy we will understand the participation, by workers' representatives, in discussions, and in the taking of certain decisions, in industrial life. It may take various forms; it may be practised at the enterprise level or at higher levels: those of the industry or those of economic life as a whole. It may refer to social questions only, including or excluding wage levels, or it may refer to economic questions as well. It may be chiefly in the sphere of discussions and less in that of decisions; or imply decisions to a larger extent. There may be a gradual development from one form to the other. In certain forms it already exists in various European countries, either in the form of works committees or of working parties for an industry as a whole, or, finally, because part of the board of directors is nominated by workers' organizations. In several countries trade union represent- atives are members of an Economic Council which advises the government on important problems of general economic policy.

6.72   The common element in all these forms of industrial democracy lies on the psychological side. The material side is much less important. Changes in the distribution of income can be brought about in much simpler ways. The social problem will not be solved, however, by mere changes of income distribution in favour of the simpler jobs. The need for self-respect and dignity is one of the basic human needs. It is continuously being suppressed in those living in the lower regions of some hierarchy unless counteracting forces are introduced. Industrial democracy is one of these counteracting forces, supplementing the regular, but often very restricted, possibilities of "climbing" on the "social ladder". Industrial democracy is probably the best way of satisfying the needs just mentioned. It is so because it has, at the same time, some natural functions to perform in a democratic society where the enterprise is gradually becoming an institution of public interest, instead of an institution to serve private interests only. The interests that an enterprise has to serve include those of consumers as well as those of the various types of producers involved, and, among the latter, the workers are one type. The fact that capital and labour, and as may be the case, land, are all factors of production supposed to co-operate in the productive process, should find its expression in the organization. The same applies for the industry and for economic life as a whole.

6.73   This does not mean that there are not also certain dangers involved. If workers or workers' representatives were inclined to use their influence in the interest of their own group only, they might threaten the sound development of the enterprise or the industry. They might claim wages too high to be borne by the enterprise or they might undermine labour productivity. Their sense of responsibility should, of course, prevent them from doing so, and usually will. But this sense is not always sufficiently developed, especially with the "rank and file". This point illustrates very well the educational side of the institution of industrial democracy. This is not restricted to the requirements necessary for the workers; very often the owners and managers are also in need of some further education. But, as in the case of every process of education, it will need to be gradual and carefully devised.

6.8. Nationalization

6.81   The most far-reaching reforms that have been proposed, and carried through in a number of countries (but to varying degrees), are those of nationalizing certain enterprises or industries. Strictly speaking, it is in their political consequences that they have been far-reaching; it does not necessarily follow that they have also been the most far-reaching reforms in terms of their economic and social consequences. Nationalization is usually taken to mean the handing over, to a country's government, of the ownership of an enterprise, or an industry's capital or its assets. This transition may be, but need not be, accompanied by the introduction of some forms of industrial democracy (cf. § 6.7). The immediate consequences of nationalization, irrespective of its precise form, are twofold: private profits are eliminated as a source of income and the possibility is opened for a centralization of production decisions (cf. § 6.6).

6.82   The reform under discussion is one of the most controversial ones, partly because of the large vested interests involved. These interests create a possible source of bias in the opinions of the interested groups. The traditional arguments in favour of, and against, nationalization may be summarized very briefly as follows. In favour of it are the arguments that the elimination of unearned income increases social justice, and that the possible centralization of production decisions may be used to avoid over-production or, more generally, economic fluctuations. Against nationalization are put the arguments that efficiency will decline because of the elimination of direct private interest in the profits to be obtained, and that dangerous concentrations of power may result.

As previously stated at the beginning of this chapter, a scientific test of these arguments is difficult to perform because of lack of precise observations. It is true that nationalization has already been carried through in a number of countries and industries; in order to determine, however, the impact on efficiency, one should be able to make comparisons between nationalized and private situations. Comparisons between the communist and non-communist countries are very difficult because a large number of other factors in economic life also differ. The simple fact that Russia's standard of life is lower than that of the United States does not, of course, prove anything at all. The fact that Russia's rate of expansion is higher than that of the U.S. does not prove anything either. Both facts are characteristic of a less developed country. Much more refined comparisons would be needed, including other relevant factors as well.

Comparisons, inside western countries, of nationalized and private industries are difficult if the nationalized industries are monopolistic, which they are, almost by definition. This means that the test of competitive power cannot be applied; in addition the question may, of course, be raised whether this test can be applied at all in "a world of polipolies".

In very few cases do nationalized enterprises compete with private ones. The Netherlands coal mining and steel industries are two cases in point. Coal mining, however, is always an industry that depends so much on geological data peculiar to each individual enterprise that comparisons are again difficult. The competition of the government-owned Dutch steel industry in the Coal and Steel Community is again complicated by Dutch wage policy.

6.83   These circumstances do not permit any definite conclusion; if the author, nevertheless, tries to formulate some tentative appraisal, he is quite aware of the reserves that have to be kept in mind. His tentative conclusion is that there are no marked differences in efficiency. This is subject to some conditions referring to other factors which seem to be more important to efficiency, such as the quality of management and the relations between management and workers. These factors should not differ too much between the enterprises compared.

The argument of power concentration does hold, of course, to some extent, but would seem to depend on other factors as well. Nazi Germany did not nationalize industry, but its political system represented much more a dangerous concentration of power than has ever been the case with the Swedish or British Labour governments.

The force of the social justice argument has also been somewhat impaired, by the invention of numerous other means of increasing social justice, particularly direct taxation and education. In addition, there is a well-known process in development which tends to reduce the importance of the shareholders as a recipient of profit income: only small percentages of total profits are nowadays paid out to these "owners".

In summary, it must be said that the significance of nationalization as a means of increasing welfare is less than its sponsors have thought.

6.84   This does not imply that there are not secondary arguments in favour of nationalization in specified circumstances. There are a number of basic activities which are so fundamental to a country's existence that they will be considered a matter of direct government responsibility everywhere. These range from defence and flood control to public utilities, transportation, and, in some countries, coal and steel. The border-line between the government sector and the private sector may be chosen differently under different circumstances. It may happen that the private capital supply is insufficient to finance the investments in these capital-intensive activities. Several of these activities, in addition, can only be carried out with heavy fixed costs, implying the tendency towards monopoly. It would not be attractive to leave such important key industries to private monopoly without control. Control may, however, require a more complicated organization than public ownership. Finally, the existence of a public sector of some size is a favourable basis for anti-cyclic policies in the field of investment.

If our analysis is correct, that is, if, on the one hand, our exact knowledge on the consequences of nationalization is restricted, whereas, on the other hand, there are some secondary arguments in its favour, all that can be recommended is to make further experiments, but carefully and gradually.

6.9. Summary and Conclusions

6.91   In the preceding chapters and sections we have discussed the various means of economic policy and their probable effects on welfare. Although we have emphasized the necessity of considering, as far as possible, economic policy as a coherent whole, we were forced to split up the discussion into a discussion of quantitative policy and one of the other types; and in the latter a further subdivision, according to the means used, was applied. The separate discussion of quantitative policy was defended by the argument that this type of policy is largely one of short-term adaptation to small current disturbances of equilibrium. The treatment, one by one, of the means of qualitative policy, and some types of reform, was defended with a reference to our lack of exact knowledge. Here the stage of analysis still cannot be concluded. Nevertheless it is necessary, in order to design these types of long-term changes, to consider them also in their mutual relations. In this section an attempt will be made to summarize the conclusions so far reached as to the probable effects of these policies.

6.92   The task which is set is a difficult one, and only a first step can be made. The subject is crowded with uncertainties. It is, moreover, almost impossible to discuss the effect of reforms in a general way, without reference to the particular situation of an individual country. The needs of one country are very different from those of other countries. The meanings of the terms used to indicate some of the most important types of reforms are vague, only; some specification will be found in the sections dealing with them. Many of them can be applied with different intensities and, in almost all cases, "too much" will do harm. The appraisal to be attempted will apply to reasonable doses applied to the average country; in a few cases some specification as to the type of country implied will be given.

Again, the meaning of the terms used to indicate certain elements of welfare is vague. We have already discussed the need for a definition of "social justice". The term "freedom" covers a wide variety of phenomena, and one man's freedom may be another man's slavery. "Cultural development" needs only to be mentioned to remind the reader of the different interpretations which are possible.

Finally, the roles these various elements have to play in welfare and, consequently, the choice to be made with regard to the intensity with which a certain reform or structural change should be carried out, are, to a large extent, of a subjective character.

6.93   The table below should, therefore, be considered with the utmost reserve and very critically. It should only be considered as an invitation to the reader to choose this form of summarizing his own appraisal of the means of economic policy considered.

Only those influences have been indicated which, in the author's opinion, are more or less clear. Their intensity is not further specified; the influences indicated by + are, however, supposed to be more intensive than the influences to which no sign has been given. A few cases of influences which are, in the author's opinion, clearly negative have also been indicated in the table. One may wonder why the number of positive signs is so much larger than the number of negative signs. This is due to the fact that, where two opposite varieties of a same policy exist, the one has been chosen with the larger number of positive signs. Instead of integration one could, for example, have chosen decentralization of international economic policy; instead of equalization of opportunities the introduction of privileges; or instead of family planning the stimulation of population increase. The appearance of relatively many +signs is also due to the exclusion of certain measures such as "quantitative restrictions", which, in the author's opinion, would have shown mainly   signs.

6.94   The author appreciates that he is expected to draw some conclusions. While doing so he wants to repeat the reservations made in

Table 6.9 Survey of probable effects of some reforms or minor structural changes on welfare as understood by the author.

Reforms or other Structural Changes	Elements of Welfare						
	Production per Capita	Social Justice	Cultural Development	Freedom	Stability	Internat. Peace	Social Peace
International Economic Integration	+	+		—		+	
International Income Transfers		+				+	
Raw Material Standard		+		+	+		
Built-in Stabilizers		+		+	+		
Equalization of Opportunities	+	+	+	+			+
Industrial Democracy		+	+				+
Family Planning	+	+	+	+		+	
Social Security Schemes		+		+	+		+
Nationalization		+		—	+		
Centralization of Production Decisions				—	+		
Direct Taxes		+			+		+

+ signs denote that more or less clearly positive influences on the various elements of welfare are to be expected from the application of the structural changes listed; the —signs negative influences.

this section as well as those already made, in the sections dealing with each of the reforms or other measures separately. It is his belief that some of the reforms listed should rank high in economic policy programs, and should be pursued with more energy than is the case at present. These are international integration, the international transfer of incomes, the introduction of built-in stabilizers and the raw material standard in the international field, and the application of family planning, of industrial democracy and the equalization of opportunities, in the national field. Social security schemes as well as direct taxes are in need of expansion in a number of less developed countries;

nationalization and the centralization of production decisions are of a less general relevance; they may be useful in isolated cases. Generally speaking the need for, or feasibility of, any of the national measures mentioned will vary greatly between individual nations. In addition, some of the simpler devices from the quantitative realm are still so much needed in a number of countries that they deserve first attention.

CHAPTER 7

UTOPIAS: MISCONCEPTION OF
HUMAN NATURE?

7.1. Introductory

In the preceding chapters we have discussed a considerable number
of means by which the situation of an economy can be influenced so
as to make it more attractive to the policy-makers; and it was assumed
that the latters' preferences represented those of the citizens. There
has been a continuous search for other and better means to "improve
society" and many more proposals have been made than have been
discussed here. Some of these proposals, although still in the minds of
many dissatisfied citizens, have been rejected by most economists or
politicians because they were not believed to be appropriate. They
have been rejected either on the basis of practical experience, or as a
result of critical analysis prior to any attempts at their realization
being undertaken. Consequences were observed, or feared, that were
neither desirable in general nor desired by the promotors of the proposals. In the opinion of most economists and politicians these promotors overlooked certain aspects of human behaviour which could
result in those undesirable consequences. In trying to construct the
optimum policy such aspects should not be disregarded. In order to
exemplify these aspects we will, in this brief chapter discuss some of
the proposals usually rejected, and also rejected by the author. They
are being presented as based on misconceptions of human nature and
are called utopias. It will already have been clear that the author is
in favour of some proposals, discussed in the preceding chapters, which
have been so far rejected by most of his colleagues. These proposals
will probably be reckoned in the utopian category by these colleagues.
This difference of opinion illustrates the margin of error, very wide
in these matters, that may exist; and the question mark behind the

title of this chapter is meant to remind the reader of the relativity of this type of opinion.

If our analysis should be more or less correct, the lessons to be learned from utopias inform us about the limits that have to be set to social reforms. These limits will depend on many circumstances, such as the education of the population, the integrity of its leaders, and many others. They may change and what would seem impossible today may become possible tomorrow.

7.2. Complete Freedom

Certain philosophers have advocated complete freedom as the governing principle of economic policy. Complete freedom has hardly ever existed in any regular society worthy of study. But is has been approached from time to time, and in widely varying degrees, either in small communities formed haphazardly, or in certain economies particularly devoted to the idea of freedom. Gold-rush communities and certain colonial areas may be examples of the former and certain phases in the history of the United States and some other western countries may be quoted as examples of the latter category. Briefly stated, complete freedom tends to resemble the state of affairs in the jungle and, as far as we know, in certain animal communities, where the strong and brutal rule. This explains why, in the oldest human societies, restrictions on freedom (often severe restrictions) were already accepted. Human intercourse has to be regulated by a large number of laws and rules in order to attain its greatest achievements. Various aspects of human nature must be held responsible for this lesson of experience. First, certain aspects of physical strength and brutality are not correlated with spiritual strength and performances, and secondly, variability in mood sometimes causes actions against which, not only society, but also the committor himself has to be protected.

Even a society like the nineteenth century European society, where so much was already regulated by law and custom, showed inacceptable exploitation of children, to quote just one example, and a degree of inequality dangerous to social stability.

7.3. Complete State Regulation

About as impossible as complete freedom, complete state regulation has hardly ever existed either. In view of the great number of members of most economies and the great numbers of acts each member has to perform to keep life it is inconceivable that it all be operated by state regulation. The closest approximation is probably obtained during war and other emergencies. Even then, a number of activities have to be done voluntarily and individually. Nevertheless war economies are not maintained even in the communist countries, where consumer rationing, for example, has been abolished. This illustrates the impossibility of complete regulation and deprives any debate on freedom or regulation of its absolute character. It is a question of degree and any choice to be made has to depend on considerations of efficiency.

7.4. Productive Co-operatives (Associations)

Attempts have been repeatedly made by idealists to substitute, for the enterprise hierarchy with its many disagreeable aspects for those at the bottom of the pyramid, forms of voluntary co-operation on an equal footing. Such organizations have sometimes been called productive co-operatives or productive associations. Their characteristic is that decisions are taken "in a democratic way", that is, in meetings of all members of the productive community in which all have equal rights and responsibilities. To the experienced business man or union leader this may seem ridiculous, but it is indicative of the deep-felt aversion against the hierarchic method. The experience made with such associations is that most of them have not survived, that very few, if any, have ever reached the size of even a medium-sized enterprise and that evidently, therefore, this form of organizing production is an impossibility. The reasons are that, as could be expected, efficiency is usually lowered, and also that difficulties between the members of the community cannot be avoided by this form of organization either. To a large extent it is therefore a technical question: in modern production processes things become so complicated that a large number of different acts are needed; these have to be co-ordinated and the natural form to do so is the hierarchy, with its system of small and large leaders each of them supervising the junctions of flows of activities whose products have to be combined and each of them having certain responsibilities. Perhaps it is significant that not only the armies and the enterprise have assumed this form, but even the most progressive political parties or workers unions.

To some extent it is, also, a human question. The majority of men need some outside stimulus for them to make their contribution to the process of production, and the question may well be put whether co-operative contacts with "equals" only are the most stimulating.

7.5. Abolition of Money

As already observed before (§ 6.5), many social and economic philoso-phers have looked at our monetary system as the root of many evils. Some of them have even gone as far as to look at money itself as that root and have proposed to abolish money at all. Evidently they have not meant to deny that money as an organizer of the exchange of goods and services is useful; for they usually have proposed that certain rationing tickets would be used in which form income would be paid out and for which consumer goods, at least, could be bought; and questions of words could be left out of consideration. Probably it is money as a means of accumulating value which was in the minds of these colleagues. It is this possibility which they want to destroy, by "abolishing" money. It cannot be denied that certain aspects of the unlimited accumulation of wealth seem to be contrary to general human wellbeing (cf. what was said in § 1.54); but there are other means that could be applied, and the elimination of money as a means to accumulate savings seems an outright error. It is not necessary to give theoretical demonstrations of the useful function of savings in order to support this thesis. Experience with our monetary system has supplied some important evidence. The situation so much desired by the sponsors of the elimination of money has been more or less ap-proached by certain war-time and post-war experiences. In such periods of extreme scarcity of goods, when rationing tickets are being distri-buted, money almost loses its significance. It cannot be spent and savings are not particularly attractive. It is well known, however, that such a situation very much reduces people's willingness to make efforts and to further efficiency. This would also be the probable consequence, then, if the possibility of accumulating savings would be eliminated. Experience in the opposite direction speaks the same language. Monetary "purges", that is, the absorption of superfluous money and its substitution by new money, whose value, it is hoped, will be maintained, generally have a very favourable influence on the activity and efficiency of the population. The German experience of 1948 is one of the best known and clearest.

7.6. Complete Equalization of Incomes

Those impressed by the sometimes appalling inequality in incomes have repeatedly suggested that there should be equality in incomes, either exact equality or at least approximate equality. For obvious reasons the idea appeals to many people. It is also clear that arguments in favour of inequality, given as they always are by people with incomes well above the average are, to the ordinary man, at least suspect. It is important, therefore, to state that some attempts at income equalization been made relatively recently and that their consequences have been observed. Russia before 1926 and Israel after 1945 made such attempts. In the Israeli case, the income of a government minister (secretary of state) was no more than 150% of the income of a huissier in the same ministry. In both countries the attempt has been given up and the income distribution in these countries does not differ much from what it is in progressive western countries generally. The consequences were exactly those foreseen by economists, namely the impossibility of attracting sufficient people for the harder jobs—harder especially in the sense of more responsibility-bearing jobs.

7.7. Completely Free Services

Another proposal meant to improve the standard of life of the low-income groups has been the supply, without any charge, of certain services or goods. The better-known modern examples are those of free education and free medical services. Completely free education hardly exists in the western world, since a student does not, as a rule, get his food, housing and clothing completely free. Free medical treatment has been applied more frequently. The experiences made do show that a certain element of waste is an almost unavoidable consequence. Even without completely free education a number of students at high schools or universities appear to be unable to complete their education. And the number of cases in which an unnecessary use is being made of free medical services is considerable. The conclusion drawn by most modern social experts is that, although the charges should certainly be very moderate, some charge, at least, seems to be advisable. The temptation to make use of a free service is too great, it seems, for human nature to permit the individual to take account of the community's interest.

CHAPTER 8

SOME REMARKS ON THE ORGANIZATION
OF ECONOMIC POLICY

8.1. Number and Nature of Agencies and Their Tasks

8.11   Economic policy, as will have become clear from the preceding analysis, is a complicated activity. Its preparation and execution require a large number of agencies, spread over the country, with many thousands of officials. In order to be well done, it requires a deliberate organization of the tasks involved. Evidently the nature and extent of such organization depend on various circumstances. One type of policy requires a much more elaborate organization than the other. In war time the number of agencies and officials is perhaps double that of a normal period. Today, in a normal period, economic policy requires a much more intricate machinery than, for example, in the nineteenth century. The degree of organization needed also depends on the quality of both the population and the officials.

An appropriate organization of any activity must be based on an analysis of its tasks. Since the tasks involved in economic policy are the handling of the various means, including, for quantitative policy, the instruments, the organization and the formation of executive agencies should be based on the various means and instruments, not on the aims or targets. The aims should, of course, be in the minds of the agencies, but they should be, at the same time, aware that other means or instruments will also exert their influence on the target variables. It is the task of the Central Bank, to give an example, to handle credit policy, not with one special aim in mind, say the defence of the gold stock or of the value of money, but with all aims together, including a stable level of employment, in mind. It is no use therefore having agencies for separate aims. Executive agencies have to act and action presupposes an instrument or a means.

8.12   Apart from executive agencies there have to be co-ordinating and supervising agencies and these will have to occupy themselves with the complete set of aims and means. To the extent that a certain group of aims can be attained by a certain group of means, without other means interfering, there may, of course, be co-ordinating agencies at an intermediate level which need only look after this group of aims, but this hardly applies to the main means of policy.

There is a correspondence between the organization of economic policy and the structure of the matrix of coefficients in the simplified version of the economic model describing the relations between target variables and instrument variables. If that matrix is partitioned there are groups of targets and instruments that can be treated independently of the others.

In the case of policy problem 162 (§ 4.23), and according to equations (4208), (4216), (4217) and (4218), there is no such partitioning, but the agency responsible for wage policy has to pay attention to two only out of the four target variables, namely employment and balance of payments deficit; the agency responsible for indirect taxes to three only: furthermore, the target for investment activity is unaffected by the level of indirect taxes.

In order to let the process of economic policy run smoothly and efficiently it is desirable that the various means are allocated to the agencies in such a way as to leave no doubt concerning competence. The instructions to each agency should be such, however, as to let all relevant aims be permitted to exert their influence (cf. § 8.2).

It follows from the preceding argument—and in fact, from the general interdependence of aims and means—that a system of autonomous ministers, each of them responsible for a certain set of aims, is incompatible with modern economic policy. This has been appreciated in most countries, and a certain degree of co-ordination usually takes place. It is doubtful, however, whether the degree of co-ordination is sufficient according to modern standards of efficiency. [1]

As was already stated in § 1.3, the process of economic policy may be decomposed into various consecutive phases, to be called planning, co-ordination and decision, execution and supervision. This decomposition is of course schematic, and the complexity of the process will

---

[1] In several countries this applies in particular to the co-ordination between the Treasury and the Central Bank.

not always permit keeping to it in detail. The phases will sometimes have to be repeated: a provisional attempt at coordinating certain elements may require a second planning phase to be inserted, etc. Co-ordination and decision have been mentioned as one single phase because of their interdependency. The various phases will be discussed in succession.

Before doing so we have to recognize that the process requires time. Certain acts of policy can be carried out in a few hours. There are others that take years; this is especially true of the decisions to carry out big investments or to set into motion a coherent program of, say, industrialization. The important element formed by a change in a tax rate usually requires several months: it has to be prepared by the Treasury experts, to be discussed by the executive officials of the Treasury, to be discussed in the Council of Ministers, perhaps to be submitted to one or more other Councils or Committees, it has to be submitted to Parliament and to be discussed in two Houses as a rule.

8.2. Planning of Economic Policy

The origin of certain acts of economic policy sometimes has to be sought for in preparatory discussions among private circles, in political parties or in research institutions. Schemes of social security, for example, were discussed for years before they entered into practical policy. Proposals to nationalize certain industries were subjects of hot controversy between citizens and experts decades before they played a practical role. Proposals for compensatory budget policies as a means of stabilizing cyclic movements were discussed long before they became parts of any government program. Often it is the underlying principles rather than the technical aspects of a policy which are discussed and worked out by the circles just indicated.

By far the largest volume of planning work, as a rule, is performed by the government agencies to whose competence the policy belongs. This is especially true for elements of current economic policy. A large number of government agencies are more or less continuously planning policy changes for the near future. One of the difficulties about the efficiency of this process is the absence of co-ordination. Even in the planning stage there should be a set of provisional directives for this work designed to avoid inconsistencies. This applies, first of all, to the basic data to be used. If the Treasury is working on tax reductions, the Minister of Social Affairs on wage policy and the Ministry of Economic Affairs on price policy there should be evidently a common basis as to what cyclical position will be probable, and the policies of these various ministries should be consistent with each other: under boom conditions, when it is desired to keep prices stable, financial policy should be directed towards a stabilization of total demand which is the driving force in short-term movements. Co-ordination is also needed as to the aims of policy: they have to be consistent in themselves. This may be facilitated by certain "declarations of intent" by the government.

Such declarations will also be of considerable help for the contacts, during the preparatory stage of policy design, with the private sector. These contacts are very desirable and almost indispensable for arriving at a reliable forecast and for creating a sphere of mutual understanding between the private sector and government agencies.

8.3. Co-ordination and Decision

As already observed, co-ordination has to start in the planning phase with the issue of directives to the agencies concerned. It is a process of mutual influence between the specialized agencies and the co-ordinating centre. The centre has to start by the sending out, on the basis of a macro-economic analysis, of provisional directives. The specialized agencies, when working out their plans, may strike elements that were unknown to the centre, or of which sufficient account had not been taken. It may then be necessary to amend the directives and start a "second round". Sometimes one round will be sufficient, sometimes even more than two rounds will be needed. The final stage of the phase under discussion consists of the decision as to aims and means and the extent to which the means need to be used.

The function of co-ordination and decision requires the existence of inter-departmental bodies, especially when instruments which exert manifold influences are involved. Changes in taxation, for example, will have to be discussed with a number of departments, because they influence the level of investment or consumption, or since they affect the competitive situation of certain industries. Wage changes will have to be discussed because of the same problems, and so on. There will have to be one central committee where economic policy generally will have to be co-ordinated; apart from the Council of Ministers which has to take the final decisions. Its decisions will have to be prepared by a central committee of high-level officials of the ministries. There will have to be staff organs for the various committees in order to carry out the investigations and to draft the necessary documents. The general design of co-ordination, based on the type of analysis presented in this book—and particularly the analysis as given in Chapters 3 and 4—will have to be the well-defined task of one well-defined unit. There should not be, in other words, any doubt as to the competence in this respect.

The pattern of organization of economic policy may have to be streamlined in some other respects as well. There will have to be clarity about the division of tasks between Parliament and Government. As a rule the details should be left to the government and the main features should be a matter for discussion in Parliament. There is a tendency to go into too many details in parliamentary debates. It requires a certain self-discipline on either side to avoid this. A well-organized debate would be made possible if there would also be some streamlining in the time schedule of economic policy. Simultaneous proposals on the more important subjects at regular intervals, e.g. once or twice a year, might be a valuable schedule. The most important features of a year's policy should, as a rule, be submitted on budget day.

Special problems of co-ordination arise when some instruments of economic policy, as, for example, wage rates or certain price and market regulations, are only supervised by the government, but largely handled by private organizations. By itself this handling by private organizations is a form of decentralization, comparable with the decentralization in local administration, which has many advantages. If, nonetheless, the instruments are considered of great importance to the general economic situation, a certain power to veto or amend their changes has to be given to the central government. It will depend on the economic situation whether these powers have to be more or less stringent. The government may permit wage changes within certain margins, for example. If, however, there is a strong upward pressure, because of, say, a boom situation, it will be certain beforehand that all wages will rise until the upper limit is reached. This may make the margin illusory.

8.4. Execution

The execution of economic policy is distributed over a large number of agencies, each of them handling certain means; often the execution will have to be subdivided according to geographical units, branches of industrial activity, social groups, and so on. In the majority of cases there wil be a hierarchic relation between the local, branch or group agencies, and the central, supervising agencies in each subject. Many well-known questions of organization and efficiency will come up and have to be solved according to business standards, although special attention has to be given to certain characteristics of the public task.

One of these special characteristics is the autonomy of local authorities. This autonomy has important human and technical aspects and should be respected as much as possible. But by its very nature, that is, by the fact that the territory covered is restricted, it will also show some of the disadvantages of decentralization, as discussed in section 5.6. Some of the decisions taken by local authorities will also very much affect the well-being of other parts of the national economy. A certain supervision and guidance of local policies has to form the counter-weight. The forms of supervision and guidance are not indifferent. Persuasion rather than orders should be the usual instrument; particularly if the policy envisaged by the central authorities is in the interest of local communities themselves, without their being aware of it. A well-known example is business-cycle policy. At a certain juncture, for example in a period of slackening of private demand, it may be desirable to increase public demand; or in another situation, namely one of brisk private demand, it may be desirable to reduce public demand. Such an anticyclic policy is not always voluntarily carried out; nevertheless it is in the interest of the economy as a whole, and also, as a rule, in the interest of local communities individually. Persuasion of local communities will have to be attempted but it may be wise to supplement it with variations in the grants-in-aid given by central authorities to local bodies. And in very urgent circumstances direct decisions by central authorities may be unavoidable. If so, the value of self-determination should, however, be taken into account.

In order that the numerous detailed decisions that have to be taken by both the agencies of the central policy-maker and the agencies of local authorities are taken in the right way, they should be taken in accordance with the aims of general policy. Exact knowledge and understanding of this general policy are among the means to obtain this parallelism of attitude.

8.5. Supervision

The execution of economic policy has to be supervised, that is, facts and figures about it have to be collected and to be critically considered against the background of the aims set. The function of such supervision is, primarily, to supply the responsible policy-makers (i.e. Government) with the means of controlling their own executive agencies. In addition, this supervision is a necessary instrument for Parliament to be able to perform its task; and, in the last ressort, also for those citizens who, individually or collectively, want to test government policy.

The function of supervision is, however, not only to appraise past acts. It also has to yield an important service in the shaping of future acts. As was discussed in § 1.3, planning has to start with an appraisal of the situation. This appraisal consists of a comparison between the actual situation prevailing and the situation considered most desirable. It will be clear that such an appraisal is identical with our definition given to supervision.

Supervision thus conceived will be largely a question of the collection of good statistics and other factual information and of their analysis. In an increasingly complicated world the role to be played by analysis is of growing importance. The task of these analytical studies may be clarified by asking why, as a rule, economic policy will not lead to the aims set. There are three groups of reasons why this is so. First, policy may not exactly have been carried out as it was intended by the policy-makers. Secondly, it may not have worked out as was expected. And, thirdly, new events or developments will have intervened.

The reasons why policy may not have been carried out exactly as was intended are themselves manifold. Minor technical obstacles may have come up during the execution. There may have been misunderstanding as to what the intentions were in detail. There may have been made errors in the execution. And there may have been lack of parallelism between the intentions at the top and the acts at the basis of the hierarchic pyramid.

There are also several reasons why a policy may not have worked out as it was supposed to. The reactions of the economy may have been different from what was known to the policy-makers, because these reactions were only superficially known, or because they were subject to conditions not realized. Since there are so many reactions involved—those represented by each of the "reaction equations" of the economy—the possible locations of divergency are numerous.

Finally, new events may have changed the situation; they may also be numerous; in the language of our models, autonomous terms may have appeared in almost any of the equations.

For all these reasons, the analysis of the data collected for the supervision of economic policy must be a careful and detailed one, requiring the application of scientific methods and of much factual knowledge about the economy concerned. This type of analysis, as so many other elements of economic policy, is in continuous development and improvement. As will be clear, it has to be developed more or less along the same lines as the design of policy itself.

8.6. International Economic Policy

Whereas economic policy inside most modern countries is beginning to be well organized, it is hardly organized at all in the international field. The outstanding factor at the basis of this situation is national autonomy, an institution with such deep roots that it is almost a datum to the economist. Since, however, several of its effects on human well-being have been proved to be disastrous, it should not actually be taken as a datum. Slow changes, only, are possible, it seems, and it will only be by a continuous process of information and education that some restrictions in autonomy will be obtained. In § 5.6 we tried to show that certain means of economic policy should indeed be centralized and it follows that accordingly a certain organization in international economic policy should be introduced.

In the present situation there is clearly a lack of agencies that can be held responsible for the fulfilment of certain aims which, in all probability, would be felt to be highly important by most citizens of the international community. In a few fields only, do international agencies, and those with a very restricted competence, exist, and there are continuous attempts on the part of national governments to reduce even these competences. In the jungle of international policy this is a self-evident feature. But, as we asserted in §§ 1.5 and 1.6, this state of affairs may well prove to be one of the biggest and most dramatic inconsistencies in the aims of economic policy, or rather policy generally. There can be no doubt about what the directives should be of all interested in world welfare.

In the actual situation a large role is played by negotiations between these autonomous policy-makers. As a consequence, the organizational picture of international economic policy is far more complicated than the already complicated subject matter would require. It is a "world of monopolies", smaller and larger ones, meeting in bilateral, or plurilateral combinations, complicated by all types of pressure groups, and their affiliations inside governmental bodies of a considerable number of countries.

There is scope for a complete reconsideration, from a truly international point of view, of this organizational pattern. There should be a few centralized agencies responsible for some of the most outstanding aims, with numerous decentralized agencies wherever that would be compatible with the vital interests or the world community. In today's jargon there is scope for much more co-ordination and integration. It is, however, beyond the scope of this chapter to give more than "some remarks" on the organization of economic policy. Some attempts at an elaboration of the remarks just made have been made elsewhere. [1]

---

[1] J. Tinbergen, International Economic Integration, Amsterdam 1954, Chapter XI.

APPENDICES

Number of Model	Brief Characteristic of Model (for fuller description see Appendix 3)	National Income Y	Expenditure X	Tax Receipts T	Total Wages L	Total Non-Labour Inc. Z	Value of Consumption C	Value of Investment J	Value of Exports E	Value of Imports I	Deficit in Bal. of Paym. D	Real National Income y	Real Expenditure x	Volume of Gross Prod ι
	Closed, static, macro													
01	Money flow	1	1											
02	Money and product flow	1	1										1	
03	Money, product and factor flow	1	1		1								1	
04	Money flow and public finance	1	1	1										
05	Money flow and assets	1	1	1										
	Closed, static, micro													
06	Horiz. money and prod. flow	1	$H+2$										H	
07	Horiz. money and prod. flow with monopolies						H						H	
08	Real income distribution 1)											1		
	Closed, dynamic, macro													
09	Development											1		
10	Cycle (money-flow, paper profits)	1	1											
	Open, static, macro													
11	Money flow	1	1						1	1				
12	Money and product flow	1	1						1	1	1		1	
13	Money, product and factor flow	1	1						1	1	1		1	
14	Money and prod. flow, exch. rate	1	1						1	1	1		1	
15	Money flow and assets	1	1								1			
	Open, static, micro													
16	Money, prod., fact. flow, publ. fin.	1			1	1	2	1	1	1	1			
17	Money flow assets and banking	1								1				
18	Horiz. money, prod. and fact. flow	1	2						2	1	1		2	
19	Horiz. money and prod. flow	1	H						H	1	1		H	H
	Open, dynamic, micro													
20	Investm. project appraisal	$2H+4$		2		$H+1$					1		1	$H-$
	Group of economies, static													
21	Money and product flow	H									H		H^2	

1) The variables of this model are explained in the description of the model itself.

X 1

ED AS EXAMPLES

urring in Model

	Depreciation	Volume of Consumption	Volume of Investment	Volume of Exports	Volume of Imports	Replacement Investm.	Real Savings	Price of Product	Price of "Other" Prod.	Wage Rate	Interest Rate	Exchange Rate	Money in Circulation	Deposits	Bonds Held	Bills and Advances	Redisc. with C. Bank	Reserves	Gold Stock	Foreign Debt	Stock of Real Cap.	Stock of Equipment
	d	c	j	e	i	r	s	p	q	l	m	k	M	M'	B	B^B	B^R	R	Au	K^i	b	w
								1														
								1														
													1									
								H														
								$H+1$														
	1	1	1			1		1													1	1
				1	1			2														
				1	1			2														
				1	1			2														
													6		6							
		1		1	1			1		1												
											2											
														1	1		1	1	1	1		
−1				2	2			$2H$														
				H	H																	
−2	1			1	$H+1$		1	2			1	1								H	$H+1$	
								H														

APPENDIX 2

PROBLEMS OF ECONOMIC POLICY TREATED WITH MODELS

Probl. No.	Nature of economy[1])	Model No.	Targets or other aims	Instruments or other means	Cf. section
011	Closed static macro	01	Full employment	Public expenditure	3.521
021		02	Full employment	Public expenditure	3.522
031		03	Full employment	Public expenditure	3.523
032		03	Full employment	Wage rate	3.523
033		03	Full employment; monetary equilibrium	Public expenditure; wage rate	3.524
041		04	Full employment	Public expenditure	3.525
042		04	Full employment	Taxes	3.525
051		05 ⎫	Full employment;	Public expenditure; ⎫	3.531
052		05 ⎬	no potential	debt policy ⎬	3.532
053		05 ⎭	inflation	⎭	3.533
054		05	Full employment	Money circulation	3.534
061	Closed static micro	06	Full employment in each industry	Public expenditure; indirect tax rates in each industry	3.535
071		07	General aims [2])	Free competition in all industries	5.52
072		07	General aims	A monopoly for one product	5.53
073		07	General aims	Vertic. integrated monopolies for all products	5.54
074		07	General aims	Cumulative monopolies for one or all final products	5.55
081		08	General aims	Tax rates, education and family allowances	6.42
091	Closed dynamic	09	Development	Investment	3.62
101	macro	10	Stabilization	Compensatory public expend.	5.32
102		10	Stabilization	Raw material standard	6.5
111	Open static macro	11	Full employment	Public expenditure	4.121
112		11	Balance of paym. equilibrium	Public expenditure	4.122
113		11	Optimum combination of full employment and balance of payments equil.	Public expenditure	4.123
121		12	Full employment	Public expenditure	4.131
131		13	Full employment and balance of payments equil.	Public expenditure and wage rate	4.141
141		14	Full employment and balance of payments equil.	Public expenditure and wage rate	4.151
142		14	Full employment and balance of payments equil.	Public expenditure and exchange rate	4.152

[1]) For fuller description cf. Appendix 3
[2]) As described in section 1.4; cf. also sections dealing with problems concerned.

Probl. No.	Nature of economy[1]	Model No.	Targets or other aims	Instruments or other means	Cf. section
143		14	Full employment, bal. of paym. eq., monetary eq.	Public expenditure, wage rate, exchange rate	4.156
151		15	Full employment and balance of payments equil.	Public expenditure and debt policy	4.161
152		15	Full employment and balance of payments equil.	Public expenditure and discount rate	4.162
161	Open static micro	16	Full employm., balance of paym. eq., investment volume, distr. of income	Public expenditure, wage rate, indirect and direct tax rate	4.221
162		16	Full employm., balance of paym. eq., investment volume, internal price level	Public expenditure, wage rate, indirect and direct tax rate	4.231
171		17	Full employment, balance of paym. equilibrium	Discount rate, reserve requirements	4.241
181		18	Full employment and bal. of paym. equil.	Productivity in two industries	4.251
191	Open static micro	19	Full employment in each industry	Public expenditure and indirect taxes	4.261
201	Open dynamic micro	20	General aims	Investment projects	5.73
211	Group of economies, static	21	Full employment and bal. of paym. equil.	Public expenditure and price levels in each country	4.43

[1] For fuller description cf. Appendix 3.

APPENDIX 3

INDIVIDUAL MODELS DEFINED [1])

Symbols for variables: see Appendix 4

MODEL 01. CLOSED, STATIC, MACRO, MONEY-FLOW MODEL

ACTORS   *Number:* 1, economy as a whole.

               Income: equal to total expenditure.

     Income behaviour: supply of commodity perfectly elastic (equation 1).

      Spending habits: see equation 2.

            Wealth: does not influence current economic process.

MARKETS   *Number:* 1, general commodity.

           Character: flow.

TECHNICAL RELATIONS   Not explicitly considered.

EQUATIONS

     Income formation: $Y = X$ (1)

      Income spending: $X = X_0 + \xi_1 Y$ (2)

               where $X_0 =$ autonomous expenditure

                      $\xi_1 =$ marginal propensity to spend

From this equation the elasticity of demand for the general commodity can be derived as follows. Equation (2) may be written as:

$$xp = X_0 + \xi_1 yp$$

$$x = \frac{X_0}{p} + \xi_1 y$$

Elasticity of demand $= -X_0$ for $x = p = 1$

By a proper choice of units we may choose two variables $= 1$; the other will then follow.

If expenditure X_0 is not autonomous, but corresponding real expenditure

$$x_0 = \frac{X_0}{p}$$

we have instead $x = x_0 + \xi_1 y$

and the elasticity of demand is zero.

If we choose $x = p = 1$ in the point of equilibrium, we have, in addition, $X = 1$, $Y = 1$, and hence $1 = X_0 + \xi_1$; also $x_0 = X_0 = 1 - \xi_1$.

---

[1] Cf. §2.14 for explanation of the terms used.

MODEL 02. CLOSED, STATIC, MACRO, MONEY AND PRODUCT FLOW MODEL

ACTORS   *Number:* 1, economy as a whole.

Income: determined by total expenditure (equation 1); supply of product not perfectly elastic.

Spending habits: expenditure dependent on income and price level (see equation 2).

Wealth: does not influence current economic process.

MARKETS   *Number:* 1, general commodity.

Character: flow

TECHNICAL RELATIONS   Not explicitly considered.

EQUATIONS

Income formation: $Y = X$ (1)

Income spending: $X = x_0 p + \xi_1 Y$ (2)

where x_0 = autonomous real expenditure

ξ_1 = marginal propensity to spend.

Price fixation: $p = p_0 + \pi x$

where p_0 = autonomous price component   (3)

π = demand sensitivity of price level.

Definition: $X = xp$ (4)

Apart from the type of calculations already made with model 01, we may add a calculation of price flexibility in this case. To this end, we have again taken the units of goods and money such as to make, in the equilibrium situation, $p = x = 1$. It follows that also $X = Y = 1$ and hence $1 = \xi_1 + x_0$ and $1 = p_0 + \pi$. And the flexibility of p is $\dfrac{\partial p}{\partial x} \dfrac{x}{p} = \pi = 1 - p_0$.

MODEL 03. CLOSED, STATIC, MACRO MONEY, PRODUCT AND FACTOR FLOW

ACTORS   *Number:* 2, wage-earners and independents.

Income: wage bill and profits.

Income behaviour: supply of labour perfectly elastic; supply of goods: see equation (3)

Spending habits: wage earners have a marginal propensity to spend of $\zeta_1 + \zeta_2$, independents of ζ_1.

Wealth: does not influence current economic process.

MARKETS   *Number:* 2, for labour and for product.

Character: both are flow markets.

Technical relations Linear relation between quantity of product produced and quantity of labour needed.

Equations

Income formation: $Y = X$ (1)

Income formation, workers: $L = la$ (2)

Income spending: $X = \xi_1 Y + \xi_2 L + X_0$ (3)

where ξ_1 = propensity to spend for independents

$\xi_1 + \xi_2$ = propensity to spend for workers

X_0 = autonomous expenditure. This was not, as in model 02, taken to vary with p, since that would make it dependent on l, which we are going to consider as an instrument competing with X_0 as an instrument [1].

Price fixation: $p = p_0 + \pi_1 l + \pi_2 x$ (4)

where p_0 = autonomous price component

π_1 = wage sensitivity of prices

π_2 = demand sensitivity of prices.

For an appropriate choice of units of goods, money and labour we may have, in the situation of equilibrium, $x = p = l = 1$. It follows that

$1 = p_0 + \pi_1 + \pi_2$ (4')

whereas π_1 may now be called the marginal labour quota, and π_2 is the flexibility of prices (cf. model 02).

Technical: $a = a_0 + ax$ (5)

where a_0 = autonomous demand for labour

$a = \pi_1$ = marginal labour quota.

Assuming that in the situation of equilibrium $a = \frac{1}{2}$, implying that labour income al is one-half of total income; and also assuming that the marginal labour quota equals 0.4 [2], we have:

$a = \pi_1 = 0.4; \ a_0 = 0.1$

A realistic value for π_2 will be 0.1 or 0.2.

Definition: $X = xp$ (6)

---

[1] Assuming X_0 to vary with p and hence with l would mean that with a wage increase X_0 would also rise; it would overestimate the positive effects of a wage rise on employment.

[2] The coefficient π_1 need not necessarily be equal to the marginal labour quota a; certain (smaller) entrepreneurs calculate a gross profit margin which is proportional to wages per unit of product, a habit which tends to increase π_1. (Cf. also model 16).

MODEL 04. CLOSED, STATIC, MACRO MONEY-FLOW AND PUBLIC FINANCE MODEL

ACTORS   *Number:* 2, government and "rest of economy".

    Income: taxes [1] and total expenditure.

    Income behaviour: inelastic supply of services in both cases.

    Spending habits: government, inelastic; rest of economy, see equation (2).

MARKETS   *Number:* 1, general commodity.

    Character of good: flow.

TECHNICAL RELATIONS   Tax revenue assumed to depend on income, for simplicity's sake according to a linear formula.

EQUATIONS

Income formation $\begin{cases} \textit{government: see equation (3)} \\ \textit{rest of economy: } Y = X^P + X^G \end{cases}$ (1)

Income spending $\begin{cases} \textit{government: } X^G \textit{ is autonomous} \\ \textit{rest of economy: } X^P = X_0^P + \xi(Y - T) \end{cases}$ (2)

Technical: $\qquad\qquad T = \tau Y + T_0$ (3)

where T_0 represents autonomous additions to tax revenue, and τ represents the marginal rate of taxation. This technical equation makes the simplest possible distinction between an "autonomous" component in taxes T_0 and an "induced" component τY. [2]

MODEL 05. CLOSED, STATIC, MACRO MONEY FLOW, PUBLIC FINANCE AND ASSETS MODEL

ACTORS   *Number:* 2, government and "rest of economy".

    Income: taxes and total expenditure.

    Income behaviour: inelastic supply of services.

---

[1] Taxes have been treated as direct taxes. It would not have been difficult to bring indirect taxes also into the picture. They are part of government income as well; in order to define income of rest of the economy they have to be deducted from total expenditure.

[2] Various authors speak of taxes T as an instrument of economic policy, a viewpoint criticized by B. Hansen (Finanspolitikens ekonomiska teori, ch. II). In principle we agree with Hansen as our choice of τ and T_0 as instruments shows. It seems permitted, however, in certain cases, and by way of approximation, to handle T, or even the surplus of T over government expenditure, as an instrument.

Spending habits: government, inelastic; rest of economy, see equation (2).

Nature and origin of wealth: wealth of rest of economy consists of accumulated investment goods stock, plus government bonds, plus money; wealth of government does not enter explicitly into model.

Investment habits: rest of economy buys all bonds issued by government for reasons of financial policy, to be discussed in applications.

MARKETS   *Number:* 1, general commodity.

           Character: flow.

TECHNICAL RELATIONS   cash balance relation for rest of economy: see equation (3), tax revenue equation (4).

EQUATIONS

Income formation, rest of economy: $Y = X^P + X^G$ (1)

Income spending, rest of economy: $X^P = \xi_1 Y + X_0{}^P (M,B)$ (2)

              where it is assumed that expenditure also depends on the quantity of liquid assets held.

Cash balance for rest of economy: $\Delta M = Y - X^P - T - \Delta B$ (3)

Tax revenue: $T = T_0 + \tau Y$ (4)

MODEL 06. CLOSED, STATIC, MICRO, HORIZONTAL MONEY AND PRODUCT FLOW MODEL WITH TAXES

ACTORS   *Number:* $H + 2$, namely H industries, the government and all households together.

         Income: *industries*, sales of their products the supply of which is supposed te be inelastic;

                government: not considered explicitly,

                households: follows from total expenditure;

                supply of services is supposed to be inelastic.

   Spending habits: *industries:* not considered explicitly;

                government: expenditure autonomous, to be used as an instrument;

                households: see equation (5).

         Wealth: not considered explicitly.

MARKETS   *Number:* H, for each of the products of the H industries.

           Character: flows.

TECHNICAL RELATIONS   Supply price of each product assumed to be given. An indirect tax (or subsidy) for each product, to be used as instruments.

EQUATIONS

Income formation: $Y = X$ (1)

Definitions: $X = X^G + X^P$ (2)

$$X^P = \overset{H}{\underset{1}{\Sigma^h}} X^h \qquad\qquad h = 1 \ldots H \qquad (3)$$

$X^h = x^h p^h$ (H eqs) (4)

Spending: $X^h = \xi_1^h Y + \xi_2^h p^h$ (H eqs) (5)

where ξ_1^h are marginal propensities to consume good h and ξ_2^h are autonomous demand coefficients for each of the goods. These spending equations are not the most general type possible; in the latter also the prices of the other goods would appear.

Price fixation: $p^h = p_0^h + \tau^h$ (H eqs) (6)

where p_0^h are the autonomous supply prices of the goods h and τ^h is an indirect tax rate (if negative, a subsidy) for each good.

MODEL 07. CLOSED, STATIC, MICRO, HORIZONTAL MONEY AND PRODUCT FLOW MODEL WITH MONOPOLIES

ACTORS   *Number:* $H + 1$, namely H industries and all households together.

Income: industries, sales of their products the supply of which is supposed to be manipulated in order to obtain a maximum income, taking account of the influence of prices (monopolistic behaviour) *households:* total expenditure; supply of services is supposed to be inelastic.

Spending habits: industries spend their incomes on services; *households* spend their incomes on products.

Wealth: not considered explicitly.

MARKETS   *Number:* H, for each of the products of the industries.

Character: flows.

TECHNICAL RELATIONS   Unit costs of production for each industry assumed to be given; and units chosen so as to make these units costs $= 1$.

EQUATIONS

Income formation: households $y = \overset{H}{\underset{1}{\Sigma^h}} x^h$ (1)

where x^h represents the values, at constant prices, of the output of each industry and y, therefore, the total value, at constant prices, of all production. This is taken to represent real income.

industries: $Z^h = (p^h - 1) x^h \quad h = 1 \ldots H \quad$ (2)

Demand: $x^h = \xi_0^h y - \xi_1^h (p^h - p) \quad\quad h = 1 \ldots H \quad$ (3)

It is assumed that $\Sigma \xi_0^h = 1$, meaning that an increase in real income as defined above will be spent completely.

Supply: expressing that industries manipulate their prices so as to obtain a maximum profit:

$$\frac{dZ^h}{dp^h} = 0 \quad\quad\quad h = 1 \ldots H \quad (4)$$

Definition: $\quad\quad p = \dfrac{\Sigma \xi_1^h \, p^h}{\Sigma \xi_1^h} \quad\quad\quad\quad (5)$

This definition of the general price level, which enters into the demand equations is admittedly intended to simplify the analysis; the weights used coincide with the coefficients in the demand function, which need not always be so. It has the consequences that the addition of all demand equations leads to

$$\Sigma \, x^h = y$$

meaning that one demand equation is dependent on the others.

MODEL 08. CLOSED, STATIC, MICRO MODEL FOR INCOME DISTRIBUTION

ACTORS   *Number:* very large, unspecified, equal to total number of employers and employees.

    Incomes: employers, product minus real wages
employees, real wage.
Income behaviour determined by supply functions described below.

Spending habits: all entirely spend their income.

    Wealth: implicitly considered to influence employers' demand for and employees' supply of labour.

MARKETS   *Number:* very large, unspecified, equal to number of "occupations".

    Character: flow of services.

TECHNICAL RELATION   production function, indicating quantity of product as a function of organization of production, occupation and personal properties.

Variables. Because of the special characteristics of this model, deviating from the usual practical models, it is desirable to describe in some more detail the concepts and variables used. This model concentrates on the labour market in the widest sense, i.e. the market for all occupations, where even being a rentier may be considered an occupation. On the product side it is held as simple as possible, i.e. one general product is supposed to be produced and consumed by all; the quantities, only, are of interest and represent the real income of employers and employees. Each employee is described by a number of personal proporties, being the intensities t_i of certain "abilities" such as force, willpower, intelligence, etc. and including wealth; property number 1 indicates the speed (or the intensity) of his work of which t_1 is the quantitative expression; as another property, not important for his work perhaps, but certainly for his well-being, we consider the (weighted) size of his family t_0. Individuals are not introduced as separate actors, but a description of the total occupied population is given by a multi-dimensional frequency distribution of the number combinations $(t_0, t_1, \ldots, t_I)$ occurring. This frequency distribution will be indicated by $n(t_0, t_1, \ldots, t_I) dt_0, dt_1, \ldots, dt_I$.

There will be another frequency distribution of the degrees of the properties, namely the one required by the organizers of production; the properties will be numbered with the same indices; and the degree desired by s_1; there will be some properties in which the organizers are not interested. In our example this will be property 0, family size. Each combination of "desired degrees" $s_1 \ldots s_I$ represents a "job". The frequency distribution of desired properties will be indicated by $m(s_1 \ldots s_I)ds_1 \ldots ds_I$. This frequency distribution will depend on, among other things, the productive result to be obtained in each job. The averages and standard deviations of the degrees s_i and t_i will be indicated by $\bar{s}_i, \bar{t}_i, \sigma_i$ and τ_i respectively. The task of income formation is to induce each individual to accept the job for which he is most appropriate under the resulting income scale and so to attribute an individual to each job as to let all jobs be filled and all individuals employed. This presupposes equality between the total frequencies M and N of m and n respectively. Indicating the income scale by $l(s_1 \ldots s_I)$ or briefly by $l(s)$ we have to find this function, which may depend on more variables than the $s_i(i = 1 \ldots I)$ alone. We assume that it will also depend on the product $p(s, t)$ obtained by a certain individual t in a job s.

The process of choice of the individual is based on certain preferences with regard to income l and job s as well as on the characteristics of the individual t. We assume the utility function ω to be of one and the same type for all individuals; the differences between individuals enter into it only in the form of the parameters t_i [1]. With a given income scale $l(s)$ each individual t chooses a job s and because of the uniqueness of ω a correspondence between s and t is established:

$$s = f(t)$$

This correspondence and hence the income scale $l(s)$ has to be so as to equate, for any set of s and t, the frequency densities of the m- and n-distribution:

$$m(s) = n(t) \frac{\partial(t)}{\partial(s)},$$

where $\dfrac{\partial(t)}{\partial(s)}$ is the Jacobian.

The process and the nature of the resulting income scale can best be clarified by considering a still more special case. To this effect the following further assumptions will be made.

In order to illustrate policy problems it will be assumed that family allowances are paid to the employees, that the income scale is made to depend on the quantity of product the individual puts out, and that taxes are paid out of which training facilities are financed.

1. The *production function* p, indicating a person's product, will be assumed to be:

$$p = \pi_1 t_1 + \sum_2^I \pi_i{}^s s_i + \sum_2^I \pi_i{}^t t_i + \pi_0\,(\bar{s}_i, \sigma_i) = p_0 + \sum_2^I \pi_i{}^s s_i \qquad (1)$$

The essence of the assumption is that p is linearly dependent on the s and t.

2. The *utility function* will be supposed to be:

$$\omega = \log \bar{\imath}_0 - \log t_0 + \log (1 - \gamma) + \log l - \sum_2^I \lambda_i\,(s_i - t_i)^2 - \varphi\,(t_1) \qquad (2)$$

This implies that utility is assumed to be a rising function of $\dfrac{(1 - \gamma)l}{t_0}$ or the income per (weighted) person after proportional taxes γl lave been paid. $\bar{\imath}_0$ represents the average family size; the corresponding term is a constant and has been added to facilitate the further analysis. It further implies that utility is negatively dependent on all $s_i - t_i$, i.e. the "tensions"

[1] It would lead us too far here to discuss the mathematical and philosophical implications of this assumption.

between the required and the actual properties—required for the job chosen and actually present with the individual. This dependency is such that both a positive and a negative deviation between required and actual properties evokes an aversion; the simplest way to represent this type of relation is to assume it to be a quadratic function. For small values of the tensions this is a perfectly general relation. The last term in the expression for ω represents an aversion from high speeds of work: φ is assumed to be increasing function of t_1 and even increasing in an accelerated way.

3. It is further assumed that the frequency distributions m and n both show two characteristics. The frequency of any one combination of degrees is the product of the frequencies of each degree separately (the properties are mutually independent):

$$m\,(s_1, s_2, \ldots, s_I) = m_1\,(s_1) \cdot m_2\,(s_2) \ldots m_I\,(s_I)\,M \qquad (3)$$

$$n\,(t_1, t_2, \ldots, t_I) = n_1\,(t_1) \cdot n_2\,(t_2) \ldots n_I\,(t_I)\,N \qquad (4)$$

Further it is assumed that all partial frequency distributions are normal:

$$m_i\,(s_i) = \frac{1}{\sigma_i\,\sqrt{2\pi}}\,e^{-\frac{(s_i-\bar{s}_i)^2}{2\sigma_i^2}} \qquad (5)$$

$$n_i\,(t_i) = \frac{1}{\tau_i\,\sqrt{2\pi}}\,e^{-\frac{(t_i-\bar{t}_i)^2}{2\tau_i^2}} \qquad (6)$$

With these hypotheses the process of income formation may be illustrated in an explicit way. We will not give the full illustration nor will we give the details of the supply of jobs. The supply of jobs will be derived by the organizers of production from a process of profit maximizing; calling the total product of all employees P and their total wages L, the organizers will so choose the frequency distribution of their jobs as to make $P - L$ a maximum with respect to their parameters s_1 and σ_i $(i = 1, 2, \ldots, I)$. We will not give the expressions for these parameters, which depend, incidentally, on the form given to the function $\pi_0(\bar{s}_i, \sigma_i)$ in equation (1).

We will, however, give the full details of the demand side. For each individual t the choice of his job s will derive from the maximization of ω as a function of t_1 (his working speed) and $s_2 \ldots s_I$:

$$\frac{\partial \omega}{\partial t_1} = \frac{\partial \omega}{\partial \log l} \frac{\partial \log l}{\partial p} \frac{\partial p}{\partial t_1} - \varphi'(t_1) = 0$$

or

$$\frac{\partial \log l}{\partial p} \pi_1 = \varphi'(t_1) \tag{7}$$

and

$$\frac{\partial \omega}{\partial s_i} = \frac{\partial \omega}{\partial \log l} \frac{\partial \log l}{\partial s_i} - 2\lambda_i (s_i - t_i) = 0, \quad i = 2 \ldots . I$$

or

$$\frac{\partial \log l}{\partial s_i} = 2\lambda_i (s_i - t_i), \quad i = 2 \ldots . I \tag{8}$$

For any conceivable income scale l these equations will determine t_1 and $s_2 \ldots s_I$. With these values there has now to be equilibrium between supply of and demand for jobs:

$$m(s_2 \ldots . s_I) = n\{t_2(s) \ldots . t_I(s)\} \frac{\partial(t)}{\partial(s)} \tag{9}$$

It is a well-known method in mathematics to try a certain solution; in the present circumstances it appears to be useful to try an income scale:

$$\log l = \psi(\log \bar{t} - \log t_0) + L_0 + L_1 p + \overset{I}{\underset{2}{\Sigma}}_i L_i s_i \tag{10}$$

With this scale equations (7) and (8) become:

$$L_1 \pi_1 = \varphi'(t_1) \tag{11}$$

$$L_1 \pi_i{}^s + L_i = 2 \lambda_i (s_i - t_i), i = 2 \ldots . I \tag{12}$$

where L_1 and L_i are constants for all individuals. Equation (12) enables us to express $t(s)$ occurring in (9) more explicitly:

$$t_i = - \frac{L_1 \pi_i{}^s + L_i}{2 \lambda_i} + s_i \tag{13}$$

This means that every t_i only depends on the corresponding s_i; implying that

$$\frac{\partial(t)}{\partial(s)} = \frac{\partial t_2}{\partial s_2} \ldots \ldots \frac{\partial t_I}{\partial s_I} = 1 \tag{14}$$

The special form chosen for m and n (cf. (3) and (4)) now enables us to "separate the variables" in (9) and to deduce that

$$m_i(s_i) = n_i \left(s_i - \frac{L_1 \pi_i^s + L_i}{2 \lambda_i} \right) \tag{15}$$

whereas the further specifications (5) and (6) transform this into

$$\frac{(s_i - \bar{s}_i)^2}{2 \sigma_i^2} = \frac{\left(s_i - \frac{L_1 \pi_i^s + L_i}{2\lambda_i} - \bar{t}_i \right)^2}{2\tau_i^2} - \log \frac{\sigma_i}{\tau_i} \tag{16}$$

We now make the further—rather stringent—hypothesis that the standard deviations of the s_i- and t_i-distributions are equal to each other: $\sigma_i = \tau_i$. It will then be possible to perform a further considerable simplification: the equality of demand for and supply of jobs now requires

$$s_i - \bar{s}_i = s_i - \frac{L_1 \pi_i^s + L_i}{2\lambda_i} - \bar{t}_i$$

or

$$L_1 \pi_i^s + L_i = 2 \lambda_i (\bar{s}_i - \bar{t}_i), \; i = 2 \ldots . I \tag{17}$$

The mathematical interpretation of this result is that the income scale (10) is, under the various assumptions as to the frequency distributions, the production function and the utility function (equations (1) to (6) inclusive) the correct one provided that its constants L_1 to L_I are not arbitrary but satisfy the relations (17). Since these relations are $I - 1$ in number, one of the L's, say L_1 can be chosen freely; the others cannot, however. The constant L_0 in (10) can also be chosen arbitrarily but will be limited by general productivity. Substituting the values from (17) for $L_2 \ldots L_I$ we arrive at the income scale:

$$\log l = \psi (\log t_0 - \log \bar{t}_0) + L_0 + L_1 p + \sum_2^I {}_i (2\lambda_i (\bar{s}_i - \bar{t}_i) - L_1 \pi_i^s) s_i$$

Substituting equation (1) for p, we get:

$$\log l = \psi (\log t_0 - \log \bar{t}_0) + L_1 \{ \pi_1 t_1 + \sum_2^I \pi_i t_i + \pi(\bar{s}_i, \sigma_i) \} +$$

$$+ \; 2 \sum_i (\bar{s}_i - \bar{t}_i) \lambda_i s_i \tag{18}$$

In this formula t_1 has to be taken from (11).

Because of the complicated nature of this model it may be as well to summarize it by enumerating the types of variables and parameters that together form its logical hierarchy. It is useful to make a distinction between four types of concepts:

1) First, there. are the *technical and natural constants* describing the framework in which society works; in this model they are the constants π_1, $\pi_i{}^s$ and $\pi_i{}^t$ $(i = 2 \ldots I)$ of the production function (1) and those hidden in π_0, also part of that function; the coefficients λ_i $(i = 2 \ldots I)$ of the ophelimity function (2) and those hidden in φ, also part of that function. We will also consider as constants the standard deviations τ_i of the frequency distributions of the "degrees" of human properties as present with the population; not, however, all of the $\bar{t}_i$, the average "degrees", since we assume some of them accessible to "education", supposed to be a government activity. We will assume t_0, family size, and some of the innate properties to be constant, however.

2) Secondly, there are the political parameters or *instruments, and the coefficients influenced by them*, considered constants by the "organizers" as well as the other citizens, but amenable to change by the government; as such we consider the tax rate γ, determining in its turn, as explained, some of the $\bar{t}_i$ (the "changeable" ones); further the coefficient L_1, to be compared to piece rates and supposed to be supervised by a centralized wage policy. This coefficient, according to equation (11), will determine the intensity t_1 of work, individually or collectively. Finally the level ψ of family allowances may be considered such an instrument.

3) The third category of parameters are those *chosen by the organizers* and considered given by the individual citizen choosing his job; as such we met $\bar{s}_i$ and σ_i, although we made the assumption that by the special form of π_0 (see category 1) each σ_i would happen to be chosen equal to τ_i. Also the coefficients L_i in the income scale may be grouped in this category, but we have found (cf. equations (17)) that these have to be chosen linearly dependent on the deviations $\bar{s}_i - \bar{t}_i$ between the average "degrees required" and "degrees present"; L_0, finally, will have to depend on the average productivity.

4) Finally, the fourth category of entities are those which have to be chosen by the individual citizens in order to maximize their satisfaction, in particular the individual s_i's defining their jobs and consequently their income level. The choice of the level of intensity t_1 is also an individual choice, although for simplicity's sake we have assumed that all individuals would make the same choice.

As a consequence of the process of government policy, organizers' choice and individual's choice a certain production P will be obtained that may be derived from (1):

$$P = M\left\{\pi_1 \bar{t}_1 + \sum_2^I \pi_i{}^s \bar{s}_i + \sum_2^I \pi_i{}^t \bar{t}_i + \pi_0\,(\bar{s}_i, \sigma_i)\right\} \tag{19}$$

and a certain income distribution, that may be derived form (18). Under the assumption of mutual independence of the various required properties s_i and family size the standard deviation of the logarithms of incomes can be calculated:

$$\sigma^2{}_{\log l} = \psi^2\,\tau_0{}^2 + L_1{}^2\,\pi_1{}^2\,\tau_1{}^2 + L_1{}^2 \sum_2^I \pi_i{}^2\,\tau_i{}^2 + 4\sum_2^I \lambda_i{}^2\,(\bar{s}_i - \bar{t}_i)^2\,\sigma_i{}^2 -$$

$$- 4\,L_1 \sum_2^I \lambda_i\,\pi_i\,(\bar{s}_i - \bar{t}_i)\,\sigma_i\,\tau_i \tag{20}$$

In this formula τ_1 will be zero if there are no individual differences in φ, and hence in t_1.

MODEL 09. CLOSED, DYNAMIC, MACRO, DEVELOPMENT MODEL

ACTORS — *Number:* 1, the national economy as a whole.

Income: net national product; the supply of services is supposed to be inelastic.

Spending habits: a fixed proportion of income is assumed to be spent on consumer goods; the remainder is invested.

Wealth: takes form of equipment and influences current economic process since equipment determines volume of production.

MARKETS — *Number:* 2, consumer goods and equipment; prices assumed to be constant and markets not considered explicitly.

Character: flow; but total stock of equipment also plays a role.

TECHNICAL RELATIONS — Life time T of equipment assumed to be constant; productivity of equipment φ also constant.

EQUATIONS

Income formation:	$y = v - d$	(1)
Income spending:	$y = c + s$	(2)
	$s = \sigma y$	(3)

Definition of gross product: $v = j + c$ (4)

Accumulation of equipment: $\dfrac{dw}{dt} = j - r$ (5)

This equation expresses that the stock of equipment available increases to the extent that new equipment is produced (j) after allowance has been made for replacement ($-r$).

Capital formation: $\dfrac{db}{dt} = s$ (6)

Technical: depreciation $d = \dfrac{w}{T}$ (7)

replacement $r = j_{-T}$ (8)

Here the symbol j_{-T} stands for j, T time units before; a more exact notation being j_{t-T}.

production $v = \varphi w$ (9)

This equation expresses the technical relation assumed to exist between production volume and stock of equipment (rather than between production volume and capital).

MODEL 10. CLOSED, DYNAMIC, MACRO, CYCLE MODEL (MONEY-FLOW PAPER PROFITS)

ACTORS *Number:* 1, the national economy.

Income: income calculations are based on the assumption that paper profits on stocks are an element of income, together with net income as usually defined by economists.

Supply of the national product is assumed not to be inelastic; supply price is assumed to lag behind money expenditure.

Spending habits: national expenditure depends on income calculation and lags.

Wealth: only element of wealth explicitly considered is commodity stocks, assumed to be equal to half the annual national product.

MARKETS *Number:* 1, the national product.

Character: flow.

TECHNICAL RELATION Stocks are supposed to have been acquired, in the average, one quarter previously.

EQUATIONS

All symbols represent *deviations from equilibrium values*. Time units are quarters.

Income calculation: $Y_t = X_t + \eta \, (p_{t+\frac{1}{2}} - p_{t-\frac{1}{2}})$ $\qquad$ (1)

In this equation $p_{t+\frac{1}{2}}$ stands for price level at end of period t and $p_{t-\frac{1}{2}}$ therefore for price level at beginning of period t. The difference indicates the value increase per unit of product since the average moment of acquisition of stocks. Taking the equilibrium value of national product equal to 1, we have an average value of stocks equal to 2 (namely equal to 2 quarters' production). The coefficient η may be different from 2 to the extent that not every producer follows the practice of including "paper profits" in his income calculation.

Demand: $X_{t+1} = \xi_1 Y_t + \xi_2 \, (p_{t+\frac{1}{2}} - p_{t-\frac{1}{2}})$ $\qquad$ (2)

Here ξ_1 represents the marginal propensity to spend; a term $\xi_2 \, (p_{t+\frac{1}{2}} - p_{t-\frac{1}{2}})$ has been added in order to account for the possibility of paper profits being spent in a different manner from normal income.

Supply: $p_t = \pi X_{t-\frac{1}{2}}$ $\qquad$ (3)

MODEL 11. OPEN, STATIC, MACRO, MONEY-FLOW MODEL

ACTORS

Number: 2, national economy and rest of the world.

Income: for national economy, net national product, of which supply perfectly elastic, for rest of the world not explicitly considered.

Spending habits: for national economy, see equation 2; for rest of the world: money flow of demand given.

Wealth: does not influence current economic process.

MARKETS

Number: 2, national product and import commodity.

Character: flows.

TECHNICAL RELATIONS Imports to be fixed proportion of national (gross or net) product.

EQUATIONS

Income formation: $Y = X + E - I$ $\qquad$ (1)

Income spending: $X = X_0 + \xi_1 Y$ $\qquad$ (2)

where X_0 = autonomous expenditure

ξ_1 = marginal propensity to spend.

The same conclusions as to the elasticity of demand can be drawn as in model 01.

Imports: $I = \iota Y$ (3)

In this simple model it does not make any difference whether we assume I to be a function of Y or of gross national product $X + E$, since either assumption would follow from the other.

Definition of balance of payments deficit:

$D = I - E$ (4)

In the simple model used here, the balance of payments consists only of the items of the balance of trade. In more general cases, other current items will have to be considered, which it will, however, be possible to include in the definitions of I and E; and capital items will have to be added (cf. model 15).

MODEL 12. OPEN, STATIC, MACRO, MONEY-AND-PRODUCT-FLOW MODEL

ACTORS   *Number:* 2, national economy and rest of the world.

Income: *national economy*, equal to net national product; supply of product not perfectly elastic; *rest of the world*, not explicitly considered; supply of import commodity not perfectly elastic.

Spending habits: expenditure of national economy dependent on income and price level; expenditures of rest of the world for national (export) product dependent on price level.

Wealth: does not influence current economic process.

MARKETS   *Number:* 3, national product sold at home and at foreign market; and import commodity.

Character: flow

TECHNICAL RELATIONS   Import volume assumed to be proportional to volume of physical production (may also be considered as a demand equation for market of import commodity).

EQUATIONS   All symbols represent deviations from initial situation.

Income formation: $Y = X + E - I$ (1)

Demand: spending of national income:

$$X = X_0 + \xi_1 Y + \xi_2 p^x \tag{2}$$

where X_0 = autonomous expenditure

ξ_1 = marginal propensity to spend

ξ_2 = price coefficient of expenditure, related to elasticity of demand;

for export product: $e = e_0 - \varepsilon_1 (p^e - p^w)$ (3)

where e_0 = autonomous export demand

ε_1 = price coefficient of demand, related to elasticity.

Supply: These will be written in the form of price fixation equations [1]

$$p^x = \pi_1{}^x v + \pi_3{}^x p^i \tag{4}$$

$$p^e = \pi_1{}^e v + \pi_3{}^e p^i + \pi_4{}^e p^w \tag{5}$$

Here the terms with p^i represent the influence of import prices as cost elements and the term with p^w, in the case of p^e, of competing export prices. The coefficients $\pi_1{}^x$ and $\pi_1{}^e$ are related to the flexibility of prices, i.e. the inverted elasticities of supply.

TECHNICAL

import demand: $i = \iota v$ (6)

volume of production: $v = x + e$ (7)

Definition: value [2]: $X = \bar{x}\, p^x + x$ (8)

$E = \bar{e} p^e + e$ (8)

$I = \bar{\imath}\, p^i + i$ (10)

balance of payments deficit: $D = I - E$ (11)

For a discussion of the numerical values assumed for the coefficients cf. model 14.

MODEL 13. OPEN, STATIC, MACRO, MONEY, PRODUCT AND FACTOR FLOW MODEL

ACTORS   *Number:* 3, wage earners, independents and rest of the world.

Income: for wage earners and independents together equal to net national product; supply of product not perfectly elastic; for rest of the world not

---

[1] Cf. e.g. J. Tinbergen, Econometrics, Philadelphia 1951, p. 29 and 166.

[2] These equations are linear approximations neglecting products of deviations and assuming that $\bar{p}^x = \bar{p}^e = \bar{p}^i = 1$.

explicitly considered; supply of import commodities not perfectly elastic.

Spending habits: expenditure of wage earners and independents together dependent on income and price level; expenditure of rest of world for national (export) product dependent on price level.

Wealth: does not influence current economic process.

MARKETS   *Number:* 4, national product sold at home and at foreign market; import commodity and labour.

Character: flow

TECHNICAL RELATIONS   Import volume proportional to volume of physical production.

EQUATIONS   All symbols represent deviations from initial situation. For simplicity's sake it has been assumed that $p^i = p^w = 0$.

Income formation: $Y = X + E - I$ (1)

Demand: spending of national income:

$$X = X_0 + \xi_1 Y + \xi_2 p^x \tag{2}$$

(for explanation cf. model 12). For simplicity's sake it has been assumed that there exists no difference in marginal propensity to spend between wage earners and independents. [1]

for export product: $e = e_0 - \varepsilon_1 p^e$ (3)

Supply: $p^x = \pi_1{}^x v + \pi_2{}^x l$ (4)

$p^e = \pi_1{}^e v + \pi_2{}^e l$ (5)

Here $\pi_2{}^x$ and $\pi_2{}^e$ indicate the influence on home and export prices respectively, exerted by a unit increase in wage rates. If prices are exactly equal to marginal costs, and if initial prices as well as wage rates are chosen equal to 1, $\pi_2{}^x$ and $\pi_2{}^e$ represent marginal labour quota. If prices are fixed in a different way—possible because of imperfect competition—, e.g. by applying profit margins, themselves proportional to certain primary cost elements, $\pi_2{}^x$ and $\pi_2{}^e$ may surpass marginal labour quota. On the other hand, export prices may, in the short run, be dependent on the price level of competing countries, which

[1] For a model where such a difference has been assumed to exist, cf. Central Economic Plan 1955, Netherlands Central Planning Bureau.

may diminish the influence of wage rates on
these prices.

Technical: import demand: $\quad i \; = \iota v$ (6)
volume of production: $\quad v \; = x + e$ (7)
Definition: value equations: $\quad X = \bar{x}p^x + x$ (8)
$\quad\quad\quad\quad\quad\quad\quad\quad\quad E = \bar{e}p^e + e$ (9)
$\quad\quad\quad\quad\quad\quad\quad\quad\quad I \; = i$ (10)
balance of payments: $\quad D = I - E$ (11)

For a discussion of the numerical values given
to the coefficients cf. model 14.

MODEL 14. OPEN, STATIC, MACRO MONEY, PRODUCT AND FACTOR FLOW MODEL WITH EXCHANGE RATES

The only difference from the preceding model is the introduction, as a separate instrument of policy, of the exchange rate of the national currency (in terms of gold, say); no general description will be given. It may be said that 5 markets are now considered, the fifth being the market for national currency; but it should be added that this latter market, as well as the labour market, are highly schematized.

Because of the similarity with the previous two models, the equations may be given without further explanation, except for the new terms.

$$Y = X + E - I \tag{1}$$
$$X = X_0 + \xi_1 Y + \xi_2 p^x \tag{2}$$
$$e = e_0 - \varepsilon_1 (p^e - p^w + k) \tag{3}$$
$$p^x = \pi_1{}^x v + \pi_2{}^x l + \pi_3{}^x (p^i - k) \tag{4}$$
$$p^e = \pi_1{}^e v + \pi_2{}^e l + \pi_3{}^e (p^i - k) + \pi_4{}^e (p^w - k) \tag{5}$$
$$i = \iota v \tag{6}$$
$$v = x + e \tag{7}$$
$$X = \bar{x}p^x + x \tag{8}$$
$$E = \bar{e}p^e + e \tag{9}$$
$$I = \bar{i}(p^i - k) + i \tag{10}$$
$$D = I - E \tag{11}$$

This model is to be considered as the general form from which 12 and 13 derive by special assumptions. The foreign price levels p^i and p^w are now being assumed to be quoted in terms of gold; the quotations in national currency will therefore be $p^i - k$ and $p^w - k$, respectively. Model 12 will be obtained by taking l and k equal to 0; indicating that these two instruments are not supposed to be used. Model 13 will be obtained by assuming both the exchange rate and the foreign prices p^i and p^w equal to 0, i.e. non-variable.

The *numerical values of the coefficients and the other constants* will now be discussed for all three models. *Initial values* of all prices have already been chosen equal to 1. [1] As a consequence, for the initial period, volume figures for each flow of goods or factors will be equal to the corresponding value figure, e.g. $\bar{x} = \bar{X}$, $\bar{i} = \bar{I}$ etc. We will assume that there is balance of payments equilibrium in the initial situation, i.e. $\bar{I} = \bar{E}$ and hence $\bar{i} = \bar{e}$. Finally we assume that national income was equal to 1, or $\bar{Y} = 1$. It follows that $\bar{x} = 1$. From the figures of the national accounts we then deduce the values that have to be given to $\bar{I}$ and $\bar{E}$, since these are expressed in the same units as Y and cannot therefore anymore be chosen freely. In the "central case" C we assume that $\bar{I} = \bar{E} = \bar{i} = \bar{e} = 0.5$, representing a country with intensive international trade, comparable to the Netherlands. In a few examples we will also consider cases where trade is less intensive (A, where it is completely absent and B, where $\bar{i} = \bar{e} = 0.25$) or more intensive (D, where $\bar{i} = \bar{e} = 1.0$).

Variations in e_0 are indicative of changes in foreign demand for the economy's products. We will not give specific numerical values to e_0, leaving this to the reader; but we will, in a number of examples where variation in foreign demand is not assumed to occur, take $e_0 = 0$.

Some of the *coefficients* will depend on the intensity of the country's international trade and others not. Apart from these variations we will consider three other types of variation. The most important aspect is the length of the period considered: a distinction will be made between *short-term* (s) and *long-term* (l) values. In a complete dynamic system the short-term values of the coefficient will indicate a variable's reaction to a simultaneous change in another variable whereas the long-term values indicate the total influence exerted by simultaneous and lagged changes in the latter variable. Another aspect to be considered is the *cyclical position:* some coefficients will be higher in boom conditions (b) than in normal (n). This reflects the curvilinearity of certain relations.

Finally we will make some incidental changes in the coefficients of the spending equation, mainly because these coefficients have a considerable influence on some results and are not too well known.

---

[1] This is only possible if for any one commodity only one price is introduced, since it can then be obtained by a proper choice of the unit of that commodity. Of course, one may, even if a price is not 1, introduce an index number, but this complicates the relations.

Variation in the *intensity of foreign trade* is only assumed in problem 121, using model 12.

The coefficients in this model varying with the intensity of a country's foreign trade are ι, π_3^x and π_3^e, which are assumed to be proportional to $\frac{\bar{\imath}}{1+\bar{\imath}}$, the ratio of imports to G.N.P.; π_1^x and π_1^e which are assumed to be proportional to $\frac{1}{1+\bar{\imath}}$, the ratio of net to gross N.P.; and ε_1, taken proportional to $\bar{e}$. If variations in the intensity of foreign trade were considered in models 13 and 14, the other coefficients appearing in the price equations would also have to be varied. This may be left to the reader.

The marginal propensity to spend ξ_1 has been assumed to be 0.8; a fixed physical expenditure ξ_2 of 0.1 and, in the initial situation, a fixed nominal expenditure X_0 of 0.1 have been assumed in addition.

The following table summarizes the values of the coefficients for the various intensities of foreign trade distinguished in the s–n examples of model 12:

Table 1 (App.) Values of coefficients in model 12·
(short-term reactions with normal cyclical position)

Case	$\bar{\imath}=\bar{e}$	$\dfrac{\bar{\imath}}{1+\bar{\imath}}$	$\iota=\pi_3^x$	π_3^e	$\dfrac{1}{1+\bar{\imath}}$	π_1^x	π_1^e	ε_1	π_4^e	ξ_1	ξ_2
Asn	0	0	0	0	1	0.15	.	.	.	0.8	0.1
Bsn	0.25	0.20	0.20	0.10	0.80	0.12	0.06	0.5	0.5	0.8	0.1
Csn	0.5	0.33	0.33	0.17	0.67	0.10	0.05	1.0	0.5	0.8	0.1
Dsn	1.0	0.50	0.50	0.25	0.50	0.08	0.04	2.0	0.5	0.8	0.1

In the problems 131, 141, 142 and 143, using models 13 and 14 respectively (cf. appendix II), a distinction between short-term and long-term reactions has been made. Short-term reactions may be said to be reactions during the same year, long-term reactions are those occurring after a few years.

The distinction applies first of all to the coefficient ε_1, related to the elasticity of demand for export products. For short-run calculations we will, in agreement with Dutch experiences, take it equal to 1, corresponding with an elasticity of 2; for long-term calculations a value of 2 will be assumed. Similarly we assume that the long-term value of π_2^x and π_2^e, the reaction of a unit change in wage rates on prices, will be higher than the short-term value: the reason being that in the long run independents tend to increase their income along with the general increase in income. The maximum value for π_2^x will be 0.67, being the total national income component in the price $\bar{p}^x$ ($= 1$). The situation as to the price formation of export products is more complicated. Short-run movements of export prices appear to react to changes in costs only half as intensively as do home price movements; in addition to this reaction there appears to be a reaction to competing prices, i.e. export prices of other, competing, countries. Accordingly the coefficients have the following short-term values:

$\pi_1^e = 0.05$ $\pi_2^e = 0.17$ $\pi_3^e = 0.17$ (being half the corresponding values for home market prices) and $\pi_4^e = 0.5$.

In the longer run it would seem probable that there be a more pronounced influence of costs, since prices cannot diverge too much from costs without causing either losses or excessive profits leading to adaptations of various types. At the same time it may, however, be maintained, that there will be a complete adaptation to competing world-market prices; this seeming contradiction being solved by a change in composition of exports tending to make both tendencies possible at the same time: those products will be preferred for which costs do not exceed world market prices and products for which costs are lowered in comparison to world market prices will be produced in increased quantities, so that costs rise again to that level. Since the essential point in our problems is to know how intensively the economy reacts upon her own instruments, we will choose the long-term values of the above coefficients equal to:

$$\pi_1^e = 0.1, \ \pi_2^e = 0.67, \ \pi_3^e = 0.33 \text{ and } \pi_4^e = 0.$$

The following table summarizes the values of the coefficients used in models 13 and 14:

Table 2 (App.) Coefficients used in models 13 and 14
(Central case C, with normal cyclical position)

Case	ξ_1	ξ_2	ε_1	π_1^x	π_2^x	π_3^x	π_1^e	π_2^e	π_3^e	π_4^e	ι
Csn	0.8	0.1	1	0.1	0.33	0.33	0.05	0.17	0.17	0.50	0.33
Cln	0.9	0.1	2	0.1	0.67	0.33	0.1	0.67	0.33	0	0.33

Variations in *cyclical positions* are assumed mostly to affect the value of coefficients π_1^x and π_1^e; in boom conditions these will become high, expressing the tendency to steep price rises if full employment of capacity is approached. They have been assumed equal to five times their value under normal cyclical conditions, i.e. $\pi_1^x = 0.5$ and $\pi_1^e = 0.25$. Accordingly the following set of coefficients has been used in examples referring to short-term boom conditions (sb):

Table 3 (App.) Coefficients used in models 12, 13 and 14 in short-term boom conditions:

Case	ξ_1	ξ_2	ε_1	π_1^x	π_2^x	π_3^x	π_1^e	π_2^e	π_3^e	π_4^e	ι
Csb	0.8	0.1	1	0.5	0.33	0.33	0.25	0.17	0.17	0.50	0.33

The *incidental variations* in ξ_1 and ξ_2 used in model 12 are found in the table below:

Table 4 (App.) Coefficients used in 2 incidental variations on model 12
(central case C, normal cyclical position, short-term reactions)

Case	ξ_1	ξ_2	ε_1	$\pi_1{}^x$	$\pi_3{}^x$	$\pi_1{}^e$	$\pi_3{}^e$	ι
C'sn	0.9	0.05	1	0.10	0.33	0.05	0.17	0.33
C''sn	0.7	0.15	1	0.10	0.33	0.05	0.17	0.33

It might have been assumed that the high value of ξ_1 in C' would also occur in boom conditions, and the lower value in C'' in a period of depression. It may be left to the reader to calculate examples with these values.

MODEL 15. OPEN, STATIC, MACRO, MONEY-FLOW AND ASSET MODEL

ACTORS   *Number:* 3, national economy excl. banks (or: "public"), banks and "rest of the world".

Income: public, net national product; supply of products inelastic; *banks*, no income; *rest of the world*, not explicitly considered; inelastic supply of imports.

Spending habits: public, as in previous models, but limited by liquid assets available; *banks*, no current expenditure; *rest of the world*, demand for exports considered given.

Nature and origin of wealth: for al three actors consisting of bonds and liquid assets. Increase in wealth results from income surplus.

Investment habits: investment into bonds and liquid assets depends on national income and interest rates.

MARKETS   *Number:* 5, one for national product (flow), and four markets for assets (stock character), namely bonds and liquidities in the national economy and the "rest of the world".

EQUATIONS

Income formation: $Y = X + E - I$ (1)

Income spending: $X = X_0 + \xi_1 Y + \xi_2 n_1 + \xi_3 n_3 + \xi_4 M_{\frac{1}{2}} + \xi_5 M_{\frac{1}{3}}$ (2)

Destination of income surplus (or financing of income deficit):

Import equation: $I = \iota Y$ (3)

Financing equation for public (i.e. non-banks), including the private non-bank and the government:

$$Y - X = n_1 \Delta B_1^1 + n_3 \Delta B_3^1 + \Delta M_2^1 + k^{-1}\Delta M_3^1 - n_1 \Delta B_1 \tag{4}$$

Financing equation for foreign countries:

$$I - E = n_1 \Delta B_1^3 + n_3 \Delta B_3^3 + \Delta M_2^3 + k^{-1}\Delta M_3^3 - n_3 \Delta B_3 - k^{-1}\Delta M_3 \tag{5}$$

Equations (4) and (5) express that a surplus of income over expenditure will be (financially) invested in increases in asset holdings, as far as not obtained by creation of assets; that is in the purchase of assets from other sectors.

Definition equation for balance of payments deficit:

$$D = I - E + n_1 \Delta B_1^1 + n_3 \Delta B_3^1 - n_1 \Delta B_1 \tag{6}$$

Definition equations for total wealth of the three sectors:

$$A^1 = n_1 B_1^1 + n_3 B_3^1 + M_2^1 + k^{-1}M_3^1 \tag{7}$$
$$A^2 = n_1 B_1^2 + n_3 B_3^2 + M_2^2 + k^{-1}M_3^2 \tag{8}$$
$$A^3 = n_1 B_1^3 + n_3 B_3^3 + M_2^3 + k^{-1}M_3^3 \tag{9}$$

Demand for the distribution of assets over the four items:

$$B_1^1/M_2^1 = \beta_1^1(A^1, n_1, n_3, k) \tag{10}$$
$$B_3^1/M_2^1 = \beta_3^1(A^1, n_1, n_3, k) \tag{11}$$
$$M_3^1/M_2^1 = \mu_3^1(A^1, n_1, n_3, k) \tag{12}$$

and similar equations with superscripts 2 and 3 (13)–(18)

Supply of assets created by sectors 2 and 3:

$$\Delta M_2 = \mu_2(Y, n_1, n_3, k) \tag{19}$$
$$\Delta B_3 = \beta_3(E, n_1, n_3, k) \tag{20}$$
$$\Delta M_3 = \mu_3(E, n_1, n_3, k) \tag{21}$$

No such equation has been introduced for sector 1, since we assume that ΔB_1 or, alternatively, n_1, is used as an instrument of policy, that is given in an analytical problem or unknown in a policy problem.

Equilibrium equations for assets:

$$B_1 = B_1^1 + B_1^2 + B_1^3 \tag{22}$$
$$M_2 = M_2^1 + M_2^2 + M_2^3 \tag{23}$$
$$B_3 = B_3^1 + B_3^2 + B_3^3 \tag{24}$$

$$M_3 = M_3^1 + M_3^2 + M_3^3 \qquad\qquad (25)$$

These equations are comparable with the equations expressing balance between supply of and demand for each of the types of assets and implicitly determine the prices n_1, n_3 and k as well as the quantity of money M_3^2 held by the banking sector.

Wherever the symbol Δ is used this represents the increase of the variable concerned during the period considered; the initial values are considered predetermined.

This model represents the simplest conceivable way of describing the flow of funds between the three sectors here distinguished, namely 1: the national economy excluding the banking system, 2: the banking system and 3: the rest of the world. The stocks to be considered must, as a minimum, be stocks of two types of assets, money M and other financial assets B, for brevity's sake to be called "bonds". It is characteristic for these assets that they can be obtained, by any of the sectors, either by exchange (purchase) or by creation (issue). We assume that sector 1 can only create "bonds", sector 2 only money and the rest of the world both. Because of this twofold possibility of obtaining assets we are forced to distinguish between the owner (upper index) and the debtor (lower index). It is also unavoidable to introduce a number of prices of assets; but they must be expressed in terms of one of them, for which we choose national money. The symbol k represents the price of national money in terms of foreign money and hence appears to the power -1 in some equations: (4), (5), (7), (8) and (9).

MODEL 16. OPEN, STATIC, MICRO, MONEY, PRODUCT AND FACTOR
      FLOW AND PUBLIC FINANCE MODEL

ACTORS   *Number:* 4, wage earners, independents, government and
                      "rest of the world".

          Income: *wage earners:* total wages; supply of labour
                      inelastic;
                      independents: net national income minus wages;
                      supply of products not inelastic;
                      government: direct and indirect tax receipts minus
                      expenditure;
                      rest of the world: not specified.

     Spending habits: *wage earners* spend all income on consumer goods;
                      independents spend all income after direct tax,
                      in a fixed proportion between consumer and
                      investment goods;
                      government spending is independent of tax

receipts (but if exact balance of payments equilibrium is a target of policy it follows that there will be equality between income and expenditure);

rest of the world: demand for export products not inelastic.

Markets   *Number:* 5, consumer goods and investment goods sold at home; export goods sold abroad, import commodity and labour.

Technical relations   Imports and labour assumed to be linearly dependent on volume of production.

Equations   All variables are deviations from initial situation.

Income formation: total income:

$$Y = C^F + J + E - I \tag{1}$$

Because of the distinction made between consumer and investment goods the term X in previous models has now been split into $C^F + J$. Because of the existence of indirect taxes (only levied from home-sold consumer goods) a distinction between the value of home-sold consumer goods at market prices C and at factor cost C^F has to be made. The relation between these two variables is given by eq. (10) and (11).

wages:
$$L = \bar{L} (a + l) \tag{2}$$

The form of this equation differs from equations like (8)–(10) in model 12 (where they first appeared), because a is not measured in the same way as e.g. x in equation (8) in model 12; $\bar{\bar{a}}$ is an index number of employment with its base value $\bar{a} = 1$.

independents' income: $\quad Z = Y - L \tag{3}$

Demand; consumer goods at home market:

$$C = C_0 + \gamma (1 - \bar{\theta}) Z - \gamma \bar{Z}\theta + L \tag{4}$$

In this equation the first term represents government expenditure and the last term consumer expenditure by workers. The two remaining terms derive from the expression for consumption expenditure by independents C_z of which the absolute amount is given by

$$\bar{\bar{C}}_z = \gamma (1 - \bar{\bar{\theta}}) \bar{\bar{Z}}$$

i.e. the proportion γ of income after direct tax. The assumptions involved are relatively simple, e.g. a proportionate tax on $\bar{\bar{Z}}$ and a fixed average propensity to consume. It would not be difficult to generalize these assumptions; this may be left to the reader.

investment goods at home market:

$$J = (1 - \gamma)(1 - \bar{\theta}) Z - (1 - \gamma) \bar{Z}\theta \qquad (5)$$

This equation expresses that the remainder of income after tax $\bar{\bar{Z}}(1 - \bar{\theta})$, after deducting consumption from income, is invested.

export goods: $e = -\varepsilon_1 p$ (6)

Here the autonomous component in export demand e_0 has been assumed to be unchanged $(e_0 = 0)$; further it is assumed that prices of all products (consumer goods, investment goods and export goods) are the same ("national price level" p) and that no indirect taxes are paid on export goods.

Supply; price fixation equation:

$$p = \pi_1 v + \pi_2 l \qquad (7)$$

Since foreign prices and the exchange rate are assumed not to vary, this equation takes its simplest form. It would not be difficult to introduce equations with different coefficients for consumer goods, investment goods and export goods.

Technical: $i = \iota v$ (8)

$a = \alpha v$ (9)

These equations express proportionality between changes in production volume on the one hand, and imports as well as volume of labour employed on the other hand.

Definition: $C^F = \bar{c}p + c$ (10)

$C = \bar{c}(p + \tau) + (1 + \bar{\tau}) c$ (11)

$J = \bar{\jmath}p + j$ (12)

$I = i$ (13)

$E = \bar{e}p + e$ (14)

$D = I - E$ (15)

$v = c + j + e$ (16)

Social equilibrium coefficient:

$$L = \lambda Z \qquad (17)$$

This equation expresses the fact that a certain preconceived ratio between increases in labour income and "non-labour" income may be aimed at.

Alternatively this equation will be replaced by another defining the home price level for consumer goods:

$$p' = p + \tau \qquad (17')$$

The numerical values of the coefficients and constants will be chosen in a way similar to the one followed with model 14, but slightly different only where the simpler structure of 16 makes this necessary. This refers primarily to the neglect of the difference between home prices and export prices, as to their response to competing prices abroad. Apart from this feature, short-term reaction coefficients have been chosen for a country with imports normally equal to one-half of net national income. Model 16 is more complicated than model 14 as regards the fiscal structure; accordingly some new assumptions as to this sector have been necessary. All price indices are equal to 1 in the base period.

We have chosen $\bar{L} = \bar{Z} = \bar{e} = 0.5$, meaning that in the base period net national income at factor cost $\bar{Y} = 1$ and is distributed in equal parts between workers and independents; in addition, exports (and imports $\bar{\imath}$) $= 0.5$. The factor value of consumption $\bar{C}^F = \bar{c} = 0.9$, that of investment $\bar{\jmath} = 0.1$. The tax rates are $\bar{\tau} = 0.1$, meaning an indirect tax of some 11 Pct on home consumption and $\bar{\theta} = 0.3$, meaning a tax of 30 Pct on non-labour income. Taxes on labour income are taken as zero. The marginal propensity to consume γ for independents, calculated on the basis of income *after* tax, $= 0.7$, and the marginal propensity to invest $= 0.3$, almost equal to the average propensity in the base period

$$\frac{0.1}{0.7 \times 0.5}$$

The elasticity of demand for export products has been again taken $= 2$, making $\varepsilon_1 = 1$; the flexibility of the home price level is taken as 0.15, equivalent with $\pi_1 = 0.1$; the wage coefficient in prices $\pi_2 = 0.33$ exactly corresponds to the average labour quota in the base period

$$\frac{\bar{L}}{\bar{v}} = \frac{0.5}{1.5}$$

The marginal import quota ι has also been taken equal to the average quota

$$0.33 \left(= \frac{0.5}{1.5} \right)$$

Finally the marginal labour quota in equation (9) has been taken less than the average labour quota, actually about 0.55 times that quota, in accordance with numerous investigations [1]; $a = 0.40$ seems to be a fair estimate. That the wage coefficient in prices is nevertheless equal to the average labour quota probably has to be explained by the custom of calculating some of the entrepreneurial income on the basis of the prevailing wage level.

MODEL 17. OPEN, STATIC, MICRO, MONEY FLOW AND BANKING MODEL

ACTORS   *Number:* 4, central bank, private banks, rest of the economy and "rest of the world".

Income: for banks not considered explicitly; for rest of the economy net national product; for rest of the world not considered explicitly.

Spending habits: for rest of the economy as in previous models (cf. model 11).

Wealth, categories considered:

Central Bank, assets: gold (Au), rediscounts (B^R); Central Bank, liabilities: money in circulation (M), Bankers' "reserves" (R). Private Banks, assets: bills and advances (B^B), reserves with Central Bank (R); Private Banks, liabilities: deposits (M'), rediscounts (B^R).

Wealth, origin: gold stock increases or decreases as a consequence of balance of payments position. Rediscounts: decision of private banks (eq. (3)). Money in circulation and deposits: decision of rest of the economy, (eqs. (6) and (7)). Bankers' reserves: balancing item with Central Bank. Bills and advances: balancing item with private banks.

MARKETS   *Number:* 3, central bank credit, private credit and national product.

[1] P. J. Verdoorn, Praeadvies 1952 voor de Vereniging voor de Staathuishoudkunde, where a slightly lower figure has been chosen. Our figure has to be considered as a round figure.

Technical relations   reserve requirements, taking the form of boundary conditions:

for Central Bank: $Au \geq aM$

for private banks: $R \geq \varrho M'$

Equations

Balance sheet,

Central Bank: $M + R = Au + B^R$ (1)

private banks: $M' + B^R = B^B + R$ (2)

These balance sheets are of course simplified. They might easily be made more complicated; an attempt is here being made to present some essential features in the simplest form conceivable.

Rediscounting decision of private banks:

$$B^R = \beta_1 (m' - m) + \beta_0 \qquad (3)$$

Here β_1 indicates the intensity with which the private banks react on an interest difference between the private discount rate m' they earn on B^B, and the official discount rate m they have to pay if they, by rediscounting with the Central Bank, are able to maintain a certain level of lending. Negative values of B^R may be interpreted as additional reserves.

Supply of credit, given the form of price fixing equation:

Central Bank: $m = \mu (aM - Au) + \mu_0$ (4)

private banks: $m' = \mu' (\varrho M' - R) + \mu'_0$ (5)

According to these equations the official discount rate is raised or lowered in parallel with the difference between required gold stock and actual gold stock. There may be an autonomous element in the rate represented by μ_0. Similarly the private discount rate, taken here to represent the whole structure of private rates, moves parallel with the difference between required reserves and actual reserves and shows an autonomous element μ'_0.

Demand for (Central-Bank) money:

$$M = \mu_1 Y - \mu_2 m + \mu_3 \qquad (6)$$

Demand for deposits: $M' = \mu'_1 Y - \mu'_2 m' + \mu'_3$ (7)

Both types of money are assumed to be demanded in quantities which depend on national income as well as on the corresponding rates of interest.

National income formation: $Y = \eta_1 X_0 - \eta_2 m' + \eta_3$ (8)

Here X_0 represents autonomous national expenditure, as far as considered a datum, and η_1 the Keynesian multiplier; it is, moreover, assumed that autonomous expenditure is negatively influenced by the private discount rate.

Gold accumulation: $Au = Au_{-1} + E - \iota Y + a' (m - m_{-1})$ (9)

The equation expresses that the increase of gold stock over its previous-year value Au_{-1} equals the balance of exports E over imports, assumed to be proportional to national income, plus an influx of foreign short-term capital, assumed to be proportional to the rise in discount rate since the previous time unit. This assumption is equivalent to supposing that holdings of national debt titles by the citizens and institutions of the "rest of the world" are dependent on the rate of interest they earn on such holdings.

About the numerical values of the coefficients much less can be said than in the preceding models. The relations in the financial sphere have not been so well investigated as those in the general models; partly because some attempts seem to have shown that their influence on the changes in the main variables is only limited. [1]

MODEL 18. OPEN, STATIC, MICRO, HORIZONTAL, MONEY, PRODUCT AND FACTOR FLOW MODEL

ACTORS   *Number:* 4, two industries, all households of the economy, "rest of the world".

Income: industries, no income; supply of products not inelastic;

households, net national product; supply of services elastic;

rest of the world, not explicitly considered;

[1] Cf. J. Tinbergen, Business Cycles in the U.S. 1919–1932, League of Nations, Geneva 1939, and Business Cycles in the United Kingdom 1870–1914, Royal Netherlands Academy of Sciences, Amsterdam 1951.

Spending habits:	households, total amount spent on each product dependent only on income (i.e. price elasticities $= 1$);	
	rest of the world, demand for export products depends on price of product.	
Wealth:	not explicitly considered.	
MARKETS *Number:*	2, each product being sold at home and abroad at the same price.	
Character:	flows.	
TECHNICAL RELATIONS	It is assumed that the quantities of imports and of labour needed per unit of product in each industry have been given, and that a given change in these constants occurs.	

EQUATIONS · Symbols indicate deviations from initial situation

Income formation:
$$Y = X^1 + X^2 + E^1 + E^2 - I \tag{1}$$

Demand:
$$X^1 = \xi^1 Y \tag{2}$$
$$X^2 = \xi^2 Y \tag{3}$$
$$e^1 = -\varepsilon^1 p^1 \tag{4}$$
$$e^2 = -\varepsilon^2 p^2 \tag{5}$$

Supply:
$$p^1 = a^1 \tag{6}$$
$$p^2 = a^2 \tag{7}$$

Technical:
$$i^1 = \iota^1 v^1 \tag{8}$$
$$i^2 = \iota^2 v^2 \tag{9}$$
$$a^1 = \bar{a}^1 v^1 + \bar{v}^1 a^1 \tag{10}$$
$$a^2 = \bar{a}^2 v^2 + \bar{v}^2 a^2 \tag{11}$$

Definition:
$$x^1 = X^1 - \bar{x}^1 p^1 \tag{12}$$
$$x^2 = X^2 - \bar{x}^2 p^2 \tag{13}$$
$$E^1 = e^1 + \bar{e}^1 p^1 \tag{14}$$
$$E^2 = e^2 + \bar{e}^2 p^2 \tag{15}$$
$$v^1 = x^1 + e^1 \tag{16}$$
$$v^2 = x^2 + e^2 \tag{17}$$
$$u = a^1 + a^2 \tag{18}$$
$$D = -E^1 - E^2 + I \tag{19}$$
$$I = i^1 + i^2 \tag{20}$$

Since in this model the coefficients a^1 and a^2 are assumed to change, we have applied the same notation as with variables, namely, $\bar{a}^1$ and $\bar{a}^2$ to indicate initial values and a^1 and a^2 to indicate changes.

MODEL 19. OPEN, STATIC, MICRO, HORIZONTAL, MONEY AND
          PRODUCT FLOW MODEL

ACTORS   *Number:* $H + 3$, namely H industries, all households of
                the economy, the government and the "rest of
                the world".

          Income: industries: sales of their products the supply of
                which is assumed to be inelastic;
                government: not considered explicitly;
                households: derives from total expenditure; the
                supply of services is supposed to be inelastic;
                rest of the world: not considered explicitly.

          Spending habits: industries: not considered explicitly;
                households: demand for the various products
                depends on income and on all prices;
                government: expenditure autonomous;
                rest of the world: demand for exports depends
                on price level of product.

          Wealth: not considered explicitly.

MARKETS   *Number:* $2H + 1$, for each of the products at home and
                abroad; and labour.

          Character: flows.

TECHNICAL RELATIONS   Imports and labour needed per unit of product
                constants for each product.

EQUATIONS   Symbols indicate deviations from initial situation

Income formation: $\quad Y = \Sigma_k (X^{Fk} + E^k) - I + X_0 \qquad\qquad$ (1)

Income spending: $\quad X^h = \xi^h Y + \Sigma_k \xi^{hk} p'^k \qquad h = 1 \ldots H \quad$ (2)

Demand for exports: $\quad e^h = -\varepsilon^h p^h \qquad\qquad h = 1 \ldots H \quad$ (3)

Supply: $\quad p'^h = \pi^h l + \tau^h \qquad\qquad h = 1 \ldots H \quad$ (4)

$\quad p^h = \pi^h l \qquad\qquad\qquad h = 1 \ldots H \quad$ (5)

Technical: $\quad i^h = \iota^h v^h \qquad\qquad\qquad h = 1 \ldots H \quad$ (6)

$\quad a^h = a^h v^h \qquad\qquad\qquad h = 1 \ldots H \quad$ (7)

Definition: $\quad x^h = X^{Fh} - \bar{x}^h p^h \qquad\quad h = 1 \ldots H \quad$ (8)

$\quad E^h = e^h + \bar{e}^h p^h \qquad\qquad h = 1 \ldots H \quad$ (9)

$\quad I = \Sigma_k i^k \qquad\qquad\qquad\qquad$ (10)

$\quad D = I - \Sigma_k E^k \qquad\qquad\qquad$ (11)

$\quad v^h = x^h + e^h \qquad\qquad\qquad h = 1 \ldots H \quad$ (12)

$\quad X^h = X^{Fh} (1 + \bar{\tau}^h) + \overline{X}^{Fh} \tau^h \quad h = 1 \ldots H \quad$ (13)

MODEL 20. OPEN, DYNAMIC, MACRO, INVESTMENT PROJECT APPRAISAL MODEL

ACTORS   *Number:* 3, program sector (consisting of a "program" of projects to be selected), rest of the economy and rest of the world.

Income: for private and public sector: net product of those sectors; for rest of the world not explicitly considered; supply of products inelastic; for private sector determined by capital available; for public sector dependent on choice of projects to be selected.

Spending habits: a fraction ξ of all income, plus capital import spent; foreign demand for national product dependent on price level.

Wealth: does not influence demand for products.

MARKETS   *Number:* 3, national product and the scarce factors, capital and foreign exchange.

Character: flow markets.

TECHNICAL RELATIONS   For private sector, factor demand assumed to be proportional to volume of production; for public sector assumed given and different for each project.

EQUATIONS   All variables in equation (1) to (15) should carry a lower index t and are supposed to apply to each time unit; the first period considered is $t = 1$.

Income formation:
$$Y^o = p\,v^o - p^i\,i^o - \delta\,p\,b^o \tag{1}$$
$$Y^h = p\,v^h - p^i\,i^h - \delta\,p\,b^h - K^{th}\,m^i \tag{2}$$

The projects of which the program sector is composed are indicated by the index h; a certain number of h's has to be selected by the policy-maker. The rest of the economy is indicated by the index 0. Equation (1) is constructed according to the usual definition of a sector's contribution to national income (where no inter-sector supplies have been assumed). The last term on the right-hand side represents depreciation allowances. Equation (2) in addition contains a deduction of interest on foreign debts K^{th} incurred for the execution of project h.

Income distribution: $Z^o = \xi^o\,Y^o$ (3)

$Z^h = \xi^h\,Y^h$ (4)

The proportion of income paid out to "independents", chosen here to represent those who save part of their income, is assumed to vary from project to project.

Demand:

$$x = \xi\ \frac{Y^o + \varSigma\,Y^h + \varSigma\,\dot{K}^{ih}}{p} \qquad (5)$$

This demand covers demand for all types of goods. It is assumed that a fraction ξ of income plus capital imports is spent.

$e = e^{*} - \varepsilon\,p$ (6)

Here e^{*} represents the autonomous component in export demand.

$S = \sigma^1\,(Z^o + \varSigma\,Z^h - T^d) + \sigma^2\,T$ (7)

Private savings are derived from private independents' income after direct taxes with a marginal propensity to save σ^1 and public saving from total taxes T with a propensity σ^2.

$i = \iota^o\,v^o$ (8)

Supply: $\beta\,v^o = b^o$ (9)

This is an approximation to the production function where β is the "capital coefficient" for gross product.

$$\dot{K}^{ih} = p^i\,i^h - \frac{K^{ih}}{\tau} \qquad (10)$$

Here $\dot{K}^{ih}$ represents net capital imports for each project, it being assumed that gross foreign credits supplied in each year are equal to the imports needed for the project.

Balance: $v^o + \varSigma\,v^h = e + x + \delta\,p\,(b^o + \varSigma b^h)$ (11)

$p\,(b^o + \varSigma'\,b^h) = S + \varSigma'\,\dot{K}^{ih}$ (12)

This equation represents the balance equation for capital; the left-hand side representing net demand for and the right-hand side net supply of savings.

Definition:
$$\tilde{Y}^o = p\,v^o - \tilde{k}^{-1}\,p^i\,i^o - \delta\,p b^o \qquad (13)$$
$$\tilde{Y}^h = p\,v^h - \tilde{k}^{-1}\,(p^i\,i^h + K^{ih}\,m^i) - \delta p\,b^h \qquad (14)$$

These expressions represent the contributions to national income of the rest of the economy and each of the projects, respectively, calculated at "accounting prices" $\tilde{k}^{-1} = \dfrac{1}{\tilde{k}}$ for foreign currency, which may differ from the official price (taken equal to 1). The accounting price has to be chosen in such a way as to equilibrate the balance of payments; since that price influences the choice of the projects and hence the imports i^h it can indeed satisfy this condition, at least within certain limits.

$$E = p\,e \qquad (15)$$
$$\tilde{Y}_o = \Sigma^h\,\tilde{Y}_o{}^h + \tilde{Y}_o{}^o \qquad (16)$$

$$\tilde{Y}_o{}^h = \sum_1^\infty{}^t \frac{\tilde{Y}_t{}^h}{\prod_{t'=2}^t (1 + n_{t'})} \qquad (17)$$

$\tilde{Y}_o{}^h$ represents the discounted value, at middle of time period 1, of all future contributions of project h to national income, at accounting prices; $\tilde{Y}_o$ represents the total for all projects chosen, plus the private sector. It is this expression which should be made by a proper choice of projects, a maximum.

MODEL 21. GROUP OF ECONOMIES, STATIC, MONEY AND PRODUCT FLOW MODEL

ACTORS   *Number:* 2H, namely H national economies and H governments.

Income: national economies: approximated by volume of production. Supply of national products inelastic; supply price considered an instrument of economic policy;

governments: not explicitly considered.

Spending habits: national economies, depending on real income; *governments:* expenditure autonomous and an instrument of economic policy.

Wealth: not explicitly considered.

MARKETS   *Number:* H, the national products, sold at one price each in all countries.

TECHNICAL RELATIONS   Each country imports the national products of all other countries and uses them as raw material to its own national product; the import quota of each country with respect to each other country, in the absence of price differences, is equal to μ; it reacts on price differences between the importing country and the country of origin with an elasticity equal for all with respect to all.

EQUATIONS   The symbol Σ' indicates summation from 1 to H inclusive, but exclusive of h.

Demand: home demand: $x^{hh} = \xi y^h + x_0{}^h$ $h = 1 \ldots H$ (1)

Here ξ stands for the propensity to spend and $x_0{}^h$ is the autonomous component of national expenditure

imports: $x^{hh'} = \mu y^{h'} + \varepsilon (p^h - p^{h'})$ $h, h' = 1 \ldots H,$ $h \neq h'$ (2)

In these equations μ indicates the import quota with respect to any one of the other countries and ε is related to the price elasticity of foreign demand.

Supply: $p^h = \mu \Sigma'_{h'} p^{h'} + p_0{}^h$ $h = 1 \ldots H$ (3)

Here $p_0{}^h$ indicates the national component in product prices, depending, among other things, of the level of efficiency incomes.

Definition: $y^h = \Sigma_{h'} x^{hh'}$ $h = 1 \ldots H$ (4)

$D^h = \Sigma'_{h'} x^{h'h} p^{h'} - p^h \Sigma'_{h'} x^{hh'}$ $h = 1 \ldots H$ (5)

In the examples to be treated with the aid of this model we choose $H = 10$, $\mu = 0.02$, $\xi = 0.7$ and $\varepsilon = -0.27$; the meaning of these figures being that there are ten countries, with total import quota of $9\mu = 0.18$, a marginal propensity to spend of 0.7 and a price elasticity of foreign demand of -2. [1]

[1] Particulars will be found in: J. Tinbergen, Centralization and Decentralization in Economic Policy, Amsterdam 1954, pp. 28–34.

APPENDIX 4

EXPLANATION OF SYMBOLS USED

Below are listed the symbols used to indicate economic variables and instrument variables. The main list does not apply to model 08, for which a separate list is added. It does not contain the Greek symbols used to indicate coefficients; these are explained in the model where they first appear. They correspond to the variable which occurs on the left-hand side of the equation in which they appear. The list below does not mention separately either the additive constants contained in a number of equations and indicated as a rule by a lower index 0 added to the symbol used for the variable on the left-hand side of the equation.

A higher index h indicates sector (industry or country) h.

Barred symbols: single bar, initial value; double bar: absolute value in problem.

In models 10, 12, 13, 14, 16, 18 and 19 symbols without bar indicate deviations from initial value; e.g. $a = \bar{\bar{a}} - \bar{a}$.

Details about the units used are to be found in the description of the model (cf. especially model 14).

Lower index added to variable (except index 0) indicates time.

Stock variables are indicated by *.

The sign $\sim$ indicates values at "accounting prices" (model 20).

LIST OF VARIABLES AND INSTRUMENTS
FOR ALL MODELS EXCEPT 08
(Alphabetical order)

*: stock variables.

$*A^h$ total wealth of sector h

a volume of employment

* Au gold stock

* b quantity of other factors of production, e.g. capital

* B quantity of bonds in circulation

* B^B bills and advances at private banks balance sheet

* B^R rediscounts at Central Bank balance sheet

$*B_h$,   amount of bonds issued by sector h

$*B_h^{h'}$ amount of bonds issued by sector h, owned by sector h'

c volume of consumption

C value of consumption at market prices

C^F value of consumption at factor cost

C^z value of consumption by independents (i.e. persons other than employees)

d depreciation allowances

D deficit on balance of payments

e volume of exports

E value of exports

h, h' number of sector (industry or country)

h'' as an index indicates average value of some variable for all values of h' except h

i volume of imports

I value of imports

j volume of gross investment

J value of gross investment

k exchange rate (price of national currency)

* K^i foreign debt

l wage rate

L total wages

m interest rate (model 17: Central Bank rate)

m' private discount rate

* M money in circulation (model 17: bank notes only)

* M' bank deposits

*M_h amount of money issued by sector h

*$M_h^{h'}$ amount of money issued by sector h, owned by sector h'

p price level of national product (excl. indirect taxes)

p' home price level of national product (incl. indirect taxes)

p^x price level of home sales

p^e export price level

p^i import price level

p^w world market price level of export goods

q price of "other" products

r volume of replacement

* R reserves of private banks with central bank

s real savings

S value of savings

t time

T tax receipts (model 09: life time of equipment)

v volume of gross product

* w stock of equipment

x real national expenditure (or home sales)

X national expenditure (at market prices)

X^G public expenditure

X^P private expenditure

y real national income

Y national income at factor cost

Z income of "independents" (before direct tax)

SYMBOLS USED IN
MODEL 08

(i) *Latin symbols*

i number of "ability" or "property" (0: family size; 1: speed or intensity of work; I: total number)

l income per occupied person

L total income paid out by production "organizers"

L_i coefficients occurring in income scale l

m frequency distribution of "required properties"

M total number of jobs $(= N)$

n frequency distribution of properties available

N total number of occupied persons $(= M)$

p product of one person

P total product of all occupied

s_i intensity or degree of property i required for job

$\bar{s}_i$ average of all s_i

t_i intensity or degree of property i available in population

$\bar{t}_i$ average of all t_i

(ii) *Greek symbols*

γ tax rate

λ_i coefficients appearing in utility function

π_i coefficients appearing in production function

σ_i standard deviation of s_i

τ_i standard deviation of t_i

φ disutility function of speed or intensity of work

ψ coefficient appearing in income scale

ω utility function

APPENDIX 5

READING SUGGESTIONS

This list does not claim to be complete, but rather indicates some of the outstanding books and reports that deal with the subject matter of economic policy and of econometric models. Further literature will be found in several of these books and reports.

Bresciani Turroni C.,	Einführung in die Wirtschaftspolitik, Berlin 1948 (Translation from Italian edition, 1942)
Central Planning Bureau	(of the Netherlands Government), Central Economic Plan 1955, the Hague 1955.
Central Planning Bureau,	Scope and Methods of the Central Planning Bureau, The Hague 1956.
Clark C.,	The Economics of 1960, London 1942.
Frisch R.,	"A Memorandum on Price-, Wage-, Tax-, Subsidy Policies as Instruments in Maintaining Optimal Employment", The University Institute of Economics, Oslo, published as an U. N. Document, April 1949 (cf. also Metroeconomica VII (1955) p. 111).
Hansen Alvin H.,	Economic Policy and Full Employment, New York–London 1947.
Hansen Bent,	Finanspolitikens ekonomiska teori, Statens offentliga Utredningar 1955: 25, Stockholm–Uppsala 1955 (to be translated into English).
Hartog F.,	Leerboek economische politiek, Leiden 1954.
Heinrich W.,	Wirtschaftspolitik, I. Band, Wien 1948.
Jöhr W. A. and Singer H. W.,	The Rôle of the Economist as Official Adviser, London 1955 (partly a translation of W. A. Jöhr, Die Beurteilung konkreter wirtschaftspolitischer Probleme, Bern 1947).
Klein L. R. and Goldberger A.S.,	An Econometric Model of the United States, 1929–1952, Amsterdam 1955.

Lampe A., (Aus dem Nachlass von): "Umrisse einer allgemeinen Theorie der Wirtschaftspolitik", Jahrbücher f. National-ökonomie u. Statistik 163 (1951), S 81, 189.

Lerner A. P.,　　　　The Economics of Control, New York 1944.

Leontief W.,　　　　The Structure of the American Economy, New York 1953.

Mahalanobis P. C.,　　"Planning in India", to appear in Sankhya, 15, 1956.

Meade J. E.,　　　　The Theory of International Economic Policy, I The Balance of Payments, Oxford 1951; II Trade and Welfare, Oxford 1955.

Palvia C. M.,　　　　An Econometric Model for Development Planning, the Hague, 1953

Polak Jacques J.,　　An International Economic System, Chicago 1953

Pütz Th.,　　　　　Theorie der allgemeinen Wirtschaftspolitik und Wirtschaftslenkung, Wien 1948.

Schumpeter J. A.,　　Capitalism, Socialism and Democracy, New York and London, 1942.

Seraphim H. J.,　　Theorie der allgemeinen Volkswirtschaftspolitik, Göttingen 1955.

Theil H.,　　　　　"Econometric Models and Welfare Maximisation", Weltw. Archiv 72 (1954) p. 60.

United Nations,　　Analyses and Projections of Economic Development (an introduction to the technique of programming, a study prepared by the Economic Commission for Latin America) New York 1955.

SUBJECT INDEX